POLITICAL VIOLENCE AND TERRORISM IN MODERN AMERICA

POLITICAL VIOLENCE AND TERRORISM IN MODERN AMERICA

A CHRONOLOGY

Christopher Hewitt

PRAEGER SECURITY INTERNATIONAL
Westport, Connecticut • London

Library of Congress Cataloging-in-Publication Data

Hewitt, Christopher.
    Political violence and terrorism in modern America : a chronology / Christopher Hewitt.
        p. cm.
    Includes bibliographical references and index.
    ISBN 0–313–33418–8 (alk. paper)
    1. Political violence—United States—History—20th century—Chronology. 2. Political violence—United States—History—21st century—Chronology. 3. Radicalism—United States—History—20th century—Chronology. 4. Radicalism—United States—History—21st century—Chronology. 5. Terrorism—United States—History—20th century—Chronology. 6. Terrorism—United States—History—21st century—Chronology. I. Title.
    HN90.V5H49 2005
    303.6′2′097309045—dc22   2005018671

British Library Cataloguing in Publication Data is available.

Library of Congress Catalog Card Number: 2005018671
ISBN: 0–313–33418–8

First published in 2005

Praeger Security International, 88 Post Road West, Westport, CT 06881
An imprint of Greenwood Publishing Group, Inc.
www.praeger.com

Printed in the United States of America

The paper used in this book complies with the
Permanent Paper Standard issued by the National
Information Standards Organization (Z39.48–1984).

10 9 8 7 6 5 4 3 2 1

CONTENTS

INTRODUCTION

This chronology was originally developed while I was writing *Understanding Terrorism in America: From the Klan to Al Qaeda* (2003). It has been updated and revised so that it now covers terrorism and other forms of organized political violence within the United States and Puerto Rico, from 1954 through early 2004. The chronology contains information on over 3000 incidents, and annual updates are planned.[1]

Terrorism is defined by the FBI as "the unlawful use of force or violence against persons or property to intimidate or coerce a government, the civilian population, or any segment thereof, in furtherance of political or social objectives." This definition is used in constructing this data set. Some writers use a more restrictive definition and consider only attacks that target civilians and non-combatants as truly "terrorist." Thus groups that attack soldiers and police are "urban guerrillas" rather than terrorists. By adding "political violence" to the title, I seek to avoid any terminological squabbles, so the chronology includes all violent incidents that were carried out for political or social objectives.

Evidence of political or social motivation includes membership in an extremist organization or other links to extremist movements, such as possession of extremist literature. In addition, an individual's statements or writings may provide evidence of political or social motivation. An incident is included in the chronology if a terrorist group claimed the attack or was identified as being responsible for the attack, or if the individual(s) carrying out the attack were members of an extremist group. In other cases, incidents can be classified as political or terrorist because the targets fit into a pattern and were apparently selected for ideological reasons. For example, even if the perpetrators are unknown, attacks in the South on blacks and civil rights activists, bombings of ROTC buildings on college campuses, or ambushes of police in black neighborhoods can be presumed to be politically motivated actions at certain periods in American history. In such cases a general category is given, such as "white racist" or "black militant," but no specific organization or individual is given.

It is often difficult to distinguish terrorism and political violence from hate crimes or from terrorist-style incidents carried out for personal reasons. Hate crimes (defined as crimes motivated by bias towards someone because of his or her "race, ethnicity, national origin, religion, sexual orientation, or disability") sometimes overlap with terrorism but are usually very different in character. In distinguishing between the two, the degree of organization and planning must be considered. If an attack is carried out by members of an organized extremist group, or if there is evidence of planning and ideological motivation on the part of the individual concerned, hate crimes are also terrorist incidents. For example, Joseph Paul Franklin had a history of involvement with racist groups, and his shooting of mixed race couples was obviously motivated by his political ideology. The sniper attacks were carefully planned rather than spontaneous, and most of his victims were ambushed. His was a campaign of premeditated violence against blacks and "race mixers." This is very different from most hate crimes, which are usually unplanned. For example, the 1982 death of Vincent Chin, a Chinese man killed in a drunken brawl with two unemployed autoworkers who thought he was Japanese, is a hate crime but is not terrorism. Similarly, the murder of Matthew Shepherd, while motivated in part by the fact that he was gay, was certainly unplanned (a robbery gone wrong), so I don't include either of these attacks as terrorist incidents.

Terrorist-style incidents carried out for personal reasons are obviously difficult to distinguish from genuine terrorist attacks. Of the presidential assassinations and attempted assassinations, several were clearly no more political than the murder of John Lennon by a deranged individual. I have, however, included quasi-terrorist incidents such as this in the chronology if the targets were selected because of their political position or political symbolism. John Hinkley shot President Reagan because he wanted to impress Jodie Foster, but he chose Reagan because he was the President. In uncertain cases I have included quasi-terrorist incidents in the chronology, such as the Alphabet Bomber, who was probably deranged rather than ideologically inspired.[2]

Some incidents, even though motivated by political or social issues, were ignored because they caused only minor damage or injury. Thus some incidents reported by the National Abortion Federation, such as "red paint flung on steps" and "fish oil sprayed through door" were excluded on these grounds.[3] However, all bombing and shooting incidents were considered non-trivial, as were kidnappings and robberies. Assaults were included if the victim was hospitalized, described as severely injured, or when serious injuries were implied (e.g., "beaten by an iron bar").

Classifying Terrorist Groups

American terrorism, that is, terrorism that occurs *within* the United States and Puerto Rico, has been remarkably diverse in terms of the causes and ideology of the terrorists and is also marked by a proliferation of organizations. Indeed many attacks have been carried out by unaffiliated freelancers, such as the Unabomber. Most incidents can be placed into one of three categories: international terrorism, émigré terrorism, and domestic terrorism. International terrorism involves attacks by foreigners on American targets, émigré terrorism involves attacks by foreigners on foreign targets in America, and domestic terrorism involves attacks by Americans on American targets.

International terrorism has come in two forms. The threat from Islamic extremists was clear even before September 11. Although they are responsible for only a handful of incidents, their willingness to attack civilian targets and their desire to maximize casualties were revealed by the 1993 bombing of the World Trade Center. In addition to the current threat from Islamic terrorism, Puerto Rican nationalists, who seek an independent Puerto Rico, carried out a wave of attacks in the 1950s and again in the 1970s. The two most important *independista* terrorist groups were the Armed Forces of National Liberation (FALN) and the *Macheteros*, the former being most active on the U.S. mainland, while the latter's attacks were concentrated in Puerto Rico. The bombing campaign of the FALN targeted banks, the corporate headquarters of organizations with economic interests in Puerto Rico, and other symbols of U.S. capitalism and imperialism. The *Macheteros* attacked and killed American sailors and local police officers.

Much foreign terrorism involves attacks on foreign targets on American soil and is linked to issues that have little or nothing to do with the United States. To take an extreme example, the Armenian who killed two Turkish diplomats on January 27, 1973, in California was taking revenge for events that occurred during World War I in the Ottoman Empire. Given the large number of immigrants and the ethnic diversity of the American population, such émigré terrorism is not uncommon with attacks involving Haitians, Sikhs, Taiwanese, Vietnamese, Croatians, Chileans, Iranians, Libyans, Nicaraguans, Palestinians, and Venezuelans on non-American targets. The most important example of émigré terrorism was the campaign waged by anti-Castro Cubans against those members of the exile community perceived to be traitors to the Cuban cause.

To be agnostic on the question of Fidel Castro, let alone to call for a renewed dialogue or an end to the U.S. trade embargo, could be danger-ous. . . . people had been killed for espousing such views. For all the talk of terrorism in the United States over the previous twenty years, Miami was the only American city to experience any significant terrorism. (Rieff, 1993:85)

However, the great majority of terrorist incidents within the United States involve attacks by Americans on American targets. This domestic terrorism has occurred in a series of waves.

The School Desegregation decision of 1954 and the civil rights campaigns of the 1960s provoked a violent response from white racists. A resurgent Ku Klux Klan burned churches, bombed homes, and shot at civil rights activists in an attempt to intimidate blacks from exercising their rights. The violence began in the 1950s, peaked in 1964, and was largely over by 1970.

Since the mid-1960s, two different types of black militants have carried out violent acts: black racist cults, such as the Black Muslims or "Nation of Islam," and black nationalists, such as the Black Panthers. The two types of groups engaged in very different forms of violence. Black nationalists carried on an urban guerrilla war against the police and killed one another in factional feuds. Black racist cults, such as the Death Angels and de Mau Mau, murdered randomly selected whites, as well as dissidents and apostates.

Revolutionary-leftist groups, such as the Weather Under-ground, turned to terrorism in 1969; their attacks peaked in 1971 and then declined erratically. The most common type of incident was bombing. They rarely attacked individuals but mostly bombed military and business targets.

Members of the Jewish Defense League and its splinter groups (Jewish Armed Resistance, Thunder of Zion, and

Save Our Israel Soil) were responsible for bombing Soviet diplomatic targets and Arab embassies, as well as for several attacks on Arab-American organizations and alleged war criminals. Five people died as a result of extremist Jewish terrorism.

Currently, three groups of domestic terrorists are active. Arson and bombings of abortion clinics, which began in 1977, increased significantly in 1984 and again after 1992. In recent years, anti-abortion violence has become more deadly, with six persons killed in the 1990s. Sabotage and arson by Animal Rights activists and Eco-terrorists are widespread, although, like revolutionary terrorism, these usually involve attacks against property and only rarely against people.

A far more serious threat is the violence by the extreme Right, which began in the late 1970s and has resulted in numerous deaths. The bombing of the Alfred P. Murrah Federal Building in Oklahoma City, which claimed 168 lives, was the most spectacular example of this new wave of terrorism, driven by hostility towards the federal government and a belief in white supremacy. A feature of this second wave of white racist terrorism is its organizational fragmentation. As well as the involvement of various Klan and Nazi groups, attacks have been carried out by the Order (or Silent Brotherhood), the White Peoples Party, the Covenant, Sword, and Arm of the Lord, and Posse Comitatus. Skinhead gangs and unaffiliated serial racist killers also play a significant role.

In order to create some order out of what would otherwise appear as a diverse and confusing variety of violent groups and individuals, they have been grouped under nine broad ideological labels and residual "other foreign" and "other domestic" categories. Groups and individuals are classified (in alphabetical order) as Anti-abortion, Black militants, Cuban, Environmental/Animal Rights, Islamic, Jewish, Puerto Rican nationalist, Revolutionary leftist, and White racist/rightist (see Table 1).

Information Given in the Chronology

In addition to giving information on the date and the place of the attack, the type of incident, and the group responsible, the chronology gives other details of the attack. However, the amount of detail given for each incident varies considerably. This reflects two factors: (1) the information that is available for each incident and (2) the significance of the incident. For the more important incidents, such as those in which somebody was killed, there is

Table 1.
Number and Percentage of Terrorist Incidents by Perpetrator

	N	%*
White Racist/Rightist	845	26.7
Revolutionary Leftist	768	24.3
Black Militants	472	14.9
Anti-abortion	242	7.7
Puerto Rican Nationalist	235	7.4
Environmental/Animal Rights	155	4.9
Cuban	141	4.5
Jewish	99	3.1
Islamic	50	1.6
Other foreign	63	2.0
Other domestic	50	1.6

*The figures do not sum to 100 percent because unknown and quasi-terrorist incidents are not included.

usually more detail, but in many cases little is known beyond the date, the place, and the target. Generally, the number of dead and injured persons is reported. If known, damage estimates are given in dollars, and for robberies, the amount stolen is given also in dollars. Wherever possible, if someone was killed in a terrorist attack, the name of the person and other salient personal characteristics are given. I have also named famous victims even if they were not killed. In the case of the Oklahoma City bombing in which 168 people perished, and the 9/11 attacks, in which almost 3000 died, space does not allow listing the victims by name.[4]

Data Sources

The chronology is based on several types of published sources. There are three chronologies that deal with terrorism and political violence in general, starting with Trick (1976) for the 1965–1976 period, those in the *Annual of Power and Conflict* (1975–1981), and the FBI's published annual reports, which begin in 1980. In addition, useful sources on particular ideological waves of terrorism include the following:

For Klan and pro-segregationist terrorism in general, sources are Holt (1965), The Southern Regional Council (1966), the House Committee on Un-American Activities Report, *The Present Day Ku Klux Klan Movement* (1967), Newton and Newton (1991), Bullard (1989), and Nelson (1993). A comprehensive chronology of leftist and black violence during the 1965–1970 period can be found in *Scanlans* (1971). Sources for particular groups include Heath (1976), Epstein (1971), and Pearson (1994) on the Black Panthers, Daley (1973) and Tanenbaum and Rosenberg (1979) on the Black Liberation Army, Howard (1979) on the Zebra killings, Castellucci (1986) on the M19CO group, and Pearsall (1974) and McLellan (1977) on the Symbionese Liberation Army. For Puerto Rican terrorism, Sater (1981) provides a chronology, and Fernandez (1987) covers the activities of the Macheteros. There are two chronologies of Jewish violence and terrorism, Sater (1996) and Russ (1981), as well as a study of the Jewish Defense League by Friedman (1990). Cuban terrorism is examined in Garcia (1996), and the Web site cuban.exile.com lists Cuban émigré actions under several headings. Anti-abortion violence is documented in detail by the National Abortion Federation. The violent activities of the extreme Right are closely monitored by watchdog groups, the most important of which are the Southern Poverty Law Center (SPLC) and the Anti-Defamation League (ADL). Their reports are the main source of information on racist and anti-Semitic violence. See, for example, *Ku Klux Klan: A History of Racism and Violence* by the SPLC and *Shaved for Battle: Skinheads Target America's Youth* and *Hate Groups in America* by the ADL. Additional sources include Melnichak (1991), Flynn and Gerhardt (1989), Hamm (1993), and Coates (1987). The U.S. Department of Energy (1997) lists anti-government terrorist incidents in the early 1990s. Information on Animal Rights and Eco-terrorism can be found on several Web sites, including Oregon Live: Sabotage 1996–2001, and Animal Extremist/Ecoterror crimes 2000–2004.

Student coders searched the *Readers Guide to Periodicals, Keesings, Facts on File,* and the *New York Times Index* for reported incidents of terrorism, arrests, and trials of terrorists. Finally, phone calls were made to local newspapers for missing and additional material. The *Cleveland Plain Dealer,* the *San Juan Star,* the *Miami Herald,* and the *Dayton Daily News* were especially helpful. The Fraternal Order of Police provided assistance in identifying police officers killed by terrorists and extremists.

Although I have attempted to make this chronology as complete as possible, it is certain that some kinds of terrorism are less likely to be included. The violence on the Pine Ridge reservation between the militants of the American Indian Movement and the supporters of the tribal council is definitely under-reported. There were probably more victims of black racist terrorism than are included in this chronology. The official total of white victims killed by the Death Angels was only 12, but San Francisco Mayor Alioto listed 57 in the Bay Area by name while Howard (1979: 34) suggests that throughout the whole of California as many as "135 white men, 75 white women, and 60 white children" were murdered. Law enforcement officials are often unaware that a particular robbery was perpetrated by a terrorist group rather than by ordinary criminals, so such incidents are also undercounted.

Notes

1. Deciding what constitutes an incident is sometimes difficult. Should the events of 9/11 be considered a single attack or three—or four—separate attacks? If several explosions took place at a given site on the same day, they were considered a single incident, but if the attacks took place on the same day but at different places, they were considered separate incidents. However, our sources sometimes describe multiple attacks without sufficient detail to distinguish them (e.g., three banks were bombed in Puerto Rico), in which case they are recorded as a single incident.

A related problem, which results from combining different sources, is one of possible duplication since the same incident may be recorded in a slightly different form in different sources. The rule adopted in such cases was to assume that two identical incidents reported within two days of one another were the same, unless there was evidence to the contrary.

2. Muharem Kurbegovic, alias "Aliens of America," carried out a series of arson and bombing attacks in Los Angeles. He was called the Alphabet Bomber because his targets were supposedly chosen in alphabetical order, beginning with a bombing at the airport, which killed three people.

3. This criterion significantly reduces the number of reported attacks against abortion clinics, although it generally agrees with what the National Abortion Federation classifies as incidents of "extreme violence."

4. A list of those killed in the Oklahoma City bombing is given in Irving (1995), while several Web sites give the names and other details of those killed in the 9/11 attacks. The official total includes 2749 names.

References

Annual of Power and Conflict: A Survey of Political Violence. (1971–1982). London: Institute for the Study of Conflict.

Bullard, S. (1989). *Free at Last: A History of the Civil Rights Movement*. Montgomery, AL: Southern Poverty Law Center.

Castellucci, J. (1986). *The Big Dance: The Untold Story of Kathy Boudin and the Terrorist Family That Committed the Brink's Robbery Murders*. New York: Dodd, Mead.

Coates, J. (1987). *Armed and Dangerous: The Rise of the Survivalist Right*. New York: Hill and Wang.

Daley, R. (1973). *Target Blue*. New York: Delacorte Press.

Epstein, E. (1971). "C. R. Garry's List of Panthers Allegedly Killed by Police." *The New Yorker*. February 13: 45–46.

Fernandez, R. (1987). *Los Macheteros*. New York: Prentice Hall.

Flynn, K. and G. Gerhardt. (1989). *The Silent Brotherhood: Inside America's Racist Underground*. New York: The Free Press.

Friedman, R. I. (1990). *The False Prophet: Rabbi Meir Kahane*. New York: Lawrence Hill Books.

Garcia, M. C. (1996). *Havana USA: Cuban Exiles in South Florida*. Berkeley: University of California Press.

Hamm, M. (1993). *American Skinheads: The Criminology and Control of Hate Crime*. Westport, CT: Praeger.

Heath, G. L. (1976). *Off the Pigs!* Metuchen, NJ: Scarecrow Press.

Hewitt, C. (2003). *Understanding Terrorism in America: From the Klan to Al Qaeda*. London, New York: Routledge.

Holt, L. (1965). *The Summer That Didn't End*. New York: Morrow.

Howard, C. (1979). *Zebra*. New York: Marek.

Irving, C. (1995). *In Their Name*. New York: Random House.

Ku Klux Klan: A History of Racism and Violence. (1997). Montgomery, AL: Southern Poverty Law Center.

McLellan, V. (1977). *The Voices of Guns*. New York: Putnam.

Melnichak J. (1991). "A Chronicle of Hate." *TVI Report*. 6: 38–42.

Nelson, J. (1993). *Terror in the Night: The Klan's Campaign against the Jews*. New York: Simon & Schuster.

Newton, M. and J. A. Newton. (1991). *Racial and Religious Violence in America*. New York: Garland.

Pearsall, R. (1974). *The Symbionese Liberation Army*. Amsterdam: Rodopi.

Pearson, H. (1994). *The Shadow of the Panther*. Reading, MA: Addison-Wesley.

Rieff, D. (1993). *The Exile: Cuba in the Heart of Miami*. New York: Simon & Schuster.

Russ, S. (1981). *Zionist Hooligans: The Jewish Defense League*. New York: City University of New York.

Sater, R. (1996). "Bombings Involving Jewish Extremists in the United States." *TVI Report*. 11:9–12.

Sater, W. (1981). *Puerto Rican Terrorists: A Possible Threat to US Energy Installations*. Santa Monica: Rand.

Shaved for Battle: Skinheads Target America's Youth. (1987). New York: Anti-Defamation League of B'Nai B'rith.

Southern Regional Council (May 1966). *The Continuing Crisis: An Assessment of New Racial Tensions in the South*. New York: American Jewish Committee.

Special Issue on Guerrilla Attacks 1968–70. (January 1971). *Scanlans*.

Tanenbaum, R. and P. Rosenberg (1979). *Badge of the Assassin.* New York: Dutton.

Trick, N. (1976). National Advisory Committee on Criminal Justice Standards and Goals, Task Force on Disorders and Terrorism, "Disorders and Terrorism." Washington, D.C.: Government Printing Office.

U.S. Department of Energy (January 1997). *Anti-Government Terrorism and Related Activities in the U.S. 1992–96.* Washington, D.C.

TYPES OF INCIDENTS AND GROUPS RESPONSIBLE

Types of Incidents

arson

assault

attempted arson

attempted assault

attempted bombing

attempted escape

attempted robbery

bio-terrorism (includes chemical terrorism and hoaxes)

bombing

bombing/explosive

bombing/incendiary

cross-burning

escape

hijacking

kidnapping

lynching

occupation

occupation/hostage taking

raid

robbery

rocket fired

sabotage

sabotage, vandalism, and property destruction

shooting

shoot-out

vandalism

Groups Responsible

Organizations are listed here by general ideological category. In the chronology, if the specific group is not known, the general category is used. To limit the number of listed organizations, name changes and aliases are included as the name of the main organization. Thus the Sam Melville–Jonathan Jackson Unit is listed as the United Freedom Front, and the International Committee against Nazism appears as the Jewish Defense League.

Anti-abortion

The Army of God

Black militant

Black Afro-militant Movement

Black Liberation Army

Black Muslims

Black Nation of New Libya

Black Panthers

Black Revolutionary Assault Team

Death Angels

de Mau Mau

MOVE

National Coalition to Combat Fascism (Black Panther splinter group)
Republic of New Africa
Student Non-violent Coordinating Committee
US (Ron Karenga's organization)
Yahweh cult

Cuban
Accion Cubana/Cuban Action Commandos
El Poder Cubano/Cuban Power
Frente de Liberacion Nacional de Cuba
Omega7
Secret Cuban Government

Environmental/animal rights
Animal Liberation Front
Earth Liberation Front
Evan Mecham Eco-terrorist International Conspiracy

Islamic
Al-Fuqra

Jewish
Jewish Armed Resistance
Jewish Defense League
Jewish Defense Organization

Puerto Rican nationalist
Armed Forces of National Liberation
Armed Independence Movement
Guerrilla Forces of Liberation
Macheteros
Pedro Albizu Campos Revolutionary Force
Volunteers for Puerto Rican Revolution

Revolutionary leftist
Continental Revolutionary Army
Emiliano Zapata Unit
George Jackson Brigade
May 19th Communist Organization

New World Liberation Front
New Years Gang
Red Guerrilla Force
Red Guerrilla Resistance
Revolutionary Force 7
Revolutionary Force 9
Sam Melville Group
Symbionese Liberation Army
United Freedom Front
Weather Underground
White Panthers

White racist/rightist
Americans for a Competent Judiciary
Aryan Nations
Aryan Republican Army
Covenant, Sword, and Arm of the Lord
Eric Rudolph
Joseph Christopher
Joseph Paul Franklin
Ku Klux Klan
Militia
Minutemen
National Socialist Liberation Front
National States Rights Party
Nazi(s)
Neal Long
Order/Silent Brotherhood
Posse Comitatus
Secret Army Organization
Skinhead(s)
Sons of the Gestapo
Up the IRS
White Aryan Resistance
White Peoples Party

Other domestic
American Indian Movement
Chicano Liberation Front
Hawaii for the Hawaiians

Latter Day Saints/Mormon Sects
Quasi-terrorist
Rajneesh
Unabomber

Other foreign
Armenian
Black September
Chilean
Croatian
Haitian

Iranian
Irish Republican Army
Justice Commandos of the Armenian Genocide
Liberian
Libyan
Mexican Revolutionary Movement
Palestine Liberation Organization
Secret Army for the Liberation of Armenia
Serbian
Taiwanese Independence Movement

THE CHRONOLOGY

March 1, 1954. *Shooting.* Puerto Rican nationalist. Washington, D.C. Puerto Rican nationalists shoot from the visitors' gallery onto the floor of the House of Representatives, wounding five congressmen.

June 27, 1954. *Bombing.* White racist. Louisville, Kentucky. A black home in a white neighborhood is bombed.

July 11, 1954. *Shooting.* White racist, Ku Klux Klan. Colbert, Georgia. One person is wounded when shots are fired at a black home.

July 14, 1954. *Bombing/explosive.* White racist. Laurel, Mississippi. A black home is bombed.

August 1954. *Bombing/explosive.* White racist. Norfolk County, Virginia. Three black properties are bombed.

May 7, 1955. *Shooting.* White racist. Belzoni, Mississippi. Rev. George Lee is killed for leading a voter registration drive.

August 13, 1955. *Shooting.* White racist. Brookhaven, Mississippi. Lamar Smith, a civil rights activist, is murdered.

August 28, 1955. *Kidnapping and shooting.* White racist. Money, Mississippi. Emmett Till, a black teenager from the North, is kidnapped and brutally murdered for allegedly whistling at a white woman.

September 1955. *Arson.* White racist, Ku Klux Klan. Lake City, South Carolina. A black minister's house is set on fire.

October 6, 1955. *Arson.* White racist, Ku Klux Klan. Lake City, South Carolina. A black church is set on fire.

October 10, 1955. *Shoot-out.* White racist, Ku Klux Klan. Lake City, South Carolina. A black minister exchanges gunfire with Klansmen.

October 22, 1955. *Shooting.* White racist. Mayflower, Texas. During a dispute over a new school for black pupils, gunmen fire into a cafe, killing John Reese and two other black teenagers.

November 26, 1955. *Shooting.* White racist. Belzoni, Mississippi. A black civil rights worker is shot and wounded.

December 7, 1955. *Assault.* White racist. Gonzales, Texas. A National Association for the Advancement of Colored People (NAACP) official is beaten to death.

January 30, 1956. *Bombing/explosive.* White racist. Montgomery, Alabama. Rev. Martin Luther King Jr.'s home is bombed.

February 1, 1956. *Bombing/explosive.* White racist. Montgomery, Alabama. The home of a civil rights worker is bombed.

February 18, 1956. *Shooting.* White racist. Columbia, Georgia. Thomas Brewer, an NAACP official, is shot and killed by a white gunman.

March 25, 1956. *Bombing/explosive.* White racist. Atlanta, Georgia. A black house is bombed.

April 11, 1956. *Assault.* White racist, Ku Klux Klan. Birmingham, Alabama. Nat King Cole is assaulted during his show.

May 28, 1956. *Cross-burning.* White racist. Tallahassee, Florida. A cross-burning occurs at a black home.

June 1956. *Arson.* White racist. Centerville, Mississippi. A black home is burned. Nine people are killed.

June 6, 1956. *Cross-burning.* White racist. Memphis, Tennessee. A cross-burning occurs at the home of a black activist.

June 15, 1956. *Shooting.* White racist. Kingstree, South Carolina. Shots are fired at a black meeting by night riders.

July 2, 1956. *Bombing/explosive.* White racist. Atlanta, Georgia. A black house is bombed.

July 13, 1956. *Cross-burning.* White racist. Camden, South Carolina. A cross-burning occurs at an integrated school.

July 23, 1956. *Bombing/explosive.* White racist. Americus, Georgia. An integrated farm commune is bombed.

August 1956. *Bombing/explosive.* White racist. Clinton, Tennessee. A black neighborhood is bombed.

August 25, 1956. *Bombing/explosive.* White racist. Montgomery, Alabama. The home of a civil rights worker is bombed.

August 28, 1956. *Cross-burning.* White racist. Mansfield, Texas. A cross-burning occurs; black dummies are hanged in effigy.

September 4, 1956. *Bombing/explosive.* White racist. Olive Springs, Tennessee. Bombs explode in a black neighborhood.

September 5, 1956. *Cross-burning.* White racist. Alvarado, Texas. A cross-burning occurs, and black dummies are hanged.

September 5, 1956. *Cross-burning.* White racist. Sturgis, Kentucky. Night riders threaten a black neighborhood.

September 18, 1956. *Shooting.* White racist. Clarendon County, South Carolina. Shots are fired at the home of an NAACP official.

September 18, 1956. *Arson.* White racist. Clarendon County, South Carolina. A black church is set on fire.

September 27, 1956. *Arson.* White racist. Mobile, Alabama. A black home is set on fire.

September 27, 1956. *Cross-burning.* White racist. San Francisco, California. A cross-burning occurs at a black home.

October 6, 1956. *Shooting.* White racist. Newton, Georgia. A black woman is shot and killed.

October 27, 1956. *Assault.* White racist. Wildwood, Florida. A black man is flogged for insulting a white woman.

November 1956. *Cross-burning.* White racist, Ku Klux Klan. Summerville, Georgia. A cross-burning occurs when a black football team is scheduled to play at a white high school.

December 1956. *Shooting.* White racist. Americus, Georgia. Shots are fired at an integrated farm commune.

December 1956. *Arson.* White racist. Kershaw, North Carolina. A black home is set on fire.

December 4, 1956. *Assault.* White racist. New Orleans, Louisiana. A white minister is beaten.

December 5, 1956. *Bombing/explosive.* White racist. Montgomery, Alabama. Rev. Martin Luther King Jr.'s home is bombed.

December 19, 1956. *Shooting.* White racist. Birmingham, Alabama. Shots are fired at a school bus.

December 24, 1956. *Bombing/explosive.* White racist. Birmingham, Alabama. The home of a black activist is bombed.

December 25, 1956. *Assault.* White racist. Montgomery, Alabama. A black girl is beaten.

December 27, 1956. *Shooting.* White racist. Montgomery, Alabama. Shots are fired at an integrated bus, wounding one.

December 28, 1956. *Assault.* White racist, Ku Klux Klan. Camden, South Carolina. A high school band director is flogged.

December 28, 1956. *Shooting.* White racist. Montgomery, Alabama. Shots are fired at an integrated bus.

December 31, 1956. *Bombing/explosive.* White racist. Birmingham, Alabama. A black home is bombed.

December 31, 1956. *Shooting.* White racist. Montgomery, Alabama. Shots are fired at an integrated bus.

January 1957. *Bombing/explosive.* White racist. Beaumont, Texas. A city auditorium is bombed.

January 1, 1957. *Cross-burning.* White racist. Montgomery, Alabama. A cross-burning occurs at a black church.

January 1, 1957. *Shooting.* White racist. Montgomery, Alabama. A black minister is shot.

January 1, 1957. *Shooting.* White racist. Montgomery, Alabama. Shots are fired at a store owned by a black activist.

January 5, 1957. *Bombing/explosive.* White racist. Clinton, Tennessee. Four integrated schools are bombed.

January 9, 1957. *Bombing/explosive.* White racist. Montgomery, Alabama. The homes of two civil rights leaders are bombed.

January 9, 1957. *Bombing/explosive.* White racist. Montgomery, Alabama. Four black churches are bombed.

January 10, 1957. *Cross-burning and bombing.* White racist. Mobile, Alabama. Attacks occur on several black homes with cross-burnings and bombings.

January 11, 1957. *Bombing/incendiary.* White racist. Chattanooga, Tennessee. An attempted bombing of a bus occurs.

January 15, 1957. *Bombing/explosive.* White racist. Americus, Georgia. An integrated farm commune is bombed, causing $5000 in damage.

January 23, 1957. *Shooting.* White racist, Ku Klux Klan. Birmingham, Alabama. A Klan leader shoots two other Klansmen.

January 23, 1957. *Bombing/explosive.* White racist. Chattanooga, Tennessee. A black home is bombed.

January 23, 1957. *Assault.* White racist, Ku Klux Klan. Montgomery, Alabama. Willie Edwards, a black man accused of accosting white women, is murdered by the Klan.

January 27, 1957. *Shooting.* White racist. Montgomery, Alabama. A TV newscaster is shot by night riders.

January 27, 1957. *Bombing/explosive.* White racist. Montgomery, Alabama. A black home is bombed.

January 28, 1957. *Bombing/explosive.* White racist. Montgomery, Alabama. A black home is bombed.

January 28, 1957. *Bombing/explosive.* White racist. Montgomery, Alabama. A black taxicab stand is bombed.

February 1957. *Bombing/explosive.* White racist. Charlottesville, North Carolina. A black school is bombed.

February 1957. *Bombing/explosive.* White racist. Knoxville, Tennessee. A city auditorium is bombed.

February 14, 1957. *Bombing/explosive.* White racist. Clinton, Tennessee. Two blacks are injured when a black neighborhood is bombed.

March 1957. *Bombing/explosive.* White racist. Mobile, Alabama. A black home is bombed.

March 1957. *Bombing/explosive.* White racist. Beaumont, Texas. Properties owned by white moderates are bombed.

March 6, 1957. *Assault.* White racist. Birmingham, Alabama. A white integrationist is assaulted.

March 22, 1957. *Shooting.* White racist. Americus, Georgia. Shots are fired at an integrated farm commune.

April 7, 1957. *Bombing/explosive.* White racist. Wilmington, Delaware. A black home is bombed.

April 26, 1957. *Shooting.* White racist. Richmond, Virginia. Six blacks are shot from a car.

April 28, 1957. *Bombing/explosive.* White racist. Bessemer, Alabama. A black union leader's home is bombed.

April 28, 1957. *Bombing/explosive.* White racist. Bessemer, Alabama. A black church is bombed.

May 1957. *Bombing/explosive.* White racist. Chattanooga, Tennessee. A black home is bombed.

May 19, 1957. *Bombing/explosive.* White racist. Americus, Georgia. Three integrated farm communes are bombed.

July 1957. *Bombing/explosive.* White racist. Birmingham, Alabama. A black home is bombed.

July 7, 1957. *Bombing/explosive.* White racist. Durham, North Carolina. A white integrationist's home is bombed.

July 23, 1957. *Assault.* White racist, Ku Klux Klan. Greenville, South Carolina. A black man is flogged.

August 1957. *Bombing/explosive.* White racist. Jersey, Tennessee. A black home is bombed.

August 2, 1957. *Bombing/explosive.* White racist. Wilmington, Delaware. A black home is bombed.

August 8, 1957. *Assault.* White racist, Ku Klux Klan. Evergreen, Alabama. Four blacks are flogged.

August 9, 1957. *Assault.* White racist, Ku Klux Klan. Maplesville, Alabama. Six blacks are beaten by night riders.

September 2, 1957. *Assault.* White racist, Ku Klux Klan. Birmingham, Alabama. A black man is castrated by Klansmen.

September 5, 1957. *Shooting.* White racist, Ku Klux Klan. Prattville, Alabama. Shots are fired at a black activist.

October 1957. *Bombing/explosive.* White racist. Chattanooga, Tennessee. Two black homes are bombed.

October 1957. *Bombing/explosive.* White racist. Greensboro, North Carolina. A black home is bombed.

November 1957. *Bombing/explosive.* White racist. Chattanooga, Tennessee. A black home is bombed.

November 1957. *Bombing/explosive.* White racist. Ringgold, Georgia. A black activist's home is bombed, and his wife is killed in the explosion.

November 1, 1957. *Bombing/explosive.* White racist. Bessemer, Alabama. A black activist's home is bombed.

November 20, 1957. *Bombing/explosive.* White racist. Gaffney, South Carolina. A white moderate's home is bombed.

November 23, 1957. *Cross-burning.* White racist. Gaffney, South Carolina. A cross-burning occurs at a white moderate's home.

December 1957. *Bombing/explosive.* White racist. Cowpens, South Carolina. A black home is bombed.

December 1957. *Bombing/explosive.* White racist. Birmingham, Alabama. Five black homes are bombed.

January 1958. *Bombing/explosive.* White racist. Little Rock, Arkansas. An NAACP official's home is bombed.

January 1, 1958. *Bombing/explosive.* White racist. Charlotte, North Carolina. An integrated theater is bombed.

January 19, 1958. *Bombing/explosive.* White racist. Tulsa, Oklahoma. A black home is bombed.

January 19, 1958. *Bombing/explosive.* White racist. Chattanooga, Tennessee. A black school is bombed, causing $1000 in damage.

January 27, 1958. *Bombing/explosive.* White racist. Chattanooga, Tennessee. An integrated YWCA is bombed.

January 27, 1958. *Bombing/explosive.* White racist. Columbus, Georgia. A black home is bombed.

February 1958. *Bombing/explosive.* White racist. Chattanooga, Tennessee. An integrated school is bombed.

February 9, 1958. *Attempted bombing.* White racist. Gastonia, North Carolina. A bombing attempt occurs at a synagogue.

February 17, 1958. *Bombing/explosive.* White racist. Atlanta, Georgia. A black home is bombed.

February 20, 1958. *Bombing.* White racist. Atlanta, Georgia. A black church is bombed.

March 16, 1958. *Bombing/explosive.* White racist. Miami, Florida. A synagogue is bombed.

March 16, 1958. *Bombing/explosive.* White racist. Nashville, Tennessee. A synagogue is bombed.

March 17, 1958. *Bombing/explosive.* White racist. Atlanta, Georgia. A black home is bombed.

April 27, 1958. *Bombing/explosive.* White racist. Jacksonville, Florida. A black school is bombed.

April 27, 1958. *Bombing/explosive.* White racist. Jacksonville, Florida. A synagogue is bombed.

May 17, 1958. *Bombing/explosive.* White racist. Bessemer, Alabama. A black home is bombed.

June 21, 1958. *Bombing/explosive.* White racist. Beaumont, Texas. A white professor's house is bombed.

June 29, 1958. *Bombing/explosive.* White racist, Ku Klux Klan. Birmingham, Alabama. A black church is bombed.

July 2, 1958. *Bombing/explosive.* White racist. Columbus, Georgia. A black home is bombed.

July 17, 1958. *Bombing/explosive.* White racist, Ku Klux Klan. Birmingham, Alabama. A black home is bombed.

August 5, 1958. *Bombing/explosive.* White racist. Memphis, Tennessee. A black church is bombed.

August 24, 1958. *Arson.* White racist. Deep Creek, North Carolina. Two integrated schools are set on fire.

September 27, 1958. *Cross-burning.* White racist. Saraland, Alabama. Cross-burnings occur at black homes.

October 5, 1958. *Bombing/explosive.* White racist. Clinton, Tennessee. An integrated school is bombed.

October 12, 1958. *Bombing/explosive.* White racist, National States Rights Party. Atlanta, Georgia. A synagogue is bombed.

October 14, 1958. *Bombing/explosive.* White racist. Chicago, Illinois. Two black homes are bombed.

October 14, 1958. *Bombing/explosive.* White racist. Peoria, Illinois. A synagogue is bombed.

October 25, 1958. *Bombing/explosive.* White racist. Clinton, Tennessee. An integrated school is bombed.

November 10, 1958. *Bombing/explosive.* White racist. Osage, West Virginia. An integrated school is bombed.

1959. *Assault.* White racist, Ku Klux Klan. Pickens County, Alabama. Two blacks are flogged.

April 7, 1959. *Bombing/explosive.* White racist. Wilmington, Delaware. A black home is bombed.

April 10, 1959. *Assault.* White racist, Ku Klux Klan. Birmingham, Alabama. A black minister is beaten by night riders.

April 25, 1959. *Lynching.* White racist. Poplarville, Mississippi. A black man suspected of raping a white woman is lynched.

April 27, 1959. *Shooting.* White racist. Richmond, Virginia. Six blacks are wounded in a drive-by shooting.

June 9, 1959. *Arson.* White racist, Ku Klux Klan. Little Rock, Arkansas. A fire occurs at the home of an anti-KKK (Ku Klux Klan) politician.

August 2, 1959. *Bombing/explosive.* White racist. Wilmington, Delaware. A black home is bombed.

August 25, 1959. *Bombing/explosive.* White racist. Little Rock, Arkansas. An integrated school is bombed.

August 27, 1959. *Bombing.* White racist. Little Rock, Arkansas. A school board meeting is teargassed.

September 7, 1959. *Bombing/explosive.* White racist. Little Rock, Arkansas. A school board office is bombed.

September 7, 1959. *Bombing/explosive.* White racist. Little Rock, Arkansas. The mayor's property is bombed.

January 28, 1960. *Bombing/explosive.* White racist. Kansas City, Missouri. A synagogue is bombed.

February 9, 1960. *Bombing/explosive.* White racist. Little Rock, Arkansas. A black home is bombed.

February 27, 1960. *Assault.* White racist, Ku Klux Klan. Montgomery, Alabama. Black demonstrators are attacked by Klansmen.

March 7, 1960. *Assault.* White racist, Ku Klux Klan. Houston, Texas. A black man is beaten with chains. The letters "KKK" are carved on his chest.

March 25, 1960. *Shooting and bombing/ incendiary.* White racist. Gadsden, Alabama. Two synagogues are shot at and firebombed.

March 27, 1960. *Cross-burning and bombing.* White racist. Anniston, Alabama. A cross-burning and bombings occur at black homes.

April 12, 1960. *Bombing/explosive.* White racist. Atlanta, Georgia. A black home is bombed.

April 15, 1960. *Arson.* White racist. Chatta-hoochee, Florida. A black home is set on fire.

April 19, 1960. *Bombing/explosive.* White racist. Nashville, Tennessee. The homes of an NAACP lawyer and a city councilman are bombed.

April 24, 1960. *Assault.* White racist. Biloxi, Mississippi. Five blacks at a segregated beach are attacked.

May 19, 1960. *Bombing/explosive.* White racist, Ku Klux Klan. Ringgold, Georgia. A black woman is killed when her home is bombed by night riders.

June 12, 1960. *Bombing/explosive.* White racist. Little Rock, Arkansas. A school warehouse is bombed.

July 15, 1960. *Arson.* White racist. Chattanooga, Tennessee. Three black school teachers' homes are set on fire.

August 13, 1960. *Bombing/explosive.* White racist. Chattanooga, Tennessee. A black neighborhood is bombed.

August 17, 1960. *Bombing/explosive.* White racist. Chattanooga, Tennessee. A white realtor is bombed.

August 21, 1960. *Bombing/explosive.* White racist. Chattanooga, Tennessee. A black home is bombed.

August 27, 1960. *Assault.* White racist, Ku Klux Klan. Jacksonville, Florida. Blacks are attacked by Klansmen.

September 9, 1960. *Arson.* White racist. Chattanooga, Tennessee. A black home is set on fire.

October 7, 1960. *Assault.* White racist, Ku Klux Klan. Whitesburg, Georgia. A black couple is flogged by Klansmen.

November 18, 1960. *Bombing/explosive.* White racist. Atlanta, Georgia. An integrated neighborhood is bombed.

November 29, 1960. *Bombing/explosive.* White racist. Austin, Texas. A white integrationist meeting is bombed.

December 12, 1960. *Bombing/explosive.* White racist. Atlanta, Georgia. A black school is bombed, causing $5000 in damage.

December 22, 1960. *Bombing.* Unknown. Van Wert, Ohio. The home of a judge is bombed, causing $10,000 worth of damage.

December 22, 1960. *Bombing/explosive.* Puerto Rican nationalist. New York City, New York. A bomb explodes in the doorway of Banco de Credito in Union Square, causing minor damage.

December 22, 1960. *Bombing/explosive.* Puerto Rican nationalist. New York City, New York. A bomb explodes at a Woolworth store, causing no injuries.

December 22, 1960. *Bombing/explosive.* Puerto Rican nationalist. New York City, New York. A bomb explodes at the offices of the Commonwealth of Puerto Rico.

January 1, 1961. *Shooting.* White racist. Greenville, Mississippi. Two blacks are wounded in a drive-by shooting.

May 13, 1961. *Assault.* White racist, Ku Klux Klan. Talladega, Alabama. Three whites are flogged by Klansmen. Their black maid had been allowed to discipline their children.

May 14, 1961. *Assault.* White racist, Ku Klux Klan. Anniston, Alabama. Freedom bus riders are attacked by Klansmen.

May 14, 1961. *Assault.* White racist, Ku Klux Klan. Montgomery, Alabama. Freedom bus riders are attacked by Klansmen.

May 14, 1961. *Assault.* White racist, Ku Klux Klan. Birmingham, Alabama. Freedom bus riders are attacked by Klansmen.

May 25, 1961. *Shooting.* White racist. Montgomery, Alabama. A black civil rights leader is wounded in a drive-by shooting.

June 15, 1961. *Assault.* White racist, Ku Klux Klan. Ocala, Florida. Freedom bus riders are attacked by Klansmen.

June 17, 1961. *Bombing/explosive.* White racist, Ku Klux Klan. Washington, D.C. Two bombs explode in roadside trash cans.

July 22, 1961. *Cross-burning.* White racist. Griffin, Georgia. A cross-burning occurs at a black home.

September 5, 1961. *Assault.* White racist. McComb, Mississippi. A black attempting to register to vote is assaulted.

September 25, 1961. *Shooting.* White racist. Liberty, Mississippi. Herbert Lee, a black civil rights worker, is shot and killed by a white legislator.

December 3, 1961. *Assault.* White racist. McComb, Mississippi. The white editor of a moderate newspaper is assaulted.

January 16, 1962. *Bombing/explosive.* White racist, Ku Klux Klan. Birmingham, Alabama. Three black churches are bombed.

February 18, 1962. *Bombing/explosive.* White racist. Shreveport, Louisiana. An NAACP official's home is bombed.

April 24, 1962. *Bombing/explosive.* White racist. Shreveport, Louisiana. A black Masonic building is bombed.

April 26, 1962. *Bombing/explosive.* White racist. Bossier City, Louisiana. An NAACP official's home is bombed.

April 27, 1962. *Shoot-out.* Black militant, Black Muslims. Los Angeles, California. In a shoot-out outside a Black Muslim mosque, a Black Muslim is killed, and 14 people are wounded; 8 of them are police officers.

July 1962. *Assault.* White racist. Greenwood, Mississippi. A Student Nonviolent Coordinating Committee (SNCC) volunteer is beaten.

August 16, 1962. *Assault.* White racist. Greenwood, Mississippi. An SNCC volunteer is beaten.

August 17, 1962. *Assault.* White racist. Greenwood, Mississippi. An SNCC office is attacked by armed men.

August 25, 1962. *Shooting.* White racist. Monroe, North Carolina. A freedom rider is wounded in a drive-by shooting.

August 27, 1962. *Shoot-out.* White racist. Monroe, North Carolina. Night riders attack a black neighborhood.

August 31, 1962. *Shooting.* White racist. Lee County, Georgia. Shots are fired at four black activists' homes.

September 5, 1962. *Shoot-out.* White racist. Dallas, Georgia. A black home is attacked by night riders. One white man is killed when the residents fire back.

September 5, 1962. *Shooting.* White racist. Dawson, Georgia. Shots are fired at a black activist's home, wounding him.

September 7, 1962. *Shooting.* White racist. New Orleans, Louisiana. A shooting occurs at an integrated school.

September 9, 1962. *Arson.* White racist. Sasser, Georgia. A black church is set on fire.

September 9, 1962. *Arson.* White racist. Chickasawatchee, Georgia. A black church is set on fire.

September 17, 1962. *Arson.* White racist. Dawson, Georgia. A black church is set on fire.

September 19, 1962. *Cross-burning.* White racist. Marksville, Louisiana. A cross-burning occurs outside a black home.

September 28, 1962. *Assault.* Rightist, Nazis. Birmingham, Alabama. Rev. Martin Luther King Jr. is assaulted by a Nazi at an NAACP meeting.

October 13, 1962. *Assault.* White racist, Ku Klux Klan. Birmingham, Alabama. A white man is beaten at a Klan rally.

November 1, 1962. *Shooting.* White racist. Pascagoula, Mississippi. Shots are fired at a liberal newspaper office.

December 14, 1962. *Bombing/explosive.* White racist. Birmingham, Alabama. A black church is bombed.

January 11, 1963. *Shooting.* White racist. Natchez, Mississippi. Shots are fired at an SNCC car.

February 24, 1963. *Shooting.* White racist. Greenville, Mississippi. Four blacks belonging to the SNCC are wounded when shots are fired at their car.

February 28, 1963. *Shooting.* White racist. Leflore, Mississippi. A black civil rights activist is shot.

March 1, 1963. *Shooting.* White racist. Greenwood, Mississippi. A black activist is shot and wounded.

March 2, 1963. *Shooting.* White racist. Greenwood, Mississippi. Shots are fired at the SNCC office.

March 6, 1963. *Shooting.* White racist. Greenwood, Mississippi. Four black civil rights activists are shot.

March 24, 1963. *Bombing/explosive.* White racist. Birmingham, Alabama. A black home is bombed, wounding two people.

March 24, 1963. *Bombing/incendiary.* White racist. Greenwood, Mississippi. The home of a black civil rights activist is bombed.

March 26, 1963. *Shooting.* White racist. Greenwood, Mississippi. A black civil rights activist is shot.

April 12, 1963. *Bombing/incendiary.* White racist. Clarksdale, Mississippi. The home of black civil rights activist is bombed.

April 23, 1963. *Shooting.* White racist. Attalla, Alabama. A white civil rights activist, William Moore, is murdered while on a one-man march to protest segregation.

April 23, 1963. *Assault.* White racist. Clarksdale, Mississippi. A black civil rights activist is beaten.

April 24, 1963. *Bombing/explosive.* White racist. Clarksdale, Mississippi. A black civil rights activist's store is bombed.

May 12, 1963. *Shooting.* White racist. Anniston, Alabama. Shots are fired at black churches.

May 12, 1963. *Bombing/explosive.* White racist. Birmingham, Alabama. Two black civil rights activists' homes are bombed.

May 13, 1963. *Shooting.* White racist. Nashville, Tennessee. Shots are fired at a black civil rights activist.

May 27, 1963. *Bombing/explosive.* White racist. Jackson, Mississippi. A black civil rights activist's home is bombed.

June 5, 1963. *Assault.* White racist. Chattanooga, Tennessee. A black civil rights activist is beaten.

June 8, 1963. *Shooting.* White racist. Clarksdale, Mississippi. Shots are fired at an NAACP member.

June 11, 1963. *Assault.* White racist. Selma, Alabama. An NAACP officer is assaulted.

June 12, 1963. *Shooting.* White racist. Jackson, Mississippi. Medgar Evers, a black civil rights leader, is assassinated by Byron de la Beckwith, who appears to have acted on his own, although he later joins the Klan.

June 17, 1963. *Bombing/explosive.* White racist. Itta Bena, Mississippi. A black church is bombed.

June 18, 1963. *Bombing/explosive.* White racist. Gillett, Arkansas. A black church is bombed.

June 23, 1963. *Cross-burning.* White racist. Biloxi, Mississippi. A cross-burning occurs at a black civil rights worker's house.

June 24, 1963. *Shooting.* White racist. Canton, Mississippi. Shots are fired at the Council of Federated Organizations (COFO) headquarters.

June 26, 1963. *Bombing/explosive.* White racist. Gulfport, Mississippi. The home of an NAACP member is bombed.

June 30, 1963. *Bombing/explosive.* White racist. Jackson, Mississippi. A black home is bombed.

July 1, 1963. *Shooting.* White racist. St. Augustine, Florida. Shots are fired at a black civil rights activist.

July 28, 1963. *Shooting.* White racist. Ocala, Florida. Shots are fired at the home of an NAACP activist.

August 10, 1963. *Shooting.* White racist. Jersey City, New Jersey. A black man is shot and killed.

August 15, 1963. *Bombing/explosive.* White racist. Birmingham, Alabama. An integrated store is bombed.

August 20, 1963. *Bombing/explosive.* White racist. Birmingham, Alabama. A black civil rights activist's home is bombed.

August 27, 1963. *Bombing/explosive.* White racist. Columbia, South Carolina. A black civil rights activist's home is bombed.

August 27, 1963. *Bombing/explosive.* White racist. Burns, Louisiana. An integrated school is bombed.

August 31, 1963. *Bombing/explosive.* White racist. Jackson, Mississippi. A black home is bombed.

September 4, 1963. *Bombing/explosive.* White racist. Birmingham, Alabama. A black civil rights activist's home is bombed.

September 8, 1963. *Bombing/explosive.* White racist. Birmingham, Alabama. A black business is bombed.

September 15, 1963. *Shooting.* White racist, National States Rights Party. Birmingham, Alabama. After attending a National States Rights Party rally, two white teenagers shoot and kill Virgil Ware, a black teenager.

September 15, 1963. *Bombing/explosive.* White racist, Ku Klux Klan. Birmingham, Alabama. A black church is bombed, killing four schoolchildren. The victims are Addie Mae Collins, Denise McNair, Carole Robertson, and Cynthia Wesley.

September 18, 1963. *Assault.* White racist, Ku Klux Klan. St. Augustine, Florida. Four blacks are attacked by Klansmen.

September 25, 1963. *Bombing/explosive.* White racist. Birmingham, Alabama. Two black homes are bombed.

October 2, 1963. *Bombing/explosive.* White racist. Birmingham, Alabama. A black business is bombed.

October 25, 1963. *Shooting.* White racist, Ku Klux Klan. St. Augustine, Florida. After night riders invade a black neighborhood, they are fired at and William Kinnard, a Klansman, is killed.

October 28, 1963. *Shooting.* White racist, Ku Klux Klan. St. Augustine, Florida. Night riders fire shots into black homes.

November 16, 1963. *Bombing/explosive.* White racist. Tuscaloosa, Alabama. An integrated university is bombed.

December 8, 1963. *Shooting.* White racist. Dawson, Georgia. Shots are fired at a black civil rights activist.

December 22, 1963. *Arson.* White racist. Hot Springs, Arkansas. A black church is set on fire.

January 1, 1964. *Arson.* White racist. St. Augustine, Florida. The home of a black integrationist is set on fire.

January 31, 1964. *Shooting.* White racist. Liberty, Mississippi. Louis Allen, a black witness to the murder of a civil rights worker, is assassinated.

February 2, 1964. *Arson.* White racist. St. Augustine, Florida. The home of a black integrationist is set on fire.

February 8, 1964. *Shooting.* White racist. St. Augustine, Florida. Shots are fired at an NAACP official's house.

February 16, 1964. *Bombing/explosive.* White racist. Jacksonville, Florida. A black integrationist's home is bombed.

February 24, 1964. *Bombing/explosive.* White racist. Princess Anne, Maryland. A black home is bombed.

February 29, 1964. *Shooting.* White racist. Centerville, Mississippi. A black soldier on leave is shot and killed.

March 23, 1964. *Shooting.* White racist. St. Augustine, Florida. A black woman, Mae Chappell, is shot and killed.

April 5, 1964. *Shooting.* White racist. Natchez, Mississippi. One black is shot and wounded.

April 18, 1964. *Assault.* White racist. Bogalusa, Louisiana. A white integrationist is attacked.

April 18, 1964. *Arson.* White racist. Notasulga, Alabama. A fire is set at a desegregated school.

April 19, 1964. *Assault.* White racist. Jackson, Louisiana. A white news reporter is assaulted.

April 28, 1964. *Bombing/explosive.* White racist. McComb, Mississippi. The NAACP office is bombed.

May 2, 1964. *Shooting.* White racist, Ku Klux Klan. Meadville, Mississippi. Two blacks, Henry Dee and Charles Moore, are murdered by the Klan.

May 10, 1964. *Bombing/explosive.* White racist. Laurel, Mississippi. The office of a moderate newspaper is bombed.

May 29, 1964. *Shooting.* White racist. St. Augustine, Florida. Shots are fired at two Southern Christian Leadership Conference (SCLC) workers.

June 1, 1964. *Cross-burning.* White racist. Canton, Mississippi. A cross-burning occurs at the house of a white integrationist.

June 8, 1964. *Bombing/explosive.* White racist. McComb, Mississippi. A black home is bombed.

June 9, 1964. *Assault.* White racist, Ku Klux Klan. St. Augustine, Florida. A black man is assaulted by Klansmen.

June 16, 1964. *Assault.* White racist. Greenwood, Mississippi. A black civil rights activist is beaten.

June 18, 1964. *Arson.* White racist. Philadelphia, Mississippi. A black church is set on fire. The church was also a Freedom School.

June 20, 1964. *Bombing/explosive.* White racist. McComb, Mississippi. Five black homes are bombed.

June 21, 1964. *Shooting.* White racist, Ku Klux Klan. Philadelphia, Mississippi. Three civil rights workers, James Chaney, Andrew Goodman, and Michael Schwerner, are killed by Klansmen.

June 21, 1964. *Shooting.* White racist, Ku Klux Klan. Athens, Georgia. Two blacks are shot.

June 21, 1964. *Bombing/incendiary.* White racist. Brandon, Mississippi. A Molotov cocktail explodes in the basement of a black church, causing minor damage.

June 22, 1964. *Bombing/explosive.* White racist. McComb, Mississippi. The homes of two black civil rights activists are bombed.

June 23, 1964. *Shooting.* White racist. Jackson, Mississippi. Shots are fired at a black minister's home.

June 23, 1964. *Bombing.* White racist. Moss Point, Mississippi. A hall used for voter registration is firebombed.

June 24, 1964. *Shooting.* White racist. Canton, Mississippi. A car driven by a civil rights worker is hit by bullets.

June 25, 1964. *Bombing/incendiary.* White racist. Longdale, Mississippi. A black church is firebombed.

June 26, 1964. *Bombing/explosive.* White racist, Ku Klux Klan. McComb, Mississippi. A newspaper office is bombed.

June 26, 1964. *Arson.* White racist. Clinton, Mississippi. A black church is firebombed and set on fire.

June 28, 1964. *Assault.* White racist. Jackson, Mississippi. A white civil rights worker is attacked when he arrives at a local train station.

June 28, 1964. *Assault.* White racist. Bateville, Mississippi. A black man is kidnapped and beaten.

June 29, 1964. *Shooting.* White racist. Hattiesburg, Mississippi. Shots are fired at a civil rights worker's car.

July 2, 1964. *Shooting.* White racist. Vicksburg, Mississippi. Whites shoot at a black motorcyclist.

July 3, 1964. *Bombing/explosive.* White racist. Soso, Mississippi. A black cafe is bombed.

July 5, 1964. *Assault.* White racist. Tougaloo, Mississippi. A black civil rights activist is assaulted.

July 5, 1964. *Assault.* White racist. Greenwood, Mississippi. A black civil rights activist is assaulted.

July 6, 1964. *Shooting.* White racist. Moss Point, Mississippi. One black is shot and wounded.

July 6, 1964. *Arson.* White racist. Raleigh, Mississippi. Two black churches are set on fire.

July 6, 1964. *Arson.* White racist. Jackson, Mississippi. A black church is set on fire.

July 7, 1964. *Arson.* White racist. Bovina, Mississippi. A black home is set on fire.

July 9, 1964. *Bombing/explosive.* White racist. McComb, Mississippi. Two people are wounded when the SNCC Freedom House is bombed.

July 10, 1964. *Assault.* White racist. Hattiesburg, Mississippi. Three white civil rights workers are assaulted.

July 11, 1964. *Shooting.* White racist, Ku Klux Klan. Colbert, Georgia. Lt. Col. Lemuel Penn, a black man, is killed while driving his car.

July 11, 1964. *Arson.* White racist. Browning, Mississippi. A black church is set on fire.

July 11, 1964. *Bombing/explosive.* White racist. Canton, Mississippi. The Freedom House is bombed.

July 11, 1964. *Assault.* White racist. Greenwood, Mississippi. A black civil rights activist is assaulted.

July 12, 1964. *Arson.* White racist. Natchez, Mississippi. A black church is set on fire.

July 12, 1964. *Arson.* White racist. Kingston, Mississippi. Two black churches are set on fire.

July 16, 1964. *Assault.* White racist. Greenwood, Mississippi. A black civil rights activist is assaulted.

July 17, 1964. *Arson.* White racist. McComb, Mississippi. A black church is set on fire.

July 17, 1964. *Assault.* White racist, Ku Klux Klan. Philadelphia, Mississippi. A civil rights worker is beaten with a lead pipe.

July 17, 1964. *Arson.* White racist. McComb, Mississippi. A church is burned to the ground.

July 19, 1964. *Arson.* White racist. Madison, Mississippi. A black church is set on fire.

July 20, 1964. *Assault.* White racist. Hattiesburg, Mississippi. A white civil rights worker is beaten.

July 20, 1964. *Shooting.* White racist. Greenville, Mississippi. Shots are fired at a car carrying civil rights workers.

July 20, 1964. *Shooting.* White racist. Greenwood, Mississippi. A shotgun is fired at a civil rights activist while he is driving a car.

July 21, 1964. *Assault.* White racist. Tchula, Mississippi. An SNCC official is assaulted.

July 21, 1964. *Assault.* White racist. Lexington, Mississippi. A black civil rights activist is assaulted.

July 22, 1964. *Arson.* White racist. McComb, Mississippi. Two black churches are set on fire.

July 24, 1964. *Bombing/explosive.* White racist, Ku Klux Klan. St. Augustine, Florida. An integrated motel is bombed.

July 25, 1964. *Bombing/incendiary.* White racist. Hattiesburg, Mississippi. The homes of the leaders of the Freedom Democratic Party are firebombed.

July 25, 1964. *Shooting.* White racist. Greenwood, Mississippi. Shots are fired at the home of a black civil rights activist.

July 26, 1964. *Bombing/explosive.* White racist. McComb, Mississippi. The home of a black civil rights activist is bombed. His wife fires at the car driven by the bombers.

July 26, 1964. *Bombing.* White racist. Batesville, Mississippi. A tear-gas grenade explodes outside the house where five civil rights workers are living.

July 26, 1964. *Arson.* White racist. Milestown, Mississippi. An SNCC car is destroyed by fire.

July 29, 1964. *Arson.* White racist. Meridian, Mississippi. A black church is burned to the ground.

July 30, 1964. *Bombing/explosive.* White racist. Batesville, Mississippi. The home of a civil rights worker is bombed.

July 30, 1964. *Arson.* White racist. Brandon, Mississippi. A black church is totally destroyed by fire.

July 31, 1964. *Assault.* White racist. Brandon, Mississippi. A white civil rights worker is badly beaten and blinded in one eye.

August 2, 1964. *Shooting.* White racist. Natchez, Mississippi. Shots are fired at a black business. The owner had participated in a voter-registration drive.

August 2, 1964. *Shooting.* White racist. Canton, Mississippi. Shots are fired from a car at the Freedom House.

August 2, 1964. *Shooting.* White racist. Greenwood, Mississippi. Shots are fired at the SNCC office.

August 4, 1964. *Shooting and arson.* White racist. Natchez, Mississippi. Shots are fired at a black church. Later that night, the church is set on fire.

August 4, 1964. *Shooting.* White racist. Jackson, Mississippi. Two shots are fired at a civil rights worker from a pickup truck.

August 9, 1964. *Bombing/explosive.* White racist. Mileton, Mississippi. A black community center is bombed.

August 9, 1964. *Bombing.* White racist. Aberdeen, Mississippi. Tear-gas canisters are thrown at the Freedom House.

August 10, 1964. *Arson.* White racist. Gluckstadt, Mississippi. A black church is set on fire. It had been the site of a Freedom School.

August 11, 1964. *Assault.* White racist, Ku Klux Klan. Oakridge, Mississippi. Three supporters of the Mississippi Freedom Democratic Party, a black alternative to the segregationist Democratic Party, were beaten by hooded Klansmen.

August 11, 1964. *Arson.* White racist. Brandon, Mississippi. The Freedom School is set on fire.

August 12, 1964. *Shooting.* White racist. Ocean Springs, Mississippi. In two separate incidents, black men are fired at from a car.

August 14, 1964. *Bombing/explosive.* White racist. McComb, Mississippi. A bomb explodes in a supermarket across from the site of a Freedom House.

August 14, 1964. *Bombing/explosive.* White racist. Natchez, Mississippi. A business belonging to an interracial married couple is bombed.

August 15, 1964. *Shooting.* White racist. Jasper, Mississippi. SNCC workers are fired at while they were driving along the highway.

August 15, 1964. *Shooting.* White racist. Greenwood, Mississippi. A black civil rights activist is shot and wounded as he sits in his parked car.

August 15, 1964. *Shooting.* White racist. Jackson, Mississippi. Shots are fired at civil rights workers.

August 16, 1964. *Assault.* White racist. Laurel, Mississippi. A white civil rights worker is beaten unconscious by two white men.

August 17, 1964. *Assault.* White racist. Gulfport, Mississippi. A civil rights worker is badly beaten.

August 18, 1964. *Bombing/incendiary.* White racist. Vicksburg, Mississippi. A business belonging to a member of the Mississippi Freedom Democratic Party is firebombed.

August 19, 1964. *Arson.* White racist. Collinsville, Mississippi. A black church is set on fire.

August 22, 1964. *Assault.* White racist. Laurel, Mississippi. A dozen armed white men beat civil rights workers with clubs and chains.

August 23, 1964. *Arson.* White racist. Tupelo, Mississippi. The voter registration headquarters is set on fire; the damage is moderate.

August 25, 1964. *Shooting.* White racist. Madison, Florida. Shots are fired at a civil rights worker.

August 26, 1964. *Shooting.* White racist. Canton, Mississippi. A civil rights worker is shot at from a car.

August 27, 1964. *Bombing/explosive.* White racist. Jackson, Mississippi. A newspaper office is bombed.

August 30, 1964. *Arson.* White racist. Sterling, Kentucky. The NAACP office is set on fire.

September 1, 1964. *Bombing/explosive.* White racist. Holly Springs, Mississippi. A black college is bombed.

September 7, 1964. *Bombing/explosive.* White racist. Summit, Mississippi. A black home is bombed.

September 7, 1964. *Bombing/explosive.* White racist. Auburn, Mississippi. A black church is bombed.

September 7, 1964. *Bombing/explosive.* White racist, Ku Klux Klan. Bogue, Mississippi. A black business is bombed.

September 7, 1964. *Shooting.* White racist, Ku Klux Klan. Pickens, Mississippi. A black teenager, Herbert Oarsby, who was a member of the Congress of Racial Equality (CORE), is killed.

September 7, 1964. *Bombing/explosive.* White racist. Magnolia, Mississippi. A black home is bombed.

September 9, 1964. *Bombing/explosive.* White racist. McComb, Mississippi. A black church is bombed.

September 10, 1964. *Bombing/explosive.* White racist. Jackson, Mississippi. A black church is bombed.

September 13, 1964. *Bombing/explosive.* White racist. Vidalia, Mississippi. The homes of white liberals are bombed.

September 14, 1964. *Bombing/explosive.* White racist. Natchez, Mississippi. The homes of white liberals are bombed.

September 19, 1964. *Bombing/incendiary.* White racist. Canton, Mississippi. Five black churches are bombed.

September 23, 1964. *Bombing/explosive.* White racist. McComb, Mississippi. A black home is bombed.

September 25, 1964. *Bombing/explosive.* White racist. Natchez, Mississippi. The homes of white liberals are bombed.

September 27, 1964. *Bombing/explosive.* White racist. Jackson, Mississippi. A black business is bombed.

October 4, 1964. *Bombing/explosive.* White racist. Vicksburg, Mississippi. A black church is bombed.

October 4, 1964. *Shooting.* White racist. Meridian, Mississippi. A civil rights worker is shot and wounded.

October 24, 1964. *Shooting.* White racist. Marks, Mississippi. Shots are fired at the Freedom Democratic Party office.

October 28, 1964. *Bombing/explosive.* White racist. Indianola, Mississippi. The SNCC Freedom House is bombed.

October 29, 1964. *Shooting.* White racist. Ruleville, Mississippi. Shots are fired at a store belonging to a black civil rights activist.

October 31, 1964. *Bombing/explosive.* White racist. Ripley, Mississippi. The Freedom School is bombed.

November 1, 1964. *Shooting.* White racist. McComb, Mississippi. Shots are fired at a newspaper office.

November 5, 1964. *Assault.* Black militant, Black Muslims. New York City, New York. Kenneth Morton, a Black Muslim who had left the group, is beaten to death.

November 17, 1964. *Assault.* White racist, Ku Klux Klan. Laurel, Mississippi. Two civil rights workers are assaulted by Klansmen.

November 29, 1964. *Bombing/explosive.* White racist. Montgomery, Alabama. A black home is bombed.

December 10, 1964. *Arson.* White racist, Ku Klux Klan. Ferriday, Louisiana. A black home is set on fire, killing Frank Morris.

January 1, 1965. *Bombing/explosive.* White racist. Charlotte, North Carolina. A civil rights worker's car is bombed.

January 15, 1965. *Assault.* White racist, Ku Klux Klan. Laurel, Mississippi. A civil rights worker is assaulted by Klansmen.

January 15, 1965. *Assault.* White racist, National States Rights Party. Selma, Alabama. Rev. Martin Luther King Jr. is assaulted by members of the National States Rights Party.

January 17, 1965. *Bombing/explosive.* White racist. Jonesboro, Louisiana. Two black churches are bombed.

January 22, 1965. *Bombing/explosive.* White racist. Brandon, Mississippi. A black church is bombed.

January 24, 1965. *Bombing/explosive.* White racist, Ku Klux Klan. New Bern, North Carolina. An NAACP meeting at a black church is bombed.

February 3, 1965. *Assault.* White racist, Ku Klux Klan. Bogalusa, Louisiana. A civil rights worker is assaulted by Klansmen.

February 12, 1965. *Shooting.* Black militant. Atlanta, Georgia. Shots are fired at police, wounding one officer.

February 14, 1965. *Bombing/explosive.* Black militant, Black Muslims. New York City, New York. Malcolm X's house is bombed.

February 16, 1965. *Attempted bombing.* Black militant. New York City, New York. Three black men and a white woman are arrested. They planned to blow up the Statue of Liberty.

February 16, 1965. *Shooting.* White racist. Mobile, Alabama. Two blacks are shot and wounded.

February 17, 1965. *Bombing/explosive.* White racist, Ku Klux Klan. Laurel, Mississippi. A bomb explodes outside COFO headquarters.

February 21, 1965. *Shooting.* Black militant, Black Muslims. New York City, New York. Malcolm X is shot and killed as he starts to address a rally of his newly formed Afro-American Unity organization. His killers are Black Muslims.

February 23, 1965. *Arson.* Black militant, Black Muslims. New York City, New York. A Black Muslim mosque is set on fire, possibly by supporters of Malcolm X in revenge for his murder.

February 23, 1965. *Arson.* Black militant, Black Muslims. San Francisco, California. A Black Muslim mosque is set on fire, possibly by supporters of Malcolm X in revenge for his murder.

February 24, 1965. *Shooting.* White racist. Mobile, Alabama. A black civil rights worker is shot.

March 1965. *Arson.* White racist, Ku Klux Klan. Laurel, Mississippi. A civil rights activist's home is set on fire.

March 2, 1965. *Shooting.* White racist, Ku Klux Klan. Bessemer, Alabama. A black worker is shot.

March 4, 1965. *Bombing/explosive.* White racist, Ku Klux Klan. Ellisville, Mississippi. A black home is bombed.

March 5, 1965. *Arson.* White racist. Indianola, Mississippi. A Freedom School is destroyed by fire.

March 6, 1965. *Shooting.* White racist, Ku Klux Klan. Bessemer, Alabama. A black worker is shot and wounded.

March 9, 1965. *Assault.* White racist. Selma, Alabama. James Reeb, a white minister and civil rights marcher, is beaten to death.

March 10, 1965. *Shooting.* White racist, Ku Klux Klan. Bessemer, Alabama. A black worker is shot.

March 13, 1965. *Assault.* Black militant, Black Muslims. New York City, New York. Louis Ameer, a supporter of Malcolm X, is found murdered in his hotel room.

March 21, 1965. *Bombing/incendiary.* White racist, Ku Klux Klan. Vicksburg, Mississippi. An integrated cafe is firebombed.

March 21, 1965. *Attempted bombing.* White racist, Ku Klux Klan. Birmingham, Alabama. Time bombs are found in black neighborhoods.

March 23, 1965. *Shooting.* White racist, Ku Klux Klan. Selma, Alabama. Viola Liuzzo is shot and killed by a passing car. She was driving back from a civil rights march with a black passenger.

March 25, 1965. *Shooting.* Black militant. Atlanta, Georgia. A sniper fires shots at the State Capitol.

March 29, 1965. *Bombing/incendiary.* White racist. Meridian, Mississippi. Two black churches are firebombed.

April 1, 1965. *Bombing/incendiary and attempted bombing.* White racist, Ku Klux Klan. Birmingham, Alabama. The Klan is suspected of bombing the home of a black accountant and the attempted bombing of the homes of the mayor and a city councilwoman.

April 2, 1965. *Shooting.* White racist, Ku Klux Klan. Bessemer, Alabama. A black civil rights worker is shot.

April 7, 1965. *Shooting.* White racist, Ku Klux Klan. Bogalusa, Louisiana. Shots are fired at black civil rights workers.

April 9, 1965. *Shooting.* Black militant. Atlanta, Georgia. Three police officers are wounded by snipers.

April 10, 1965. *Shooting.* White racist. Jonesboro, Louisiana. A black motorist is shot.

April 23, 1965. *Arson.* White racist, Ku Klux Klan. Ellisville, Mississippi. A black home is set on fire.

May 1, 1965. *Bombing/incendiary.* White racist. Indianola, Mississippi. Three black homes are bombed.

May 1, 1965. *Bombing/incendiary.* White racist. Indianola, Mississippi. The Freedom House is bombed.

May 9, 1965. *Assault.* White racist, Ku Klux Klan. Bogalusa, Louisiana. Black civil rights demonstrators are assaulted.

May 11, 1965. *Bombing/incendiary.* White racist, Ku Klux Klan. New Orleans, Louisiana. A Unitarian church is bombed.

May 12, 1965. *Bombing/incendiary.* White racist, Ku Klux Klan. New Orleans, Louisiana. An American Civil Liberties Union (ACLU) car is bombed.

May 13, 1965. *Bombing/explosive.* White racist. Oxford, Alabama. A black church is bombed.

May 16, 1965. *Arson.* White racist, Ku Klux Klan. Laurel, Mississippi. A black store is set on fire.

May 16, 1965. *Shooting.* White racist, Ku Klux Klan. Laurel, Mississippi. Shots are fired at a black nightclub.

May 16, 1965. *Shooting.* White racist, Ku Klux Klan. Laurel, Mississippi. Shots are fired at an NAACP official.

May 17, 1965. *Arson.* White racist, Ku Klux Klan. Laurel, Mississippi. Two businesses owned by opponents of the Klan are set on fire.

May 26, 1965. *Assault.* White racist, Ku Klux Klan. Crawfordsville, Georgia. A black civil rights worker is assaulted.

May 29, 1965. *Bombing/explosive.* Revolutionary leftist. Lebanon, Missouri. Radio station KLWT is bombed, causing an estimated damage of $3000.

June 2, 1965. *Shooting.* White racist, Ku Klux Klan. Bogalusa, Louisiana. A black deputy sheriff, Oneal Moore, is killed, and another deputy is wounded.

June 14, 1965. *Bombing/incendiary.* White racist. Vicksburg, Mississippi. A white integrationist's home is bombed.

June 15, 1965. *Shooting.* White racist. Laurel, Mississippi. Shots are fired at the home of a civil rights leader, wounding two people.

June 19, 1965. *Arson.* White racist, Ku Klux Klan. Jones County, Mississippi. A black home is set on fire.

July 1, 1965. *Arson.* White racist, Ku Klux Klan. Jones County, Mississippi. An integrated restaurant is set on fire.

July 1, 1965. *Arson.* White racist. Mount Olive, Mississippi. Three white moderates' homes are set on fire.

July 1, 1965. *Bombing/explosive.* White racist, Ku Klux Klan. Sharon, Mississippi. A Klan opponent's barn is bombed.

July 1, 1965. *Arson.* White racist, Ku Klux Klan. Laurel, Mississippi. Three civil rights activists' homes are set on fire.

July 1, 1965. *Arson.* White racist, Ku Klux Klan. Laurel, Mississippi. COFO headquarters is set on fire.

July 3, 1965. *Arson.* White racist, Ku Klux Klan. Laurel, Mississippi. A black activist's home is set on fire.

July 15, 1965. *Shooting.* White racist. Anniston, Alabama. Willis Brewster, a black man, is shot dead by whites in a passing car.

July 18, 1965. *Arson.* White racist. Elmwood, Alabama. A black church is set on fire.

July 18, 1965. *Arson.* White racist. Greensboro, Alabama. Two black churches are set on fire.

July 19, 1965. *Arson.* White racist, Ku Klux Klan. Laurel, Mississippi. A Klan opponent's home is set on fire.

July 20, 1965. *Arson and shooting.* White racist, Ku Klux Klan. Columbia, Mississippi. The headquarters of COFO, a civil rights group, is damaged by fire and riddled with bullets.

July 27, 1965. *Bombing/explosive.* White racist. New Orleans, Louisiana. The offices of CORE are bombed.

July 27, 1965. *Bombing/incendiary.* White racist. Ferriday, Louisiana. Firebombs are thrown into two black homes.

July 31, 1965. *Shooting.* White racist. Columbia, Mississippi. Shots are fired at the civil rights headquarters.

August 3, 1965. *Arson.* White racist. Slidell, Louisiana. Two black churches are burned.

August 7, 1965. *Shooting.* White racist. Jackson, Alabama. Shots are fired at integrated restaurants.

August 8, 1965. *Shooting.* White racist, Ku Klux Klan. West Point, Mississippi. Shots are fired at a civil rights activist's home.

August 8, 1965. *Arson.* White racist, Ku Klux Klan. Valewood, Mississippi. The Head Start office is set on fire.

August 10, 1965. *Shooting.* White racist, Ku Klux Klan. Sharon, Mississippi. Shots are fired at a white minister's home. He had spoken out against the Klan.

August 11, 1965. *Bombing/explosive.* White racist. Baton Rouge, Louisiana. A motel housing civil rights workers is bombed.

August 16, 1965. *Assault.* White racist, Ku Klux Klan. Meadville, Mississippi. An informer is beaten to death.

August 18, 1965. *Shoot-out.* Black militant, Black Muslims. Los Angeles, California. A clash at a mosque between Black Muslims and police leaves four people injured.

August 20, 1965. *Shooting.* White racist, Ku Klux Klan. Hayneville, Alabama. Two white civil rights workers are shot.

August 22, 1965. *Assault.* Black militant. Greensboro, Alabama. An elderly black man opposed to civil rights demonstrations is found beaten and his tongue cut out.

August 22, 1965. *Shooting.* White racist. Jackson, Mississippi. A white minister active in the civil rights campaign is seriously wounded by shotgun blasts at his apartment.

August 25, 1965. *Bombing/explosive.* White racist. Baton Rouge, Louisiana. A black nightclub is bombed.

August 26, 1965. *Assault.* White racist, Ku Klux Klan. Plymouth, North Carolina. Civil rights workers are beaten after a Klan rally.

August 27, 1965. *Bombing/explosive.* White racist. Natchez, Mississippi. A bomb explodes in an NAACP leader's car, seriously injuring him.

September 2, 1965. *Bombing/explosive.* White racist. Laurel, Mississippi. A COFO truck is bombed.

September 5, 1965. *Shooting.* White racist. Forrest, Mississippi. Shots are fired at a black integrationist's home.

September 7, 1965. *Shooting.* White racist, Ku Klux Klan. Aberdeen, Mississippi. Shots are fired at a black home. The parents had enrolled their son in a previously all-white school.

September 9, 1965. *Bombing/explosive.* White racist. McComb, Mississippi. A hand grenade is thrown at two black workers who were building a patio.

September 14, 1965. *Arson.* White racist, Ku Klux Klan. Sandersville, Mississippi. A black home is set on fire.

September 16, 1965. *Shooting.* White racist. Laurel, Mississippi. Shots are fired at an NAACP official's home.

September 26, 1965. *Arson.* White racist. Jones County, Mississippi. A black church is set on fire.

September 29, 1965. *Assault and cross-burning.* White racist. Conway, North Carolina. A local union official active in voter registration is beaten, and a cross is burned outside his house.

October 1965. *Arson.* White racist. Wetumpka, Alabama. The home of a black woman who was active in school desegregation is burned to the ground.

October 4, 1965. *Assault.* White racist, Ku Klux Klan. Crawfordville, Georgia. A black demonstrator is assaulted by Klansmen.

October 5, 1965. *Bombing/explosive.* White racist. Swansboro, North Carolina. A migrant workers' dormitory is dynamited.

October 10, 1965. *Arson.* White racist. Lakewood, New Jersey. Two black homes in a white neighborhood are set on fire.

October 11, 1965. *Shooting.* White racist. Laurel, Mississippi. Shots are fired at a black home.

October 12, 1965. *Assault.* White racist, Ku Klux Klan. Crawfordville, Georgia. A Klansman assaults an SCLC photographer.

October 12, 1965. *Arson.* White racist. Colerain, North Carolina. An integrated school is set on fire.

October 16, 1965. *Bombing/explosive.* White racist. Wise Forks, North Carolina. A dynamite blast occurs outside a black home.

October 17, 1965. *Assault.* White racist, Ku Klux Klan. Crawfordville, Georgia. A black motorist is assaulted by Klansmen.

October 25, 1965. *Bombing/explosive.* White racist. Smithfield, North Carolina. A black school is dynamited.

October 26, 1965. *Shooting.* White racist. Laurel, Mississippi. Shots are fired at a black school.

October 31, 1965. *Shooting.* White racist. Norfolk, Virginia. Two black men are wounded by a shotgun blast fired from a passing car as they leave a civil rights rally.

October 31, 1965. *Bombing/explosive.* White racist. Vanceboro, North Carolina. A black church is dynamited.

November 7, 1965. *Shooting.* White racist. Detroit, Michigan. A black man is shot and killed by white youths in a car.

November 8, 1965. *Arson.* White racist. Georgia. Three black churches are burned down.

November 8, 1965. *Shooting.* Black militant. Fayetteville, North Carolina. Three heavily armed black Marines belonging to the "National Abolitionist Forces" terrorize the area for several hours before being arrested.

November 8, 1965. *Bombing/explosive.* White racist, Ku Klux Klan. Baton Rouge, Louisiana. A printing shop is destroyed by an explosion, shortly after the owner refused to print literature for the Klan.

November 18, 1965. *Shooting.* White racist. Victoria, Virginia. Shots are fired at civil rights workers, wounding one.

November 19, 1965. *Shooting.* White racist. Livingston, Louisiana. White men in a car shoot at a black man in a car.

November 21, 1965. *Bombing/incendiary.* White racist. Ferriday, Louisiana. A gasoline bomb damages a civil rights leader's home.

November 22, 1965. *Bombing/explosive.* White racist. Charlotte, North Carolina. The homes of four black activists are bombed.

November 26, 1965. *Bombing/incendiary.* Revolutionary leftist. Salem, Indiana. The homes of two John Birch Society officials are bombed.

November 29, 1965. *Bombing/explosive.* White racist. Vicksburg, Mississippi. The car bombing of a black grocery store injures three.

December 15, 1965. *Shooting.* White racist, Ku Klux Klan. Hamburg, Arkansas. A black man, Lee Culbreath, is murdered by the Klan.

December 15, 1965. *Shooting.* White racist. Meridian, Mississippi. Shots are fired at the home of a black student who enrolled in a previously all-white school.

December 19, 1965. *Shooting.* Unknown. Marin City, California. Shots are fired at a police car.

December 25, 1965. *Shooting.* White racist. Deerfield, Florida. Three whites in a car drive by a black tavern and spray it with gunfire, wounding seven persons.

December 31, 1965. *Arson.* White racist, Ku Klux Klan. Natchez, Mississippi. A business belonging to a white opponent of the Klan is burned down.

January 2, 1966. *Arson.* White racist. Newton, Georgia. A black church is burned.

January 3, 1966. *Cross-burning.* White racist, Ku Klux Klan. Mississippi. Cross-burnings occur in nine counties.

January 3, 1966. *Shooting.* White racist. Tuskegee, Alabama. Samuel Younge, a black civil rights activist, is killed in a dispute over a whites-only restroom.

January 10, 1966. *Bombing/incendiary.* White racist, Ku Klux Klan. Hattiesburg, Mississippi. Vernon Dahmer, a black civil rights leader, is killed by a firebomb.

January 23, 1966. *Shooting.* White racist. Camden, Alabama. David Colston, a black man, is shot and killed.

February 2, 1966. *Shooting.* White racist, Ku Klux Klan. Kosciusco, Mississippi. The home of civil rights workers is the target of shotgun blasts.

February 6, 1966. *Bombing/explosive.* White racist. Zachary, Louisiana. A black home is bombed.

February 19, 1966. *Bombing/explosive.* White racist. Neshoba, Mississippi. A black church is dynamited.

February 21, 1966. *Shooting.* White racist. Birmingham, Alabama. Shots fired by a white motorist wound five blacks who were picketing a store.

February 24, 1966. *Bombing/explosive.* White racist. Elba, Alabama. A bomb explodes at an integrated school.

April 2, 1966. *Bombing/explosive.* White racist. Baton Rouge, Louisiana. An integrated pool is bombed.

April 2, 1966. *Bombing/explosive.* Cuban. Miami, Florida. The editor of an anti-Castro newspaper, *Patria,* is injured when his car is bombed.

April 9, 1966. *Bombing/explosive.* White racist. Ernul, North Carolina. A black church is bombed.

April 18, 1966. *Bombing/explosive.* Cuban. Miami, Florida. An explosion blows out the windows of the home of the ex-minister of finance in the Cuban government.

May 1966. *Shooting.* Rightist, Nazis. Michigan. Leo Bernard, a Socialist Workers Party member, is murdered.

May 21, 1966. *Arson.* Revolutionary leftist. Washington, D.C. The American Nazi Party headquarters is damaged by fire.

May 21, 1966. *Shooting.* Black militant. Chicago, Illinois. Two police officers are wounded by snipers.

June 6, 1966. *Shooting.* White racist. Hernando, Mississippi. An ambush wounds a black civil rights marcher.

June 10, 1966. *Shooting.* White racist, Ku Klux Klan. Natchez, Mississippi. Ben Chester White, a black man, is killed by the Klan.

June 21, 1966. *Shooting.* White racist. Philadelphia, Pennsylvania. Shots are fired at four black homes.

June 22, 1966. *Bombing/explosive.* White racist. Canton, Mississippi. The civil rights headquarters is bombed.

June 24, 1966. *Arson.* White racist. Carthage, Mississippi. A Catholic church is set on fire.

June 28, 1966. *Shoot-out.* White racist. Cordele, Georgia. There is a shoot-out between blacks and whites over a desegregated swimming pool.

July 1, 1966. *Bombing/explosive.* White racist, Ku Klux Klan. Milwaukee, Wisconsin. A store owned by a civil rights leader is bombed.

July 9, 1966. *Shooting.* White racist. Grenada, Mississippi. Two white civil rights workers are shot entering a black church.

July 19, 1966. *Shooting.* White racist. Cleveland, Ohio. A black man is killed by sniper fire.

July 20, 1966. *Bombing/explosive.* White racist, Ku Klux Klan. Jacksonville, Florida. A black store is bombed.

July 22, 1966. *Shooting.* White racist. Cleveland, Ohio. A black man is shot by whites in a passing car.

July 30, 1966. *Shooting.* White racist. Bogalusa, Louisiana. A black man, Clarence Triggs, is killed by night riders.

August 6, 1966. *Shooting.* Black militant. Chicago, Illinois. Police are fired on by snipers; there are no injuries.

August 9, 1966. *Bombing.* White racist. Milwaukee, Wisconsin. The NAACP office is bombed.

August 10, 1966. *Shooting.* White racist. Detroit, Michigan. One black is wounded in a drive-by shooting.

August 11, 1966. *Bombing/explosive.* White racist. Carthage, Mississippi. A black civil rights worker's home is bombed.

August 15, 1966. *Bombing/incendiary.* White racist. Providence, Rhode Island. A black church is bombed.

August 30, 1966. *Shooting.* White racist. Benton Harbor, Michigan. A black man is wounded in a drive-by shooting.

September 1, 1966. *Shooting.* White racist. Dayton, Ohio. Lester Mitchell, a black man, is killed when shots are fired from a passing car driven by whites.

September 10, 1966. *Shooting.* White racist. Atlanta, Georgia. One black is killed and another is wounded by a white gunman.

September 17, 1966. *Assault.* White racist. New Rochelle, New York. Rev. Melvin Dewitt Bullock, an NAACP leader, is beaten to death.

September 24, 1966. *Arson.* White racist. Cleveland, Ohio. A black home is set on fire.

October 5, 1966. *Bombing/explosive.* White racist. Richmond, Virginia. A black church is bombed.

January 3, 1967. *Bombing/explosive.* Revolutionary leftist. Cincinnati, Ohio. A bomb explodes in the Delta Savings and Loan Company bank.

January 15, 1967. *Arson.* White racist. New York City, New York. A black home is set on fire.

January 21, 1967. *Arson.* White racist. Collins, Mississippi. A black church is burned down.

January 23, 1967. *Arson.* White racist. Grenada, Mississippi. A black church is set on fire.

January 29, 1967. *Shooting.* White racist. Atlanta, Georgia. A black woman is shot and killed.

January 29, 1967. *Bombing/explosive.* Croatian. Washington, D.C. The Yugoslav Embassy is bombed.

February 6, 1967. *Bombing/explosive.* Croatian. Washington, D.C. The Yugoslav Embassy is bombed.

February 11, 1967. *Shooting.* White racist, Ku Klux Klan. Meridian, Mississippi. Shots are fired at an ex-Klansman's house.

February 27, 1967. *Bombing/explosive.* White racist, Ku Klux Klan. Natchez, Mississippi. Wharlest Jackson, an NAACP official, is killed by a bomb. He had just been promoted to a "white job."

March 4, 1967. *Arson.* White racist. Grenada, Mississippi. A black church is set on fire.

March 12, 1967. *Arson.* White racist. Hayneville, Mississippi. A black church is set on fire.

March 13, 1967. *Bombing/explosive.* White racist. Liberty, Mississippi. The Head Start office is bombed.

March 13, 1967. *Arson.* White racist. Fort Deposit, Alabama. A black church is set on fire.

April 3, 1967. *Bombing/explosive.* Cuban. New York City, New York. One person is wounded by a bombing at the Cuban Mission to the United Nations (UN).

April 25, 1967. *Bombing/explosive.* White racist. Montgomery, Alabama. The home of the mother of a desegregation judge is bombed.

May 14, 1967. *Bombing/incendiary.* White racist. Cleveland, Ohio. A black home is firebombed.

May 16, 1967. *Shoot-out.* Black militant. Houston, Texas. Police officer Louis Kuba is shot to death in a gun battle at Texas Southern University.

June 5, 1967. *Escape.* Other foreign. Tierra Amarilla, New Mexico. The courthouse is raided by armed men who free 11 prisoners who had been arrested when they tried to regain control of land granted to their ancestors by the Spanish crown.

June 11, 1967. *Shooting.* Black militant. Prattville, Alabama. Gunfire is exchanged between police and snipers.

June 20, 1967. *Bombing/explosive.* White racist, Ku Klux Klan. McComb, Mississippi. Bombs explode at four black homes and a barbershop.

June 28, 1967. *Bombing/explosive.* White racist. Mobile, Alabama. A black civil rights worker's home is bombed.

June 28, 1967. *Bombing/explosive.* Revolutionary leftist. Berkeley, California. The Berkeley draft board is bombed, causing an estimated damage of $500.

July 16, 1967. *Bombing/incendiary.* Black militant. Chicago, Illinois. A police car is firebombed and destroyed.

July 18, 1967. *Shooting.* Black militant. Cairo, Illinois. A police car is hit by sniper fire.

July 19, 1967. *Bombing/explosive.* White racist, Ku Klux Klan. Baton Rouge, Louisiana. The home of an anti-Klan labor leader is bombed.

July 19, 1967. *Bombing/explosive.* White racist. Port Allen, Louisiana. A black civil rights worker's home is bombed.

August 4, 1967. *Shooting.* White racist. Wichita, Kansas. Twenty blacks are wounded in a shotgun ambush.

August 12, 1967. *Arson.* White racist. Milwaukee, Wisconsin. The NAACP headquarters is set on fire.

August 25, 1967. *Shooting.* Rightist, Nazis. Arlington, Virginia. George Lincoln Rockwell, a Nazi leader, is killed by an ex-follower.

September 18, 1967. *Bombing/explosive.* White racist, Ku Klux Klan. Jackson, Mississippi. A dynamite blast causes serious damage to Temple Beth Israel. The bombing is carried out by the White Knights of the KKK.

October 6, 1967. *Shooting.* White racist. Carthage, Mississippi. A black civil rights worker is shot.

October 6, 1967. *Bombing/explosive.* White racist. Jackson, Mississippi. A black college is bombed.

October 16, 1967. *Bombing/explosive.* Unknown. New York City, New York. An explosion occurs near the UN Building.

October 22, 1967. *Shooting.* Revolutionary leftist. Chicago, Illinois. Shots are fired in the student center, the dining hall, and the auditorium of the University of Chicago after a recent anti-war protest.

October 28, 1967. *Shoot-out.* Black militant, Black Panthers. Oakland, California. One police officer, John Frey, is killed and another is wounded in a gun battle between police and Black Panthers.

November 15, 1967. *Shooting.* Black militant. San Francisco, California. Two police officers are injured by sniper fire at Hunters Point Police Station.

November 15, 1967. *Bombing/explosive.* White racist. Laurel, Mississippi. An NAACP official's home is bombed by the White Knights of the KKK.

November 19, 1967. *Bombing/explosive.* White racist. Jackson, Mississippi. A dynamite bomb explodes on the front porch of a white civil rights activist.

November 21, 1967. *Bombing/explosive.* White racist, Ku Klux Klan. Jackson, Mississippi. A powerful explosion destroys a rabbi's home. The White Knights of the KKK are responsible.

December 16, 1967. *Bombing/incendiary.* Black militant. Washington, D.C. The home of the president of Howard University is firebombed.

December 24, 1967. *Bombing/explosive.* Black militant. San Francisco, California. Park Police Station is bombed.

December 25, 1967. *Shooting.* White racist, Ku Klux Klan. Louisburg, North Carolina. Shots are fired at a black civil rights worker's home.

1968. *Bombing/explosive.* Revolutionary leftist, White Panthers. Detroit, Michigan. At least eight bombings are claimed by the White Panthers.

January 16, 1968. *Shooting.* Black militant. Nashville, Tennessee. Police officer Thomas Johnson is killed and another officer is wounded by black militants.

January 19, 1968. *Assault.* Black militant, Black Muslims. New York City, New York. A white school principal is assaulted by Black Muslims.

January 20, 1968. *Bombing/explosive.* Black militant. Walnut Creek, California. A police station is bombed.

January 25, 1968. *Bombing/explosive.* Cuban, El Poder Cubano/Cuban Power. Miami, Florida. A package en route to Cuba explodes.

January 31, 1968. *Bombing/incendiary.* Revolutionary leftist. Kalamazoo, Michigan. A National Guard storage building is bombed, causing an estimated damage of $12,000.

February 1968. *Shooting.* White racist. Hattiesburg, Mississippi. Shots are fired at the home of an NAACP official.

February 1, 1968. *Bombing/explosive.* Cuban. Miami, Florida. The Mexican Consulate is bombed.

February 8, 1968. *Bombing/explosive.* Cuban, El Poder Cubano/Cuban Power. Miami, Florida. The British Consulate is bombed.

February 19, 1968. *Shooting.* Black militant. San Diego, California. A sniper shoots at a police car.

February 25, 1968. *Shooting.* Black militant. San Diego, California. A sniper shoots at a police car.

March 3, 1968. *Shoot-out.* White racist. Jackson, Mississippi. Shots are fired at an NAACP official's home; he returns fire.

March 12, 1968. *Bombing/explosive.* Revolutionary leftist. New York City, New York. The General Telephone headquarters building is bombed, causing heavy damage.

March 12, 1968. *Bombing/explosive.* Cuban. Florida. A Cuban restaurant is bombed.

March 13, 1968. *Bombing/explosive.* Cuban. Miami, Florida. The Chilean Consulate is bombed.

March 17, 1968. *Arson.* White racist. Gainesville, Florida. Eighteen black homes are the targets of arsonists.

March 19, 1968. *Bombing/explosive.* Black militant. Norwalk, Connecticut. A bomb explodes outside the police department.

March 20, 1968. *Bombing/explosive.* Revolutionary leftist. Berkeley, California. An electric tower in Tilden Park is dynamited.

March 23, 1968. *Bombing/explosive.* Revolutionary leftist. Berkeley, California. Telephone trunk lines are dynamited.

March 25, 1968. *Bombing/explosive.* Revolutionary leftist. Juneau, Alabama. There is an explosion on the Coast Guard Cutter *Barataria*, which had just returned from Vietnam.

March 26, 1968. *Attempted bombing.* Revolutionary leftist. Oakland, California. An attempted bombing occurs at an induction center.

March 31, 1968. *Bombing/explosive.* Revolutionary leftist. New York City, New York. A dynamite blast occurs at an induction center.

April 1, 1968. *Bombing/incendiary.* Revolutionary leftist. New York City, New York. Bloomingdale's, S. Klein's, Montgomery Ward, and Gimbel's department stores are the targets of arson attacks. Fires started by Molotov cocktails cause $20 million in damage.

April 2, 1968. *Bombing/explosive.* Cuban, El Poder Cubano/Cuban Power. New York City, New York. A pharmaceutical company that sends drugs to Cuba is bombed.

April 4, 1968. *Shooting.* White racist. Memphis, Tennessee. Rev. Martin Luther King Jr. is shot and killed. His assassin, James Earl Ray, was a petty criminal who allegedly anticipated getting money from a rich Southern racist.

April 4, 1968. *Shooting.* Black militant. Greensboro, North Carolina. Three policemen are wounded by a shotgun blast. One officer is in critical condition.

April 4, 1968. *Shooting.* Black militant. Memphis, Tennessee. Three police officers are the targets of snipers.

April 5, 1968. *Shooting.* Revolutionary leftist. Tallahassee, Florida. A sniper fires at police officers on a university campus.

April 5, 1968. *Shooting.* Black militant. Pine Bluff, Arkansas. A police officer is hit by sniper fire.

April 5, 1968. *Shooting.* Black militant. Wilmington, North Carolina. A police car is the target of snipers.

April 5, 1968. *Shooting.* Black militant. High Point, North Carolina. Shots are fired at a police car.

April 5, 1968. *Sabotage.* Revolutionary left-ist. San Francisco County, California. A bulldozer topples a Pacific Gas and Electric Company (PG and E) tower, causing a series of utility outages.

April 6, 1968. *Shoot-out.* Black militant, Black Panthers. Oakland, California. Policemen are wounded in a shoot-out.

April 7, 1968. *Shooting.* Black militant. East Albany, Georgia. A police car is the target of an ambush.

April 7, 1968. *Shooting.* Black militant. Malvern, Arkansas. Shots are fired at a police car.

April 11, 1968. *Shoot-out.* Black militant. St. Louis, Missouri. A black man is killed in a gunfight with police.

April 18, 1968. *Bombing/explosive.* Cuban, El Poder Cubano/Cuban Power. New York City, New York. The Mexican Consulate is bombed.

April 22, 1968. *Bombing/explosive.* Cuban, El Poder Cubano/Cuban Power. New York City, New York. The Spanish tourist office is bombed.

May 1, 1968. *Shoot-out.* Black militant. Philadelphia, Pennsylvania. Police officers are fired at with shotguns.

May 4, 1968. *Sabotage.* Revolutionary left-ist. San Francisco, California. The telephone company is the target of sabotage, causing $400 in damage.

May 4, 1968. *Shooting.* Black militant. Chicago, Illinois. A police car is the target of a sniper from a nearby apartment house.

May 5, 1968. *Bombing/explosive.* Revolutionary leftist. San Francisco, California. PG and E towers are bombed.

May 5, 1968. *Bombing/explosive.* Cuban, El Poder Cubano/Cuban Power. Miami, Florida. The British ship *Greenwood* is bombed.

May 8, 1968. *Arson.* Revolutionary leftist. Palo Alto, California. The Reserve Officers' Training Corps (ROTC) building at Stanford University is set on fire, causing $75,000 in damage.

May 15, 1968. *Bombing/explosive.* White racist. Hattiesburg, Mississippi. An NAACP official's car is bombed.

May 16, 1968. *Arson.* Revolutionary leftist. Washington, D.C. Catholic University's theater, museum, and other buildings are the targets of arson fires, causing $150,000 in damage.

May 18, 1968. *Sabotage, vandalism, and property destruction.* Revolutionary leftist. Catonsville, Maryland. Philip Berrigan and other anti-war radicals damage files at the local induction center.

May 25, 1968. *Bombing/explosive.* Cuban, El Poder Cubano/Cuban Power. Miami, Florida. The Japanese ship *Aroka Maru* is bombed.

May 26, 1968. *Bombing/explosive.* Cuban, El Poder Cubano/Cuban Power. Miami, Florida. The Mexican Consulate is bombed.

May 28, 1968. *Bombing/explosive.* White racist. Meridian, Mississippi. A synagogue is bombed by the White Knights of the KKK.

May 30, 1968. *Bombing/explosive.* Cuban, El Poder Cubano/Cuban Power. New York City, New York. The Spanish tourist office is bombed.

June 1, 1968. *Shooting.* Black militant. Philadelphia, Pennsylvania. A police officer is wounded by gunfire.

June 2, 1968. *Shooting.* Black militant. East St. Louis, Illinois. Shots are fired at plain-clothes police officers.

June 5, 1968. *Shooting.* Islamic. Los Angeles, California. Robert F. Kennedy, Democratic Party presidential candidate, is assassinated by Sirhan Sirhan, and five bystanders are wounded. In his diary Sirhan wrote that he hated Kennedy because of his support for Israel and his pledge to give jet bombers to Israel.

June 5, 1968. *Shooting.* Black militant. Chicago, Illinois. Police officer Henry Peeler is shot and killed.

June 6, 1968. *Bombing/explosive.* White racist. Florence, Mississippi. A black home is bombed, injuring one person.

June 21, 1968. *Bombing/explosive.* Cuban, El Poder Cubano/Cuban Power. New York City, New York. The Spanish tourist office is bombed.

June 23, 1968. *Shooting.* Black militant. South Bend, Indiana. A police car is the target of sniper fire.

June 23, 1968. *Bombing/explosive.* Cuban, El Poder Cubano/Cuban Power. New York City, New York. The Mexican tourist office is bombed.

June 27, 1968. *Shooting.* Black militant. Owensboro, Kentucky. A police car is the target of sniper fire.

June 27, 1968. *Bombing/explosive.* Cuban, El Poder Cubano/Cuban Powe. New York City, New York. A bomb explodes in the Mexican consul's garage.

June 29, 1968. *Attempted bombing and shoot-out.* White racist, Ku Klux Klan. Meridian, Mississippi. Kathy Ainsworth, a Klanswoman, is shot to death in a police ambush when she and Thomas Tarrants attempt to blow up the house of a Jewish businessman. The ambush was set up by two Klansmen who were bribed with money provided by the Anti-Defamation League of B'nai B'rith (ADL).

July 3, 1968. *Bombing/explosive.* Revolutionary leftist. Berkeley, California. The University of California campus police station is bombed. Firebombs are thrown at Berkeley High School and at the Veterans Administration building.

July 4, 1968. *Bombing.* Cuban, El Poder Cubano/Cuban Power. New York City, New York. The Canadian Consulate and the tourist office are bombed.

July 5, 1968. *Arson.* Revolutionary leftist. Palo Alto, California. The office of the president of Stanford University is set on fire, causing $300,000 in damage.

July 7, 1968. *Bombing.* Cuban, El Poder Cubano/Cuban Power. New York City, New York. The Japanese tourist office is bombed.

July 9, 1968. *Bombing/explosive.* Cuban, El Poder Cubano/Cuban Power. New York City, New York. The Yugoslav Mission to the UN is damaged by a bomb that explodes outside the Cuban Mission.

July 11, 1968. *Bombing/incendiary.* Black militant. Topeka, Kansas. The police information center is the target of a firebomb.

July 12, 1968. *Bombing/incendiary.* Revolutionary leftist. Denver, Colorado. The Denver police garage is the target of an incendiary device.

July 14, 1968. *Bombing/explosive.* Cuban, El Poder Cubano/Cuban Power. Chicago, Illinois. The Mexican tourist office is bombed.

July 15, 1968. *Bombing/explosive.* Revolutionary leftist. Denver, Colorado. A dynamite blast at the police department causes only minor damage.

July 15, 1968. *Bombing.* Cuban, El Poder Cubano/Cuban Power. New York City, New York. The French tourist office is bombed.

July 16, 1968. *Bombing.* Cuban, El Poder Cubano/Cuban Power. Newark, New Jersey. The Mexican Consulate is bombed.

July 17, 1968. *Bombing/explosive.* Cuban. New York City, New York. A Cuban diplomat's home is bombed.

July 19, 1968. *Bombing/explosive.* Cuban, El Poder Cubano/Cuban Power. Los Angeles, California. The Mexican tourist office is bombed.

July 19, 1968. *Bombing/explosive.* Cuban, El Poder Cubano/Cuban Power. Los Angeles, California. The Shell Oil office is bombed.

July 19, 1968. *Bombing/explosive.* Cuban, El Poder Cubano/Cuban Power. Los Angeles, California. A Japanese airline office is bombed.

July 19, 1968. *Bombing/explosive.* Cuban, El Poder Cubano/Cuban Power. Los Angeles, California. A French airline office is bombed.

July 21, 1968. *Bombing/explosive.* Revolutionary leftist. San Francisco, California. A military uniform factory is destroyed by an explosion.

July 21, 1968. *Bombing/incendiary.* Revolutionary leftist. Benton Harbor, Michigan. A police car is firebombed.

July 22, 1968. *Shooting.* Black militant. New Orleans, Louisiana. A police car is the target of sniper fire.

July 22, 1968. *Shooting.* Black militant. Newark, New Jersey. A police director is shot at his home.

July 23, 1968. *Shooting.* Black militant. South Bend, Indiana. Shots are fired at a police car.

July 23, 1968. *Shoot-out.* Black militant, Black Nation of New Libya. Cleveland, Ohio. According to police, a squad car was fired on from the headquarters of the Black Nation of New Libya (BNNL). In a gun battle between police and black nationalists, seven people are killed. The dead include three police officers, Willard Wolff, Louis Golonka, and Leroy Jones, three BNNL members, and James Chapman, a black man described as "helping police." Another three people are shot and killed in separate incidents later that night.

July 24, 1968. *Shoot-out.* White racist. Cleveland, Ohio. In the aftermath of the gun battle between black nationalists and police, a black man is shot from a car while he is waiting at a bus stop.

July 26, 1968. *Bombing/explosive.* Cuban, El Poder Cubano/Cuban Power. Chicago, Illinois. The Mexican tourist office is bombed.

July 27, 1968. *Bombing/incendiary.* Black militant, Black Panthers. New York City, New York. A police car is destroyed by a firebomb.

July 28, 1968. *Shooting.* Black militant. Gary, Indiana. A policeman is the target of a sniper.

July 29, 1968. *Shooting.* Black militant. Seattle, Washington. Three policemen are wounded by sniper fire.

July 30, 1968. *Bombing/explosive.* Cuban, El Poder Cubano/Cuban Power. Los Angeles, California. The British Consulate is bombed.

July 31, 1968. *Shooting.* Black militant. New York City, New York. A rifle is fired at a police car on Harlem River Drive.

August 1968. *Shoot-out.* Black militant. Memphis, Tennessee. A shoot-out occurs between police and black militants.

August 1, 1968. *Shooting.* Black militant. Marin City, California. The sheriff's office is the target of rifle fire.

August 2, 1968. *Shooting.* Black militant, Black Panthers. Brooklyn, New York. Two policemen are seriously injured by shotgun blasts.

August 2, 1968. *Bombing/incendiary.* Black militant. St. Petersburg, Florida. A police car is firebombed and destroyed.

August 3, 1968. *Bombing/explosive.* Cuban, El Poder Cubano/Cuban Power. New York City, New York. A Japanese bank is bombed.

August 3, 1968. *Shooting.* Revolutionary leftist. Las Vegas, Nevada. A policeman is shot.

August 5, 1968. *Bombing/explosive.* Cuban, El Poder Cubano/Cuban Power. Los Angeles, California. The British Consulate is bombed.

August 5, 1968. *Shoot-out.* Black militant. Watts, California. In a shoot-out between Black Panthers and police, three Panthers are killed. The dead men are Thomas Lewis, Steven Bartholemew, and Robert Lawrence.

August 6, 1968. *Attempted bombing.* Black militant. Lexington, Kentucky. The police department is the target of an attempted bombing.

August 6, 1968. *Shooting.* Black militant. Dolton, Illinois. A police car is the target of sniper fire; no injuries are reported.

August 6, 1968. *Shoot-out.* Black militant. Chicago, Illinois. Six policemen are injured in a shoot-out with the "Black Elephants."

August 7, 1968. *Shooting.* Black militant. Jackson, Michigan. A police car is fired at, but no injuries are reported.

August 8, 1968. *Bombing/explosive.* Cuban, El Poder Cubano/Cuban Power. Miami, Florida. A British ship, *Caribbean Venture,* is bombed.

August 8, 1968. *Shooting.* Black militant. Inkster, Michigan. A sniper shoots at police, wounding two and killing police detective Robert Gonser. James Mather, a black militant, is shot and killed by police.

August 8, 1968. *Bombing/explosive.* Cuban, El Poder Cubano/Cuban Power. Los Angeles, California. The British Consulate is bombed.

August 8, 1968. *Shoot-out.* Black militant, Black Panthers. Los Angeles, California. A shoot-out occurs between Black Panthers and police.

August 8, 1968. *Shoot-out.* Black militant. Miami, Florida. Three blacks are killed in a gunfight with police.

August 9, 1968. *Bombing/explosive.* Cuban, El Poder Cubano/Cuban Power. Miami, Florida. The Mexican consul's home is bombed.

August 11, 1968. *Shooting.* Black militant, Black Panthers. New York City, New York. Snipers shoot at a police car.

August 11, 1968. *Shooting.* Black militant. East Chicago, Illinois. A police officer is wounded by sniper fire.

August 12, 1968. *Shooting.* Black militant. Little Rock, Arkansas. A police car is the target of gunshots; no injuries are reported.

August 14, 1968. *Shooting.* Black militant. St. Bernard, Louisiana. A shotgun is fired at the sheriff.

August 14, 1968. *Bombing/explosive.* White racist. Louisville, Kentucky. A black church is bombed.

August 17, 1968. *Shooting.* Revolutionary leftist. Waterloo, Iowa. Police cars are the targets of snipers.

August 17, 1968. *Bombing/explosive.* Cuban, El Poder Cubano/Cuban Power. Miami, Florida. A Mexican airline office is bombed.

August 20, 1968. *Shooting.* Black militant. Wichita, Kansas. Three policemen are wounded by gunfire.

August 22, 1968. *Bombing/incendiary.* Revolutionary leftist. Detroit, Michigan. The Army recruiting office is firebombed; no damages are reported.

August 23, 1968. *Bombing/incendiary.* Revolutionary leftist. Chicago, Illinois. The Army recruiting office is the target of a Molotov cocktail explosion, which slightly damages the office.

August 24, 1968. *Shooting.* Black militant. Memphis, Tennessee. A police car is the target of shots fired from a .30 caliber rifle, wounding one officer in the leg.

August 24, 1968. *Shoot-out.* Rightist, Minutemen. Voluntown, Connecticut. A gun battle between a group of Minutemen and state troopers leaves one state trooper and five Minutemen injured.

August 24, 1968. *Shooting.* Black militant. Evansville, Indiana. A policeman is shot in the back by a sniper.

August 26, 1968. *Arson.* Black militant. Oakland, California. The Police Information Center in East Oakland is the target of arsonists.

August 28, 1968. *Shooting.* Black militant. Chicago, Illinois. A police car is the target of gunfire, which injures one officer.

August 28, 1968. *Shoot-out.* Black militant, Black Panthers. Los Angeles, California. A shoot-out occurs between police and Black Panthers.

August 29, 1968. *Shooting.* Black militant. San Francisco, California. Shots are fired at the Hunters Point Police Station from cars.

August 30, 1968. *Shoot-out.* Black militant. Berkeley, California. Two police officers are wounded by gunfire.

August 30, 1968. *Bombing/explosive.* Black militant. Detroit, Michigan. A police car is dynamited outside the Woodward Police Station.

August 31, 1968. *Shooting.* Black militant. San Francisco, California. Hunters Point Housing Authority Police Station is the target of shotgun fire.

September 1968. *Shoot-out.* White racist, National States Rights Party. Berea, Kentucky. After a National States Rights Party rally, gunfire leaves two people dead, John Boggs, a black man, and Elza Rucker, a white man.

September 1, 1968. *Bombing/explosive.* Revolutionary leftist. Ann Arbor, Michigan. The Central Intelligence Agency (CIA) is bombed; no damage is reported.

September 3, 1968. *Bombing/explosive.* Revolutionary leftist. Macomb, Michigan. Two Selective Service offices are bombed; no injuries are reported.

September 3, 1968. *Bombing/explosive.* Black militant. Oakland, California. The police headquarters in the Oakland Hall of Justice is bombed.

September 4, 1968. *Shooting.* Black militant. Seattle, Washington. A police car is the target of sniper fire.

September 4, 1968. *Bombing/explosive.* Revolutionary leftist. Long Beach, California. Southern California Edison Company is bombed.

September 6, 1968. *Bombing/explosive.* Revolutionary leftist. Elmhurst, Michigan. Police officers' private cars are dynamited.

September 7, 1968. *Shooting.* Black militant. Pittsburgh, Pennsylvania. A police car is the target of sniper fire.

September 8, 1968. *Shooting.* Black militant. Seattle, Washington. A police car is hit by sniper fire.

September 10, 1968. *Shooting.* Black militant. Summit, Illinois. Three police cars are shot at by sniper fire.

September 10, 1968. *Bombing/explosive.* Revolutionary leftist. Oakland, California. A stick of dynamite is thrown into an Army Recruiter's car from a passing car.

September 10, 1968. *Bombing/explosive.* Revolutionary leftist. Van Nuys, California. Five Army trucks are dynamited.

September 10, 1968. *Bombing/explosive.* Black militant. Detroit, Michigan. Police cars parked at the Woodward Police Station are dynamited.

September 10, 1968. *Bombing/explosive.* Revolutionary leftist. Detroit, Michigan. An Army Recruiter's car is dynamited.

September 12, 1968. *Shooting.* Black militant, Black Panthers. Brooklyn, New York. Two policemen are wounded by sniper fire while they are stopped at a red light.

September 13, 1968. *Shooting.* Black militant. Waterloo, Iowa. Two police officers are the targets of sniper fire.

September 13, 1968. *Bombing/explosive.* Revolutionary leftist. Berkeley, California. The ROTC building at the University of California is bombed, causing extensive damage.

September 13, 1968. *Shooting.* Black militant. San Francisco, California. A police car is the target of sniper fire.

September 16, 1968. *Shooting.* Cuban, El Poder Cubano/Cuban Power. Miami, Florida. A Polish ship is shot at with a bazooka.

September 16, 1968. *Bombing/explosive.* Cuban, El Poder Cubano/Cuban Power. Puerto Rico. A bomb explodes aboard the Spanish ship *Satrustequi.*

September 19, 1968. *Bombing/incendiary.* Black militant. New York City, New York. The firebombing of a police communications truck wounds two.

September 19, 1968. *Bombing/explosive.* Cuban, El Poder Cubano/Cuban Power. Miami, Florida. The Mexican consul's home is bombed.

September 20, 1968. *Assault.* Black militant, Black Panthers. Seattle, Washington. A police detective is assaulted by a Black Panther.

September 20, 1968. *Bombing/explosive.* Revolutionary leftist. Chicago, Illinois. Illinois Bell Telephone Company is bombed, causing one death.

September 22, 1968. *Bombing/explosive.* Revolutionary leftist. Roseville, Michigan. The Macomb County draft board is the target of a bomb, which blows a hole in the front wall.

September 22, 1968. *Shooting.* Black militant. York, Pennsylvania. Shots are fired at a police department.

September 23, 1968. *Shooting.* Black militant. Chicago, Illinois. A shotgun is fired at a police car.

September 24, 1968. *Shooting.* Black militant, Black Panthers. Jersey City, New Jersey. Three police officers are injured by sniper fire.

September 25, 1968. *Bombing/incendiary.* Revolutionary leftist. Jefferson City, Missouri. The ROTC building at Lincoln University is the target of two Molotov cocktails, which cause a fire.

September 25, 1968. *Arson.* Revolutionary leftist. Milwaukee, Wisconsin. Selective Service office files are burned in a protest over the Vietnam War.

September 28, 1968. *Shooting.* Black militant. New York City, New York. A police car is hit by gunfire, wounding two officers.

September 29, 1968. *Bombing/explosive.* Revolutionary leftist. Ann Arbor, Michigan. The CIA recruiting office is bombed.

September 30, 1968. *Shooting.* Black militant. Kandakee, Illinois. A policeman is injured by a sniper.

September 30, 1968. *Bombing/explosive.* Revolutionary leftist. Eugene, Oregon. The Naval and Marine Training Center is bombed, causing $106,000 in damage.

October 1968. *Shooting.* Black militant. St. Petersburg, Florida. Snipers fire at police.

October 2, 1968. *Bombing/incendiary.* Revolutionary leftist. Washington, D.C. The Selective Service office is firebombed, causing $1000 in damage.

October 2, 1968. *Bombing.* Black militant. Oakland, California. The Oakland Police Station is bombed; the explosion occurs in the restroom.

October 2, 1968. *Bombing/incendiary.* Revolutionary leftist. Madison, Wisconsin. An explosion at the Selective Service office destroys files.

October 5, 1968. *Shoot-out.* Black militant, Black Panthers. Seattle, Washington. Welton Armstead, a Black Panther, is killed in a shoot-out with police.

October 6, 1968. *Shooting.* Black militant. Seattle, Washington. Two policemen are injured by sniper fire to their car.

October 9, 1968. *Shooting.* Black militant. Norfolk, Virginia. A police car is hit by sniper fire.

October 13, 1968. *Shooting.* Black militant. Brooklyn, New York. A police patrol is the target of sniper fire.

October 14, 1968. *Shooting.* Black militant. Seattle, Washington. A police car is the target of sniper fire.

October 14, 1968. *Bombing/incendiary.* Revolutionary leftist. San Francisco, California. The ROTC building at San Francisco State College is set on fire.

October 15, 1968. *Bombing/explosive.* Revolutionary leftist. Ann Arbor, Michigan. The University of Michigan's Institute of Science and Technology is bombed. The explosion causes heavy damage.

October 17, 1968. *Shooting.* Black militant. Miami, Florida. A police paddy wagon is the target of sniper fire.

October 20, 1968. *Attempted bombing.* Cuban, El Poder Cubano/Cuban Power. New York City, New York. An attempted bombing occurs at a theater where a Cuban actress is performing.

October 23, 1968. *Shooting.* Cuban, El Poder Cubano/Cuban Power. New York City, New York. An attempted assassination of the Cuban ambassador to the UN occurs.

October 24, 1968. *Shooting.* Black militant. San Diego, California. A sniper fires a shot at a police car.

October 28, 1968. *Bombing.* Black militant. Oakland, California. The highway patrol parking lot is bombed.

October 29, 1968. *Bombing/explosive.* Black militant. San Francisco, California. Richmond District Police Station is destroyed by dynamite.

November 12, 1968. *Shoot-out.* Black militant, Black Panthers. Carbondale, Illinois. A gun battle occurs between four patrolmen and Black Panther Party (BPP) members. Ten people are wounded, four of whom are police officers.

November 12, 1968. *Bombing/explosive.* Black militant. New York City, New York. A police station is bombed.

November 13, 1968. *Shoot-out.* Black militant. Boston, Massachusetts. In a dispute between two black factions, three men are killed and two are wounded. The shoot-out takes place at the office of the New England Grass Roots Organization.

November 13, 1968. *Shooting.* Black militant, Black Panthers. Berkeley, California. A policeman is wounded by sniper fire.

November 16, 1968. *Shooting.* Black militant. St. Louis, Missouri. The police department is the target of sniper fire; no injuries are reported.

November 19, 1968. *Shoot-out.* Black militant, Black Panthers. San Francisco, California. Three police are wounded in a shoot-out with Black Panthers following a robbery at a gas station.

November 23, 1968. *Shooting.* Black militant. Pittsburgh, Pennsylvania. Two policemen are wounded by a shotgun blast.

November 29, 1968. *Shooting.* Black militant, Black Panthers. Jersey City, New Jersey. The 5th Precinct Police Station of the Jersey City Police Department is machine-gunned.

December 7, 1968. *Shooting.* Black militant, Black Panthers. Denver, Colorado. Rifle shots are fired at a police cruiser from a passing car.

December 10, 1968. *Attempted bombing.* Black militant. Pittsburgh, Pennsylvania. An attempted bombing occurs at a police station.

December 19, 1968. *Shooting.* Black militant, Black Panthers. Watts, California. Frank Diggs is shot and killed in what appears to be a feud between Black Panther factions.

December 24, 1968. *Shooting.* White racist, Ku Klux Klan. Monroe, Louisiana. Shots are fired into the home of a black official who works for the Office of Equal Opportunity.

January 1969. *Bombing/explosive.* Rightist. Puerto Rico. A car belonging to the leader of the Puerto Rican Independence Party is bombed by rightists.

January 1, 1969. *Bombing/explosive.* Black militant. Jersey City, New Jersey. An explosive device detonates in the 5th Precinct of the Jersey City Police Department, causing minor property damage.

January 2, 1969. *Shooting.* Black militant. Chicago, Illinois. A shotgun is fired at a police station.

January 2, 1969. *Arson.* White racist. New York City, New York. A Jewish center is set on fire.

January 3, 1969. *Arson.* White racist. Far Rockaway, New York. A Jewish synagogue is set on fire.

January 7, 1969. *Bombing/incendiary.* Revolutionary leftist. Santa Barbara, California. Two Molotov cocktails are thrown at the ROTC building at the University of California, causing $1200 in damage.

January 10, 1969. *Shooting.* Black militant. Plainfield, New Jersey. A police officer is shot and wounded by a sniper.

January 11, 1969. *Shooting.* Black militant, Black Panthers. Seattle, Washington. A police car is the target of gunfire.

January 14, 1969. *Bombing/incendiary.* Revolutionary leftist. Chicago, Illinois. A Molotov cocktail is thrown into the Selective Service board office, causing minor damage.

January 17, 1969. *Shooting.* Black militant, US. UCLA, California. Two Black Panthers, Apprentice Carter and John Huggins, are shot by members of US, a rival black nationalist faction, in a dispute over who should control the black studies program at the university.

January 17, 1969. *Bombing/explosive.* Black militant, Black Panthers. New York City, New York. The police station in the Highbridge Section is shaken by an explosion.

January 17, 1969. *Shooting.* Black militant, Black Panthers. New York City, New York. A police car is hit by gunfire.

January 18, 1969. *Bombing/incendiary.* Revolutionary leftist. Washington, D.C. National Selective Service headquarters is the target of a Molotov cocktail, causing extensive damage.

January 20, 1969. *Bombing/explosive.* Revolutionary leftist. Colorado. The Public Service Company of Colorado electric transmission towers are damaged by an explosion.

January 26, 1969. *Shooting.* White racist. Seattle, Washington. Edwin T. Pratt, a civil rights leader, is shot and killed at his home.

January 30, 1969. *Bombing/incendiary.* Revolutionary leftist. Kalamazoo, Michigan. The Michigan National Guard is firebombed, damaging five jeeps and the building.

February 3, 1969. *Bombing/explosive.* Revolutionary leftist. San Rafael, California. The Selective Service office and the Army recruiting office are damaged by explosive devices.

February 6, 1969. *Shooting.* Black militant. St. Paul, Minnesota. A police car is the target of shotgun blasts.

February 10, 1969. *Arson.* Revolutionary leftist. Athens, Georgia. The ROTC building at the University of Georgia is set on fire.

February 11, 1969. *Bombing/explosive.* Revolutionary leftist. Minneapolis, Minnesota. The U.S. Air Force recruiting office is bombed.

February 17, 1969. *Bombing/explosive.* Puerto Rican nationalist. San Juan, Puerto Rico. Police cars outside a police station are the targets of three bombs, which destroy 21 cars and a Howard Johnson's restaurant.

February 21, 1969. *Bombing/incendiary.* Revolutionary leftist. Lawrence, Kansas.

The ROTC building at the University of Kansas is the target of four Molotov cocktails.

February 21, 1969. *Bombing/incendiary.* Black militant. St. Louis, Missouri. The 9th District Police Station is the target of two firebombs, which cause minor damage.

February 22, 1969. *Bombing/explosive.* Revolutionary leftist. Seattle, Washington. There is an explosion outside the Armed Forces Entrance and Examining Station.

February 24, 1969. *Bombing/explosive.* Puerto Rican nationalist. San Juan, Puerto Rico. The draft board is bombed.

March 5, 1969. *Bombing/explosive.* Revolutionary leftist. San Francisco, California. A pipe bomb explodes on the San Francisco State College campus.

March 7, 1969. *Bombing/explosive.* Revolutionary leftist. Los Angeles, California. The computer center at Loyola University is bombed.

March 7, 1969. *Bombing/explosive.* Revolutionary leftist. San Francisco, California. The creative arts building at San Francisco State College is bombed.

March 10, 1969. *Bombing/incendiary.* Revolutionary leftist. Waltham, Massachusetts. The history building at Brandeis University is firebombed, causing $5000 in damage.

March 12, 1969. *Bombing/explosive.* Revolutionary leftist. Los Angeles, California. At Los Angeles Valley College a Molotov cocktail is thrown through a window into an office in the administration building.

March 13, 1969. *Shooting.* Black militant. Greensboro, North Carolina. A police car is fired at by a sniper on campus.

March 13, 1969. *Shooting.* Black militant. Durham, North Carolina. A police car is fired at by a sniper.

March 13, 1969. *Bombing/incendiary.* Revolutionary leftist. Tuscaloosa, Alabama. Several buildings on Stillman College campus are firebombed.

March 13, 1969. *Shooting.* Revolutionary leftist. Durham, North Carolina. There is sniper fire at Duke University.

March 13, 1969. *Shooting.* Revolutionary leftist. Greensboro, North Carolina. Police at the North Carolina Agricultural & Technical (A&T) State University are the target of sniper fire.

March 15, 1969. *Bombing/explosive.* Revolutionary leftist. Compton, California. A pipe bomb explodes at the U.S. Naval and Marine Corps Training Center.

March 17, 1969. *Bombing.* Black militant. Los Angeles, California. A bomb explodes in a police station parking lot.

March 17, 1969. *Bombing/explosive.* Revolutionary leftist. Contra Costa County, California. A Shell Oil Company pipeline is ruptured by an explosion, which kills one man and injures five others.

March 20, 1969. *Sabotage, vandalism, and property destruction.* Revolutionary leftist. Fairfield, California. Southern Pacific Railway is the target of sabotage, which causes 30 railway cars to crash.

March 20, 1969. *Bombing/incendiary.* Revolutionary leftist. Jackson, Tennessee. The science building at Lane College is destroyed by a firebomb.

March 21, 1969. *Bombing/incendiary.* Black militant. Cleveland, Ohio. Three police cars are firebombed.

March 22, 1969. *Shooting.* Revolutionary leftist. Eugene, Oregon. A police car is the target of sniper fire.

March 22, 1969. *Bombing.* Black militant. Long Beach, California. An undercover police car is destroyed by a bomb.

March 25, 1969. *Bombing.* Black militant. Long Beach, California. A police car is bombed.

March 29, 1969. *Shoot-out.* Black militant, Republic of New Africa. Detroit, Michigan. In a church a gun battle follows after a meeting of The Republic of New Africa, a black separatist group. One police officer is killed and one is wounded. Five black militants are wounded.

March 31, 1969. *Shooting.* White racist. Cairo, Illinois. Night riders invade a black neighborhood, wounding one man.

April 1, 1969. *Arson.* White racist. Lorman, Mississippi. Arsonists set fires at a black college.

April 1, 1969. *Shooting.* Black militant. Gainesville, Florida. A police car is the target of shotgun fire.

April 2, 1969. *Shooting.* Black militant, Black Panthers. New York City, New York. Two policemen are wounded in an ambush.

April 5, 1969. *Shooting.* Black militant, Black Panthers. Oakland, California. Ron

Black is gunned down on the street, an apparent victim of the feud between Black Panther factions.

April 6, 1969. *Bombing/incendiary.* Revolutionary leftist. Melvindale, Michigan. The police station parking lot is bombed.

April 11, 1969. *Bombing/explosive.* Revolutionary leftist. Santa Barbara, California. The Faculty Club at the University of California is bombed.

April 14, 1969. *Shooting.* Revolutionary leftist. Las Vegas, Nevada. Police are the target of a sniper.

April 17, 1969. *Bombing/explosive.* Revolutionary leftist. Tulsa, Oklahoma. The residence of the National Tank Company's executive vice president is bombed.

April 18, 1969. *Shooting.* Black militant. Port Gibson, Mississippi. Two state patrolmen are shot and injured.

April 19, 1969. *Bombing/incendiary.* Revolutionary leftist. Buffalo, New York. The University of Buffalo is firebombed.

April 21, 1969. *Shooting.* Black militant. Chicago, Illinois. One policeman is injured by gunfire from a group of black youths.

April 23, 1969. *Shooting.* Black militant. Pittsburgh, Pennsylvania. A police car is the target of sniper fire.

April 25, 1969. *Shooting.* Black militant, Black Panthers. Oakland, California. A Black Panther is shot and seriously wounded near his home, an apparent victim of the feud between Black Panther factions.

April 26, 1969. *Shooting.* Black militant. Chicago, Illinois. Two police lieutenants are shot and wounded by a shotgun blast.

April 26, 1969. *Bombing/explosive.* Black militant, Black Panthers. Des Moines, Iowa. Two people are injured in an explosion at a BPP office. It is suspected that the office was a bomb factory.

April 28, 1969. *Shooting.* Black militant. Chicago, Illinois. A sniper fires at a police car, wounding one officer.

April 29, 1969. *Shooting.* Black militant. Linden, New Jersey. A police car is hit by sniper fire.

May 2, 1969. *Shooting.* Black militant. Charlestown, South Carolina. Two police cars are the targets of sniper fire.

May 5, 1969. *Bombing/incendiary.* Revolutionary leftist. Cambridge, Massachusetts. The ROTC building at Harvard University is firebombed, causing minor smoke and fire damage.

May 5, 1969. *Arson.* Revolutionary leftist. Kalamazoo, Michigan. The ROTC building at Western Michigan University is set on fire, causing $3000 in damage.

May 6, 1969. *Bombing/incendiary.* White racist. Brooklyn, New York. A Jewish synagogue is firebombed.

May 7, 1969. *Bombing/incendiary.* Revolutionary leftist. Palo Alto, California. The ROTC building is set on fire by a Molotov cocktail.

May 7, 1969. *Shooting.* Black militant. Chicago, Illinois. A policeman is wounded by a sniper at 6147 South University Avenue.

May 7, 1969. *Shooting.* Black militant. Chicago, Illinois. A policeman is wounded by a sniper at 47th and Drexal streets.

May 8, 1969. *Bombing/incendiary.* Black militant. Washington, D.C. Howard University buildings are firebombed.

May 10, 1969. *Bombing/incendiary.* Revolutionary leftist. Denton, Texas. The ROTC building at North Texas State University is the target of a Molotov cocktail, causing $8000 in damage.

May 12, 1969. *Bombing/incendiary.* Revolutionary leftist. Chicago, Illinois. The ROTC building at Loyola University is firebombed.

May 14, 1969. *Arson.* Revolutionary leftist. Chicago, Illinois. The ROTC building at DePaul University is set on fire, causing $10,000 in damage.

May 14, 1969. *Assault.* Black militant, Black Muslims. Atlanta, Georgia. Black Muslims assault a policeman.

May 17, 1969. *Bombing/explosive.* Revolutionary leftist. Seattle, Washington. Seattle Center Coliseum is bombed during a military display for Armed Forces Week, causing $500 in damage.

May 17, 1969. *Shooting.* Black militant. Chicago, Illinois. Two teenagers fire at a police car.

May 18, 1969. *Shooting.* Black militant. Burlington, North Carolina. Police officers are the targets of sniper fire.

May 18, 1969. *Shooting.* Black militant. Durham, North Carolina. Shots are fired at a police car.

May 20, 1969. *Bombing/explosive.* Revolutionary leftist. Coquille, Oregon. A bomb explodes on the Coos Bay County Courthouse lawn.

May 20, 1969. *Bombing/explosive.* Revolutionary leftist. Oakland, California. The PG and E transmission tower is damaged by a dynamite blast.

May 20, 1969. *Bombing/explosive.* Revolutionary leftist. Eugene, Oregon. The Registrar's Office at the University of Oregon and the university branch of First National Bank are dynamited.

May 20, 1969. *Arson and shoot-out.* Revolutionary leftist. Jefferson City, Missouri. Arson is reported and state troopers exchange gunfire with snipers on a college campus.

May 20, 1969. *Bombing/explosive.* Revolutionary leftist. Eugene, Oregon. The university branch of the First National Bank is dynamited.

May 21, 1969. *Shooting.* Black militant, Black Panthers. New Haven, Connecticut. Black Panthers torture and kill Alex Rackley, a suspected informer.

May 22, 1969. *Bombing.* Black militant. Los Angeles, California. A pipe bomb explodes on the roof of the 77th Division Police Station.

May 23, 1969. *Shooting.* Black militant, US. San Diego, California. A Black Panther, John Savage, is shot by gunmen belonging to the US Cultural Organization.

May 23, 1969. *Shooting.* Black militant. Greensboro, North Carolina. On the North Carolina Agricultural & Technical State University campus, a police officer is wounded by a sniper.

May 24, 1969. *Shoot-out.* Black militant, US. San Diego, California. Four are wounded in a shoot-out between Black Panthers and US.

May 24, 1969. *Attempted bombing.* Revolutionary leftist. Portland, Oregon. The National Bank of Oregon and the U.S. Navy recruiting station are the targets of dynamite packages that fail to explode.

May 25, 1969. *Arson.* Revolutionary leftist. Chicago, Illinois. The Selective Service office is set on fire, and files are destroyed.

May 26, 1969. *Bombing/incendiary.* Revolutionary leftist. Los Angeles, California. The roof of Mayor Yorty's house is firebombed, causing $5000 in damage.

May 26, 1969. *Shooting.* Black militant. Cairo, Illinois. Shots are fired at police headquarters.

May 26, 1969. *Arson.* Revolutionary leftist. Los Angeles, California. Los Angeles City College is the target of arsonists. The fires cause $2000 in damage.

May 28, 1969. *Attempted bombing.* Revolutionary leftist. Los Angeles, California. A Safeway store is the target of a TNT device, but it does not explode.

May 28, 1969. *Bombing/explosive.* Revolutionary leftist. Los Angeles, California. A pipe bomb explodes at Los Angeles City College, causing minor damage.

May 29, 1969. *Bombing/incendiary.* Revolutionary leftist. Evanston, Illinois. A Molotov cocktail is thrown at the ROTC building at Northwestern University, causing a small fire with minor damage.

June 1, 1969. *Bombing/explosive.* Revolutionary leftist. Ann Arbor, Michigan. The ROTC building at the University of Michigan is bombed, causing $25,000–$30,000 in damage.

June 1, 1969. *Assault.* Jewish, Jewish Defense League. New York City, New York. Jewish Defense League (JDL) marchers beat up Nazis.

June 2, 1969. *Shooting.* Black militant. Charlestown, South Carolina. Police cars are hit by sniper fire.

June 3, 1969. *Bombing/explosive.* Revolutionary leftist. Louisville, Kentucky. Two bombs explode at Dupont College.

June 4, 1969. *Shoot-out.* Black militant, Black Panthers. Santa Ana, California. Nelson Sasscer, a police officer, is shot and killed by a sniper.

June 7, 1969. *Shooting.* Black militant. Macon, Georgia. Two police officers are wounded by sniper fire.

June 7, 1969. *Shooting.* Black militant. Greensboro, North Carolina. Two police officers are wounded by a sniper.

June 7, 1969. *Shooting.* Black militant, Black Muslims. Bronx, New York. A black militant is shot and wounded by Black Muslims.

June 8, 1969. *Shooting.* Black militant. Indianapolis, Indiana. A police officer is injured by sniper fire.

June 8, 1969. *Bombing/explosive.* Cuban, Accion Cubana/Cuban Action Comman-

dos. New York City, New York. A Loew's theater is bombed.

June 10, 1969. *Bombing.* Black militant. Denver, Colorado. The Denver Police Station is the target of a dynamite explosion, causing minor damage.

June 12, 1969. *Bombing/explosive.* Revolutionary leftist. Van Nuys, California. A military installation is bombed from an airplane.

June 13, 1969. *Shooting.* Black militant. Roxboro, North Carolina. A police car is the target of sniper fire.

June 14, 1969. *Arson.* Revolutionary leftist. New Haven, Connecticut. Yale University's art and architecture building is set on fire, causing $1 million in damage.

June 14, 1969. *Attempted bombing.* Revolutionary leftist. Vancouver, Washington. A bombing attempt occurs at the Bonneville Power administration substation.

June 15, 1969. *Shooting.* Black militant. Cairo, Illinois. Police are the target of sniper fire.

June 15, 1969. *Shoot-out.* Black militant, Black Panthers. Sacramento, California. A shoot-out occurs between police and Black Panthers.

June 17, 1969. *Bombing/incendiary.* Black militant. Springfield, Ohio. A police car is firebombed.

June 18, 1969. *Bombing/incendiary.* Black militant. Cleveland, Ohio. A police car is firebombed.

June 18, 1969. *Bombing/explosive.* Revolutionary leftist. Seattle, Washington. An explosion at the State Multiservice Center causes $1500 in damage.

June 20, 1969. *Shooting.* Black militant. Pittsburgh, Pennsylvania. A police officer is hit by sniper fire.

June 23, 1969. *Shooting.* Black militant. Cleveland, Ohio. Three police officers are shot.

June 26, 1969. *Shooting.* Black militant. Denver, Colorado. A police station is hit by sniper fire.

June 27, 1969. *Bombing/incendiary.* Black militant. St. Louis, Missouri. A police car is firebombed.

June 27, 1969. *Bombing/explosive.* Revolutionary leftist. Powers, Oregon. An explosion at the ranger station causes minor damage.

June 29, 1969. *Bombing/explosive.* Revolutionary leftist. Seattle, Washington. The University of Washington administration building is bombed, causing an estimated $300,000 in damage.

July 1969. *Shooting.* Black militant, Black Panthers. Baltimore, Maryland. A suspected informer, Eugene Anderson, is murdered by the Black Panthers.

July 1, 1969. *Bombing.* Black militant. Wichita, Kansas. A bomb explodes on the roof of Razooks Thrift Market.

July 2, 1969. *Bombing/incendiary.* Revolutionary leftist. San Rafael, California. The sheriff's office is firebombed.

July 4, 1969. *Bombing.* Black militant. San Francisco, California. Mission District Police Precinct Station is bombed, causing minor damage.

July 4, 1969. *Bombing/explosive.* Revolutionary leftist. Aspen, Colorado. Explosions in the Aspen area cause no injuries.

July 5, 1969. *Shooting.* White racist, Ku Klux Klan. Middleton, North Carolina. Following a Klan rally, a black woman is wounded in a drive-by shooting.

July 5, 1969. *Shooting.* Black militant. Tampa, Florida. A police officer is wounded by sniper fire.

July 5, 1969. *Shooting.* Black militant. Camden, New Jersey. Two police officers, George Schultz and Charles Sutman, are shot and killed by sniper fire.

July 7, 1969. *Shooting.* Black militant. Arlington, Virginia. A police car is the target of sniper fire and Molotov cocktails.

July 11, 1969. *Shooting.* White racist. Evansville, Indiana. A sniper kills Jeffrey Taylor, a black man.

July 11, 1969. *Bombing/explosive.* Revolutionary leftist. Cleveland, Ohio. The Collingwood National City Bank is bombed.

July 15, 1969. *Bombing/explosive.* Revolutionary leftist, Sam Melville Group. New Jersey. A grenade arsenal is bombed.

July 15, 1969. *Bombing/incendiary.* Revolutionary leftist. Seattle, Washington. The Gompers branch of Seattle Community College is firebombed.

July 15, 1969. *Bombing/incendiary.* Revolutionary leftist. Pittsburgh, Pennsylvania.

The tower on the University of Pittsburgh campus is firebombed, causing $500 in damage.

July 16, 1969. *Shoot-out.* Black militant, Black Panthers. Chicago, Illinois. Larry Roberson, a Black Panther, is killed in a shoot-out with police.

July 17, 1969. *Arson.* Revolutionary leftist. Berkeley, California. The student union at the University Hall and Dwinelle Hall at the University of California are set on fire.

July 19, 1969. *Shooting.* Black militant. Denver, Colorado. A police officer is shot while he is sitting in his car.

July 22, 1969. *Bombing/incendiary.* Revolutionary leftist. Monterey, California. The National Guard Armory is hit by a firebomb that does not ignite.

July 25, 1969. *Shooting.* Black militant, Black Panthers. Los Angeles, California. A police officer is wounded by sniper fire.

July 25, 1969. *Bombing/incendiary.* Revolutionary leftist. Cincinnati, Ohio. A judge's home is firebombed.

July 26, 1969. *Bombing.* Revolutionary leftist. Prichard, Alabama. A bomb explodes on the steps of city hall.

July 27, 1969. *Bombing/explosive.* Revolutionary leftist, Sam Melville Group. New York City, New York. The United Fruit Company pier is bombed.

July 31, 1969. *Shoot-out.* Black militant, Black Panthers. Chicago, Illinois. Five police officers are wounded in a gun battle with Black Panthers. John Soto, a Black Panther, is killed.

July 31, 1969. *Bombing/explosive.* Revolutionary leftist. Seattle, Washington. The State Multiservice Center is damaged by a small explosion.

August 4, 1969. *Shooting.* Black militant. Chicago, Illinois. A police car is shot at in the area of 18th and Wabash streets.

August 6, 1969. *Bombing.* Revolutionary leftist. Denver, Colorado. Five Points Police Substation is bombed.

August 8, 1969. *Shooting.* Black militant. Michigan. A police officer is shot in an ambush.

August 10, 1969. *Bombing/incendiary.* Black militant. Seattle, Washington. A firebomb destroys a police car.

August 13, 1969. *Shooting.* Black militant. Chicago, Illinois. Shots are fired at a police car.

August 13, 1969. *Shooting.* Black militant. St. Louis, Missouri. A police car is fired at by an automatic weapon.

August 15, 1969. *Arson.* Revolutionary leftist. Stroudsberg, Pennsylvania. Selective Service office files are destroyed by a fire at the local draft board.

August 15, 1969. *Shooting.* Black militant, Black Panthers. San Diego, California. Sylvester Bell is shot and killed while distributing Black Panther newspapers. His killers are believed to be members of US, a rival black militant group.

August 16, 1969. *Bombing/explosive.* Black militant. Chicago, Illinois. Youth are arrested for throwing a black powder bomb under a police car.

August 18, 1969. *Shooting.* Black militant. Tacoma, Washington. A police car is fired on by a sniper.

August 20, 1969. *Bombing/explosive.* Revolutionary leftist, Sam Melville Group. New York City, New York. A bombing at the Marine Midland Bank Building injures 19 people.

August 24, 1969. *Bombing/incendiary.* Revolutionary leftist. Modesto, California. The National Guard Armory is bombed.

August 25, 1969. *Bombing/incendiary.* Black militant. Denver, Colorado. The district police station is firebombed.

August 30, 1969. *Bombing/explosive.* Black militant, Black Panthers. San Diego, California. The new headquarters of US is bombed.

August 31, 1969. *Shooting.* Black militant. Lawrence, Kansas. A shotgun is fired at a police car.

September 4, 1969. *Shooting.* Black militant. St. Louis, Missouri. A police car is hit by gunshots.

September 5, 1969. *Shooting.* Black militant. St. Louis, Missouri. Shots are fired from an apartment building, wounding three police officers.

September 7, 1969. *Shoot-out.* Black militant, Black Panthers. Gardena, California. A shoot-out occurs between the police and Black Panthers.

September 15, 1969. *Shooting.* Black militant. Chicago, Illinois. A policeman is shot by a sniper.

September 15, 1969. *Shooting.* Black militant. St. Louis, Missouri. Police are the target of snipers.

September 15, 1969. *Bombing.* Black militant. Chicago, Illinois. Offices are attacked with Molotov cocktails.

September 16, 1969. *Shooting.* White racist. Cairo, Illinois. A black woman is wounded in a drive-by shooting.

September 16, 1969. *Shooting.* White racist. Sandersville, Georgia. A black civil rights leader is shot and wounded.

September 17, 1969. *Arson.* Revolutionary leftist. Berkeley, California. The University of California Institute of International Relations is set on fire.

September 17, 1969. *Shooting.* White racist. Cairo, Illinois. A black teenager is wounded in a drive-by shooting.

September 19, 1969. *Bombing/explosive.* Revolutionary leftist, Sam Melville Group. New York City, New York. A federal office is bombed.

September 20, 1969. *Assault.* Jewish, Jewish Defense League. New York City, New York. JDL marchers beat up Nazis.

September 24, 1969. *Bombing/explosive.* Revolutionary leftist. Milwaukee, Wisconsin. A federal office is bombed.

September 24, 1969. *Bombing/incendiary.* Revolutionary leftist. Madison, Wisconsin. The ROTC building at the University of Wisconsin is firebombed.

September 24, 1969. *Shooting.* Black militant. St. Louis, Missouri. A police car is the target of sniper fire.

September 24, 1969. *Bombing/explosive.* Revolutionary leftist. Chicago, Illinois. The Civic Center is bombed.

September 25, 1969. *Bombing/explosive.* Revolutionary leftist. El Sobrante, California. Pacific Gas and Electric is bombed.

September 25, 1969. *Shooting.* Black militant. Fort Lauderdale, Florida. Twelve shots are fired by a sniper at the police department.

September 26, 1969. *Shooting.* Black militant. Chicago, Illinois. A police car is the target of sniper fire.

September 26, 1969. *Bombing/explosive.* Revolutionary leftist. Madison, Wisconsin. An explosion at the Wisconsin National Guard Armory causes $25,000 in damage.

September 26, 1969. *Bombing/explosive.* Revolutionary leftist. Milwaukee, Wisconsin. The Selective Service office is bombed. The explosion causes almost $100,000 in damage.

September 26, 1969. *Bombing/explosive.* Revolutionary leftist. Bowling Green, Kentucky. An explosion damages a TV tower.

September 26, 1969. *Arson.* Revolutionary leftist. Akron, Ohio. The Selective Service office is the target of arsonists. Fire destroys records with an estimated damage of $15,000.

September 26, 1969. *Shooting.* Revolutionary leftist. Champlain, New York. Police customs agents are injured by gunfire.

September 27, 1969. *Shooting.* Black militant. Pontiac, Michigan. A sniper shoots at police.

September 27, 1969. *Bombing/explosive.* Revolutionary leftist. Syracuse, New York. A bomb explodes at Syracuse University.

September 29, 1969. *Robbery.* Black militant, Black Panthers. Los Angeles, California. A security guard is killed during a robbery by Black Panthers.

September 29, 1969. *Bombing/explosive.* Revolutionary leftist. Ann Arbor, Michigan. The CIA building is bombed.

September 29, 1969. *Shooting.* Black militant. Dallas, Texas. A black sniper wounds three police officers.

October 1, 1969. *Shooting.* Black militant. St. Petersburg, Florida. A police car is hit by sniper fire.

October 4, 1969. *Shoot-out.* Black militant, Black Panthers. Chicago, Illinois. A police officer is wounded in a gun battle with Black Panthers.

October 4, 1969. *Bombing/incendiary.* Revolutionary leftist. New York City, New York. The ROTC building at Columbia University is damaged by a Molotov cocktail.

October 4, 1969. *Shooting.* Revolutionary leftist. Chicago, Illinois. Police are hit by sniper fire.

October 6, 1969. *Bombing/explosive.* Black militant. Philadelphia, Pennsylvania. Hand grenades are thrown into a police parking lot.

October 6, 1969. *Bombing/explosive.* Revolutionary leftist, Weather Underground. Chicago, Illinois. An explosion in Haymarket Square damages a statue commemorating the violent clash between police and trade unionists in 1886.

October 7, 1969. *Bombing/explosive.* Revolutionary leftist, Sam Melville Group. New York City, New York. A bomb explodes at the entrance to the Armed Forces Examining Station.

October 7, 1969. *Shooting.* Black militant. Sanford, North Carolina. A police officer is hit by sniper fire.

October 7, 1969. *Bombing/incendiary.* Revolutionary leftist. College Station, Texas. The ROTC headquarters at Texas A&M is bombed.

October 8, 1969. *Bombing.* Revolutionary leftist. Chicago, Illinois. The Weathermen confront police with guns, clubs, tear gas, and Molotov cocktails.

October 8, 1969. *Bombing/incendiary.* Revolutionary leftist. Chicago, Illinois. A police car is firebombed.

October 9, 1969. *Bombing/explosive.* Revolutionary leftist. West Point, Nebraska. A power transformer is bombed, causing an estimated damage of $8000.

October 9, 1969. *Bombing/incendiary.* Revolutionary leftist. Chicago, Illinois. An incendiary device is thrown into the office of Chicago Alderman George McCutcheon.

October 10, 1969. *Shooting.* Revolutionary leftist. Chicago, Illinois. A police car is the target of shotgun fire.

October 11, 1969. *Bombing/incendiary.* Revolutionary leftist. Chicago, Illinois. Navy and U.S. Air Force recruiting offices are firebombed; minor damage is reported.

October 13, 1969. *Shooting.* Black militant. St. Louis, Missouri. Shots are fired at the 9th District Police Station.

October 14, 1969. *Bombing/incendiary.* Revolutionary leftist. New York City, New York. Macy's Herald Square store is bombed six times in four days, causing an estimated damage of thousands of dollars.

October 14, 1969. *Bombing/incendiary.* Revolutionary leftist. Indiana, Pennsylvania. The ROTC building at the Indiana campus of the University of Pennsylvania is firebombed.

October 14, 1969. *Bombing/explosive.* Black militant. Dallas, Texas. An explosion occurs at police headquarters.

October 15, 1969. *Bombing/incendiary.* Revolutionary leftist. Philadelphia, Pennsylvania. A Molotov cocktail thrown at Pennsylvania State University Research Lab causes minor damage.

October 17, 1969. *Shooting.* Black militant. Compton, California. A police officer is shot and wounded.

October 18, 1969. *Shoot-out.* Black militant, Black Panthers. Los Angeles, California. Two police officers are wounded in a shoot-out with Black Panthers. Walter Pope, a Black Panther, is killed.

October 18, 1969. *Arson.* Revolutionary leftist. Chapel Hill, North Carolina. Four buildings at the University of North Carolina are set on fire.

October 21, 1969. *Arson.* Revolutionary leftist. Lorain, Ohio. The Selective Service office is the target of arsonists who destroy files.

October 22, 1969. *Arson.* Revolutionary leftist. Painesville, Ohio. The Selective Service office is set on fire, causing $5000 in damage.

October 26, 1969. *Shooting.* Black militant. Chicago, Illinois. A police officer is shot and wounded by a sniper.

October 30, 1969. *Shooting.* Black militant. Chicago, Illinois. A police car is the target of a sniper.

October 30, 1969. *Arson.* Black militant. Alexandria, Virginia. The Sunshine Supermarket is set on fire, causing several thousand dollars of damage.

November 2, 1969. *Bombing.* Revolutionary leftist. Beverly, Massachusetts. An explosion occurs in the rear of a police station.

November 3, 1969. *Shooting.* Black militant. Wheaton, Illinois. Five police cars are the targets of snipers.

November 8, 1969. *Shooting.* Revolutionary leftist, Weather Underground. Cambridge, Massachusetts. A sniping occurs at police headquarters by the Weathermen.

November 10, 1969. *Bombing/incendiary.* Revolutionary leftist. New York City, New York. Incendiary bombs cause slight damage to the New York Public Library.

November 11, 1969. *Bombing/explosive.* Revolutionary leftist, Sam Melville Group. New York City, New York. Chase Manhattan Bank headquarters is bombed.

November 11, 1969. *Bombing/explosive.* Revolutionary leftist, Sam Melville Group. New York City, New York. General Motors Corporation and Rockefeller Center are bombed.

November 12, 1969. *Bombing/explosive.* Revolutionary leftist, Sam Melville Group. New York City, New York. An explosion occurs at the criminal courts building near police headquarters.

November 12, 1969. *Bombing/explosive.* Revolutionary leftist. Seattle, Washington. An explosion at the Electric Power Co. building causes minor damage.

November 12, 1969. *Attempted bombing.* Revolutionary leftist. Seattle, Washington. A bomb is found in the First National Bank building.

November 12, 1969. *Attempted bombing.* Revolutionary leftist. Seattle, Washington. Two unexploded bombs are found at the telephone company building.

November 12, 1969. *Bombing/incendiary.* Revolutionary leftist. New York City, New York. The Brooklyn branch of the Hanover Trust Co. Bank is firebombed.

November 12, 1969. *Attempted bombing.* Black militant. New York City, New York. The police find men placing dynamite charges in the armory.

November 12, 1969. *Bombing/explosive.* Revolutionary leftist. St. Louis, Missouri. Mosley Square Shopping Center in Creve Coeur is bombed.

November 12, 1969. *Attempted bombing.* Black militant. New York City, New York. A bomb is found in a National Guard truck.

November 13, 1969. *Bombing/explosive.* Revolutionary leftist. Franklin, Missouri. The Franklin County Courthouse is bombed, causing an estimated damage of $173,000, and 10 people are injured.

November 13, 1969. *Shoot-out.* Black militant, Black Panthers. Chicago, Illinois. Two police officers, Frank Rappaport and John Gilhooly, are shot and killed in a gun battle with Black Panthers. Jake Winters, a Black Panther, is also killed.

November 14, 1969. *Shooting.* Black militant. Hartford, Connecticut. A police car is hit by gunfire.

November 17, 1969. *Bombing/incendiary.* Revolutionary leftist. Lafayette, Indiana. The Selective Service office is firebombed.

November 17, 1969. *Shooting.* Black militant. Chicago, Illinois. A police car is hit by sniper fire.

November 17, 1969. *Bombing/explosive.* Revolutionary leftist. Sioux City, Nebraska. An explosion occurs in front of the county sheriff headquarters.

November 18, 1969. *Bombing.* Black militant. Seattle, Washington. The bombing of a Safeway store injures two.

November 21, 1969. *Shooting.* Revolutionary leftist. Cambridge, Massachusetts. A police station is hit by gunfire.

November 25, 1969. *Shooting.* Black militant. St. Louis, Missouri. A police car is fired at by snipers.

November 26, 1969. *Shooting.* White racist. Sandersville, Georgia. Shots are fired at the home of a black civil rights leader.

November 29, 1969. *Shooting.* Black militant. Jackson, Michigan. Police headquarters is the target of sniper fire.

December 2, 1969. *Shooting.* Black militant. St. Louis, Missouri. A police car is fired at by snipers.

December 4, 1969. *Shoot-out.* Black militant, Black Panthers. Chicago, Illinois. Fred Hampton and Mark Clark are killed in a pre-dawn police raid on an apartment occupied by Black Panthers. Four other Panthers are wounded. Although police claim that the Panthers fired first, forensic evidence shows that only one shot was fired by the Panthers and more than 80 by the police. It is likely that Hampton was sleeping when he was shot by police.

December 6, 1969. *Shooting.* Black militant. Chicago, Illinois. A police car is the target of sniper fire.

December 8, 1969. *Shoot-out.* Black militant, Black Panthers. Los Angeles, California. Following a raid on the BPP office, three police and three Black Panthers are wounded in a four-hour gun battle.

December 9, 1969. *Arson.* White racist. Pell City, Alabama. Fire damages the property of a white businessman who sold land to Black Muslims.

December 9, 1969. *Bombing.* Revolutionary leftist. Huntsville, Texas. A bomb explodes at Sam Houston State University.

December 10, 1969. *Bombing/incendiary.* Revolutionary leftist. Salt Lake City, Utah. A police car is destroyed by a firebomb.

December 10, 1969. *Bombing/incendiary.* Revolutionary leftist. New Brunswick, New Jersey. The Rutgers University administration building is firebombed.

December 11, 1969. *Bombing/explosive.* Puerto Rican nationalist, Armed Independence Movement. San Juan, Puerto Rico. The Sheraton, Hilton, San Jeronimo, Chez Bamboo, Americana, and Howard Johnson's hotels are bombed.

December 12, 1969. *Attempted bombing.* Black militant. Denver, Colorado. A dynamite stick is thrown at a police car, but it fails to explode.

December 13, 1969. *Shooting.* Black militant. St. Louis, Missouri. Two shots are fired at the 9th District Police Station.

December 13, 1969. *Shooting.* Black militant. St. Louis, Missouri. Shots are fired at a police car.

December 18, 1969. *Shooting.* Black militant. Chicago, Illinois. A police car is hit by gunfire.

December 21, 1969. *Shooting.* Black militant. St. Louis, Missouri. A police car is hit by sniper fire.

December 21, 1969. *Bombing/explosive.* Puerto Rican nationalist. New York City, New York. A bank and department stores are bombed.

December 21, 1969. *Bombing/incendiary.* Revolutionary leftist. Chicago, Illinois. A firebombing of the 6th Ward Democratic headquarters causes minor damage.

December 28, 1969. *Bombing/incendiary.* Revolutionary leftist, New Years Gang. Madison, Wisconsin. A ROTC classroom is firebombed.

December 29, 1969. *Sabotage, vandalism, and property destruction.* Jewish, Jewish Defense League. New York City, New York. Soviet Airline offices are vandalized.

December 31, 1969. *Attempted bombing.* Revolutionary leftist, New Years Gang. Baraboo, Wisconsin. The New Years Gang attempts to bomb the Badger Army Ammunition Plant by dropping mayonnaise jars filled with explosives from a plane.

January 1970. *Bombing/explosive.* White racist. West Point, Mississippi. Clay County Courthouse is bombed.

January 1, 1970. *Shooting.* Black militant, US. Los Angeles, California. Shots are fired at police from the headquarters of US.

January 1, 1970. *Shooting.* Black militant. Cairo, Illinois. Shots are fired at police headquarters.

January 2, 1970. *Bombing/explosive.* Revolutionary leftist. Oakland, California. An explosion at a Pacific Gas and Electric Company substation causes an estimated damage of $20,000–$25,000.

January 3, 1970. *Bombing/incendiary.* Revolutionary leftist, New Years Gang. Madison, Wisconsin. ROTC offices are firebombed.

January 6, 1970. *Bombing/incendiary.* Revolutionary leftist. Denver, Colorado. A

Molotov cocktail causes minor damage at the Army recruiting office.

January 9, 1970. *Bombing/incendiary.* Revolutionary leftist. Detroit, Michigan. The Packard Properties building that houses federal employees is firebombed; no injuries are reported.

January 11, 1970. *Bombing.* Revolutionary leftist. Emory, Virginia. An explosion occurs in the unoccupied car of the dean of Emory & Henry College.

January 14, 1970. *Bombing/incendiary.* Black militant. Champaign, Illinois. The firebombing of the Champaign Police Department severely injures a patrolman.

January 15, 1970. *Shooting.* Black militant. Lima, Ohio. The police department building is the target of sniper fire.

January 15, 1970. *Shooting.* Black militant. Jacksonville, Florida. A police car is the target of a sniper.

January 19, 1970. *Bombing/explosive.* Revolutionary leftist. Seattle, Washington. An explosion occurs in the Seattle University liberal arts building.

January 19, 1970. *Arson.* White racist. New York City, New York. Arson occurs at a Jewish synagogue.

January 19, 1970. *Attempted bombing.* Revolutionary leftist. Seattle, Washington. An attempted bombing of the Seattle University Air Force ROTC building occurs.

January 22, 1970. *Bombing/explosive.* Revolutionary leftist. Bloomington, Indiana. Two explosions in the Coca-Cola Bottling Plant cause $10,000–$15,000 in damage.

January 25, 1970. *Shooting.* Black militant. New York City, New York. Two policemen are shot from behind.

January 26, 1970. *Bombing/explosive.* White racist. West Point, Mississippi. An explosion in the Clay County Courthouse shatters windows.

January 29, 1970. *Bombing/incendiary.* Revolutionary leftist. Coral Gables, Florida. The dean's office at the University of Miami is firebombed.

January 30, 1970. *Shooting.* Black militant. Philadelphia, Pennsylvania. A police officer, Frederick Cione, is shot and killed by sniper fire.

January 31, 1970. *Bombing.* Black militant. Denver, Colorado. A bomb blast damages the police band building.

January 31, 1970. *Shooting.* Black militant. Chicago, Illinois. A police officer is wounded by snipers at the Mother Cabrini Housing Project.

February 1, 1970. *Shooting.* Black militant. Cairo, Illinois. Police are shot by snipers.

February 2, 1970. *Bombing/explosive.* Black militant. Cleveland, Ohio. An explosion to the Cleveland Municipal Building causes $800,000 in damage.

February 6, 1970. *Bombing/explosive.* White racist. Denver, Colorado. School buses are destroyed by bombs.

February 6, 1970. *Bombing/incendiary.* Puerto Rican nationalist. Dorado, Rio Piedras, and Isla Verde, Puerto Rico. The Selective Service office in Dorado, General Electric offices in Rio Piedras, and Hotel San Juan in Isla Verde are firebombed.

February 6, 1970. *Bombing/incendiary.* Revolutionary leftist. Boston, Massachusetts. Molotov cocktails are thrown at the University of Boston ROTC office.

February 7, 1970. *Arson.* Revolutionary leftist. Whitewater, Wisconsin. Old Mail Hall of Wisconsin State College is destroyed by fire, causing an estimated damage of $1 million.

February 9, 1970. *Bombing/explosive.* Puerto Rican nationalist, Armed Independence Movement. New York City, New York. General Electric service centers in Woodside, Queens, and the Atlantic Terminal section of Brooklyn are bombed.

February 11, 1970. *Bombing/incendiary.* Revolutionary leftist. Ypsilanti, Michigan. A firebombing at Washtenaw Community College causes $2500 in damage.

February 13, 1970. *Bombing/explosive.* Black militant. Berkeley, California. Two explosions in the parking lot of the Berkeley Police Department injure six officers.

February 13, 1970. *Bombing/explosive.* Revolutionary leftist. Danbury, Connecticut. A police station is bombed, injuring 23 people. The bombing is a diversionary tactic during a robbery, when $40,000 is stolen from a downtown bank.

February 16, 1970. *Bombing/explosive.* Black militant, Black Liberation Army. San Francisco, California. San Francisco Park Police Station is bombed, killing Sergeant Brian McDonnell and injuring eight others.

February 16, 1970. *Bombing/explosive.* Black militant, Black Liberation Army. Berkeley, California. Department stores are bombed.

February 17, 1970. *Bombing/explosive.* Revolutionary leftist. Buckeyesville, Maryland. An explosion at an electric tower causes power outages.

February 18, 1970. *Shooting.* Black militant. Wilmington, Delaware. A police car is the target of sniper fire.

February 18, 1970. *Shooting.* Revolutionary leftist. Portland, Oregon. A police officer is wounded by a sniper.

February 20, 1970. *Bombing/explosive.* Revolutionary leftist. Seattle, Washington. An explosion is set off at the site of the new University of Washington architecture building.

February 20, 1970. *Bombing/incendiary.* Revolutionary leftist. Hartford, Connecticut. A Molotov cocktail is thrown at the federal building housing the U.S. Courthouse, causing minor damage.

February 21, 1970. *Bombing/incendiary.* Revolutionary leftist. New York City, New York. The Army recruiting office is firebombed.

February 21, 1970. *Bombing/incendiary.* Black militant, Black Panthers. New York City, New York. The home of State Supreme Court Judge John M. Murtaugh is the target of three gasoline bombs. Judge Murtagh is presiding over the trial of Black Panthers.

February 21, 1970. *Bombing/incendiary.* Revolutionary leftist. Carbondale, Illinois. The ROTC building at Southern Illinois University is firebombed, causing an estimated $100,000 in damage.

February 22, 1970. *Bombing/incendiary.* Revolutionary leftist. New York City,

New York. Columbia University Law School is firebombed, causing minor damage.

February 23, 1970. *Bombing/explosive.* Revolutionary leftist. Tucson, Arizona. An explosion occurs at the Selective Service office.

February 23, 1970. *Shooting.* Black militant. Cleveland, Ohio. A police car is the target of a sniper.

February 23, 1970. *Bombing/explosive.* Revolutionary leftist. Dakota City, Nebraska. Dynamite explosions damage four separate power transmission poles in Dakota City and Sioux City.

February 24, 1970. *Bombing/incendiary.* Revolutionary leftist. Champaign, Illinois. A Molotov cocktail is thrown at the armory, which houses the ROTC office, at the University of Illinois.

February 25, 1970. *Bombing/incendiary.* Black militant. Santa Barbara, California. A police car is firebombed.

February 25, 1970. *Arson.* Revolutionary leftist. Isla Vista, California. The Vista branch of the Bank of America is destroyed by arson, causing damage estimated at $330,000.

February 26, 1970. *Bombing/incendiary.* Revolutionary leftist. St. Louis, Missouri. The firebombing of the ROTC building at Washington University destroys 90 percent of the building.

February 27, 1970. *Bombing/explosive.* Revolutionary leftist. Boulder, Colorado. A bomb explodes at the Institute of Behavioral Sciences of the University of Colorado.

March 1, 1970. *Bombing/incendiary.* Revolutionary leftist. Boulder, Colorado. A campus police car is firebombed.

March 1, 1970. *Bombing/incendiary.* Revolutionary leftist. Boulder, Colorado. The Selective Service office and the ROTC offices are firebombed.

March 2, 1970. *Bombing/incendiary.* Revolutionary leftist. Cleveland, Ohio. The home of the president of Cleveland's Fraternal Order of Police is firebombed, causing an estimated damage of $200.

March 4, 1970. *Attempted bombing.* Revolutionary leftist. Oakland, California. An explosive device is discovered at the Oakland Army Terminal.

March 5, 1970. *Shooting.* Puerto Rican nationalist, Armed Independence Movement. Puerto Rico. Two U.S. sailors are shot and wounded.

March 6, 1970. *Bombing/explosive.* Revolutionary leftist, Weather Underground. New York City, New York. An explosion destroys a townhouse that was a Weatherman bomb factory, killing Diana Oughton, Ted Gold, and Terry Robbins. Two other people ran away from the house.

March 6, 1970. *Attempted bombing.* Black militant. Detroit, Michigan. A bomb is found in the Detroit Police Department headquarters.

March 9, 1970. *Bombing/incendiary.* Revolutionary leftist. Champaign, Illinois. The firebombing of a federal building causes $2500 in damage.

March 9, 1970. *Arson.* Revolutionary leftist. Berkeley, California. A fire destroys a portion of the main library at the University of California, causing $320,000 in damage.

March 9, 1970. *Arson.* Revolutionary leftist. Seattle, Washington. Parrington Hall at the University of Washington is set on fire, causing $6000 in damage.

March 10, 1970. *Bombing/explosive.* Black militant, Student Non-Violent Coordinating Committee. Bel Air, Maryland. Two blacks, William Payne and Ralph Featherstone, are killed when a bomb in their car explodes. They were members of SNCC, and evidence suggests that they were carrying the bomb.

March 10, 1970. *Arson.* Revolutionary leftist. Berkeley, California. Wheeler Hall at the University of California is set on fire, causing $5000 in damage.

March 10, 1970. *Bombing/incendiary.* Revolutionary leftist. San Francisco, California. The office of Dr. S. I. Hayakawa, president of San Francisco State College, is firebombed.

March 10, 1970. *Bombing.* Revolutionary leftist. Cambridge, Maryland. Dorchester County Courthouse is bombed; no injuries are reported.

March 11, 1970. *Bombing/incendiary.* Revolutionary leftist. Urbana, Illinois. The U.S. Army recruiting office is destroyed by a firebomb.

March 11, 1970. *Bombing/explosive.* Black militant, Student Non-Violent Coordinating Committee. Cambridge, Maryland. The courthouse where SNCC leader Rap Brown was due to go on trial is bombed.

March 12, 1970. *Bombing/incendiary.* Black militant. Chicago, Illinois. A police car is firebombed.

March 12, 1970. *Bombing/explosive.* Revolutionary leftist, Revolutionary Force 9. New York City, New York. Revolutionary Force 9 claims credit for an explosion in the Sylvania Electric Division at the General Telephone Company building.

March 12, 1970. *Bombing/explosive.* Revolutionary leftist, Revolutionary Force 9. New York City, New York. Revolutionary Force 9 claims credit for an explosion on the 12th floor of the IBM building.

March 12, 1970. *Bombing/explosive.* Revolutionary leftist, Revolutionary Force 9. New York City, New York. Revolutionary Force 9 claims credit for an explosion on the 34th floor of the Mobil Oil Co. building.

March 13, 1970. *Bombing/incendiary.* Revolutionary leftist. Appleton, Wisconsin. The ROTC building at Lawrence University is firebombed.

March 13, 1970. *Bombing/incendiary.* Black militant, Black Afro-militant Movement. Miami, Florida. A store is firebombed by the Black Afro-Militant Movement.

March 16, 1970. *Bombing/explosive.* Revolutionary leftist. Billings, Montana. A parked police car is destroyed by a bomb.

March 16, 1970. *Bombing/explosive.* Puerto Rican nationalist. Puerto Rico. A department store is bombed.

March 17, 1970. *Bombing.* Puerto Rican nationalist. New York City, New York. An Army recruiting center is bombed.

March 18, 1970. *Shooting.* Black militant. Chicago, Illinois. A shotgun is fired at a police car.

March 18, 1970. *Bombing/explosive.* Revolutionary leftist. Cincinnati, Ohio. An explosion at the Cincinnati Gas & Electric Co. causes extensive damage.

March 20, 1970. *Bombing/incendiary.* Revolutionary leftist. Portland, Oregon. The firebombing of two trucks at the U.S. Army Reserve training center causes an explosion.

March 21, 1970. *Bombing/incendiary.* Revolutionary leftist. New York City, New York. Bloomingdale's Department Store is firebombed.

March 21, 1970. *Bombing/incendiary.* Revolutionary leftist. New York City, New York. Alexander's Department Store is firebombed.

March 22, 1970. *Bombing/explosive.* Revolutionary leftist. New York City, New York. A stockbrokers office, Nagler, Weissman & Co., Inc., is the target of a pipe bomb.

March 23, 1970. *Arson.* Revolutionary leftist. Oakland, California. A garage at the Oakland Army Base is set on fire, causing an estimated damage of $5000.

March 28, 1970. *Bombing/explosive.* Black militant. New York City, New York. An explosion in a bomb factory kills one Black Panther and injures another.

March 28, 1970. *Arson.* Revolutionary leftist. Seattle, Washington. Parrington Hall at the University of Washington is set on fire, causing an estimated damage of $20,000.

March 31, 1970. *Bombing.* Revolutionary leftist. Seattle, Washington. Two jeeps are bombed at the University of Washington.

April 1, 1970. *Arson.* Revolutionary leftist. Houston, Texas. A fire set by kerosene at Rice University causes damage to the outer wall of the ROTC building.

April 1, 1970. *Attempted bombing.* Revolutionary leftist. Washington, D.C. A bomb is mailed from Seattle to the Director of the Selective Service, but it does not detonate.

April 1, 1970. *Bombing.* Revolutionary leftist. East Lansing, Michigan. The bombing of the administration building at Michigan State University causes slight damage.

April 3, 1970. *Shooting.* Black militant. Chicago, Illinois. Police officers are wounded by gunfire from the vicinity of Altgeld Gardens.

April 4, 1970. *Arson.* Revolutionary leftist. Pullman, Washington. Roger's Field Stadium at Washington State University is set on fire, causing damage of $700,000.

April 5, 1970. *Bombing/explosive.* Revolutionary leftist. Trona, California. A dynamite blast shatters a power line.

April 5, 1970. *Bombing/incendiary.* Revolutionary leftist. Houston, Texas. The firebombing of the office of the dean of students at Rice University causes an estimated damage of $50,000.

April 7, 1970. *Arson.* Revolutionary leftist. New Orleans, Louisiana. The ROTC building at Tulane University is set on fire and is completely destroyed.

April 8, 1970. *Bombing/explosive.* Revolutionary leftist. Lawrence, Kansas. A pipe bomb explodes in the Anchor Savings & Loan Co.

April 11, 1970. *Bombing/explosive.* Revolutionary leftist. San Diego, California. An explosion at the Imperial Beach Naval Air Station damages the barracks building.

April 11, 1970. *Bombing/incendiary.* Revolutionary leftist. Freeport, Texas. The Dow Chemical plant is the target of a firebomb, causing an estimated $250,000 in damage.

April 12, 1970. *Bombing/explosive.* Revolutionary leftist. Atlanta, Georgia. Citizens and Southern National Bank is bombed.

April 12, 1970. *Bombing/incendiary.* Revolutionary leftist. Ithaca, New York. Several buildings at Cornell University, including Olin Library, are targets of Molotov cocktails.

April 13, 1970. *Bombing/explosive.* Black militant. Kansas City, Missouri. The Kansas City Police Academy is bombed.

April 13, 1970. *Bombing/explosive.* Revolutionary leftist. Berkeley, California. A bomb explosion at the University of California topples an 80-foot tower.

April 15, 1970. *Shooting.* Black militant. Durham, North Carolina. Three white college students are shot and wounded by three black males.

April 15, 1970. *Arson.* Revolutionary leftist. Eugene, Oregon. Fires are set at the University of Oregon's ROTC building.

April 16, 1970. *Shooting.* Black militant. Detroit, Michigan. Shots are fired at a police officer.

April 17, 1970. *Shooting.* Black militant, Black Panthers. Oakland, California. A police van is ambushed by Black Panthers firing automatic weapons.

April 18, 1970. *Bombing/incendiary.* Revolutionary leftist. Baraboo, Wisconsin. The Badger Army Ammunition Plant is damaged by a firebomb, causing an estimated damage of $150,000.

April 20, 1970. *Bombing/incendiary.* Revolutionary leftist. Los Angeles, California. Two firebombs are thrown in the window of a Bank of America branch, causing an estimated damage of $25,000.

April 20, 1970. *Bombing/explosive.* Revolutionary leftist. Lawrence, Kansas. Two explosions at the student union building at the University of Kansas cause an estimated damage of $1 million.

April 22, 1970. *Bombing/incendiary.* Revolutionary leftist. Milwaukee, Wisconsin. A firebomb damages the Schmidt Building federal government offices.

April 22, 1970. *Bombing/incendiary.* Revolutionary leftist. Redlands, California. A firebombing of the Hall of Letters at Redlands University causes minor damage. The administrative offices are also targeted, causing $40,000 in estimated damage.

April 22, 1970. *Bombing/incendiary.* Revolutionary leftist. Berkeley, California. A firebomb explodes at the University of California.

April 24, 1970. *Shooting.* Black militant, Black Panthers. Baltimore, Maryland. Shots are fired at police, killing Donald Sager and wounding another officer.

April 24, 1970. *Arson.* Revolutionary leftist. Palo Alto, California. A fire at Stanford University causes an estimated $100,000 in damage.

April 25, 1970. *Bombing/explosive.* White racist. Seattle, Washington. Four bombs explode in black neighborhoods.

April 25, 1970. *Bombing/explosive.* Revolutionary leftist. East Lansing, Michigan. Three explosions at East Lansing banks cause an estimated damage of $1000.

April 25, 1970. *Bombing/explosive.* Revolutionary leftist. New York City, New York. An explosion at an Army recruiting office causes heavy damage.

April 25, 1970. *Bombing/incendiary.* Revolutionary leftist. Philadelphia, Pennsylvania. Molotov cocktails explode in College Hall at the University of Pennsylvania.

April 26, 1970. *Bombing/explosive.* Black militant. Baton Rouge, Louisiana. A dynamite explosion occurs at the State Capitol Building.

April 26, 1970. *Bombing/explosive.* Revolutionary leftist. Robbinsdale, Minnesota. A bomb explodes outside the Selective Service office, Local Board Number 51.

April 26, 1970. *Bombing/explosive.* Black militant. Baton Rouge, Louisiana. A bomb explodes at the Baton Rouge Country Club.

April 26, 1970. *Bombing.* Revolutionary leftist. East Lansing, Michigan. The bombing of three banks causes minor damage.

April 27, 1970. *Arson.* Revolutionary leftist. Los Angeles, California. A Bank of America branch in East Los Angeles is set on fire, causing an estimated damage of $25,000.

April 27, 1970. *Arson.* Revolutionary leftist. New Haven, Connecticut. The Yale Law School library is set on fire, causing considerable damage.

April 27, 1970. *Arson.* Revolutionary leftist. Evanston, Illinois. The department of linguistics building at Northwestern University is set on fire, causing an estimated damage of $15,000.

April 27, 1970. *Bombing.* Revolutionary leftist. Evanston, Illinois. A stink bomb set off at the new library at Northwestern University causes an estimated damage of $7000.

April 29, 1970. *Bombing/incendiary.* Revolutionary leftist. Seattle, Washington. Xavier Hall at Seattle University is firebombed, causing an estimated damage of $1000.

April 30, 1970. *Attempted bombing.* Revolutionary leftist. New York City, New York. A pipe bomb is found in a canvas bag in front of the New York Police Station.

April 30, 1970. *Bombing/incendiary.* Revolutionary leftist. East Lansing, Michigan. First National Bank is firebombed.

May 1, 1970. *Bombing/incendiary.* Revolutionary leftist. College Park, Maryland.

The University of Maryland ROTC building is firebombed, causing extensive damage.

May 1, 1970. *Bombing/incendiary.* Revolutionary leftist. Geneva, New York. A firebomb destroys the ROTC building at Hobart College.

May 1, 1970. *Bombing/incendiary.* Revolutionary leftist. East Lansing, Michigan. The Michigan State University ROTC building is firebombed.

May 1, 1970. *Bombing/incendiary.* Revolutionary leftist. Princeton, New Jersey. The ROTC building is firebombed.

May 1, 1970. *Bombing/incendiary.* Revolutionary leftist. West DePere, Wisconsin. Firebombs are thrown at the ROTC rifle range at St. Norbert College.

May 1, 1970. *Bombing/explosive.* Revolutionary leftist. Greencastle, Indiana. An explosion and an ensuing fire damage the ROTC office at DePauw University.

May 1, 1970. *Bombing/incendiary.* Black militant. Detroit, Michigan. The police recruiting office is firebombed.

May 1, 1970. *Bombing/incendiary.* Revolutionary leftist. Corvallis, Oregon. Two firebombs are thrown at the Oregon State University ROTC building.

May 1, 1970. *Bombing/explosive.* Revolutionary leftist. New Haven, Connecticut. A bomb explodes in the ROTC building at Yale University, but no serious injuries are reported.

May 2, 1970. *Bombing/incendiary.* Revolutionary leftist. New York City, New York. A firebomb heavily damages the U.S. Army recruiting office.

May 2, 1970. *Bombing/incendiary.* Revolutionary leftist. Princeton, New Jersey. The armory at Princeton University is firebombed.

May 2, 1970. *Bombing/incendiary.* Revolutionary leftist. Seattle, Washington. Thompson Hall at the University of Washington is firebombed, causing an estimated $750 in damage.

May 3, 1970. *Bombing/incendiary.* Revolutionary leftist. Kent State, Ohio. The Army ROTC building at Kent State University is firebombed and totally destroyed. Other buildings on campus also suffer fire damage.

May 3, 1970. *Bombing/incendiary.* Revolutionary leftist. New Brunswick, New Jersey. The ROTC building at Rutgers College is firebombed.

May 3, 1970. *Shooting and robbery.* Black militant. Fort Lauderdale, Florida. A white insurance agent is killed during a robbery by three black males. The three youths go on a shooting spree through three states.

May 3, 1970. *Bombing/incendiary.* Revolutionary leftist. Milwaukee, Wisconsin. Two buildings at Marquette University are firebombed, causing extensive damage.

May 3, 1970. *Arson.* Revolutionary leftist. New Paltz, New York. New Paltz State College is the target of arson, causing moderate damage.

May 4, 1970. *Bombing/incendiary.* Revolutionary leftist. Norman, Oklahoma. The Selective Service office is firebombed.

May 4, 1970. *Bombing/incendiary.* Revolutionary leftist. Madison, Wisconsin. The ROTC building at the University of Wisconsin and the home of a military instructor are firebombed.

May 4, 1970. *Shooting.* Black militant. Brooklyn, New York. A police patrol is hit by sniper fire.

May 4, 1970. *Bombing/incendiary.* Revolutionary leftist. Berkeley, California. The ROTC building at the University of California is firebombed, causing minor damage.

May 4, 1970. *Bombing/incendiary.* Revolutionary leftist. Maryville, Missouri. Molotov cocktails are thrown at Missouri National Guard vehicles.

May 4, 1970. *Bombing/incendiary.* Revolutionary leftist. Chapel Hill, North Carolina. The ROTC office at the University of North Carolina is firebombed.

May 5, 1970. *Bombing/incendiary.* Revolutionary leftist. Lewiston, Idaho. The National Guard Armory is firebombed, causing an estimated damage of $250,000.

May 5, 1970. *Bombing/incendiary.* Revolutionary leftist. Moscow, Idaho. A firebomb damages the ROTC building at the University of Idaho.

May 5, 1970. *Bombing/incendiary.* Revolutionary leftist. St. Louis, Missouri. The ROTC building at Washington University is firebombed.

May 5, 1970. *Shooting.* Black militant. Chicago, Illinois. Two police officers are fired on by snipers.

May 5, 1970. *Bombing/incendiary.* Revolutionary leftist. New York City, New York. A fire is set at the ROTC building of City College.

May 5, 1970. *Bombing/incendiary.* Revolutionary leftist. Davis, California. A Molotov cocktail explodes at the ROTC building at the University of California.

May 5, 1970. *Bombing/incendiary.* Revolutionary leftist. Orange, New Jersey. The ROTC building at Seton Hall University is firebombed.

May 5, 1970. *Bombing/incendiary.* Revolutionary leftist. Lexington, Kentucky. A firebomb destroys the ROTC building at the University of Kentucky.

May 5, 1970. *Bombing/explosive.* Black militant, Black Afro-militant Movement. Coral Gables, Florida. A university computer center is bombed by the Black Afro-Militant Movement.

May 5, 1970. *Bombing.* Revolutionary leftist. Hazard, Kentucky. A police car is bombed; the estimated damage is $500.

May 5, 1970. *Arson.* Revolutionary leftist. Evanston, Illinois. Northwestern University Traffic Institute is the target of arsonists, causing an estimated damage of $80,000.

May 6, 1970. *Arson.* Revolutionary leftist. Greencastle, Indiana. The Air Force ROTC building at DePauw University is set on fire.

May 6, 1970. *Bombing/incendiary.* Revolutionary leftist. Columbia, Missouri. Molotov cocktails are thrown through the window of the ROTC building, causing an estimated damage of $150.

May 6, 1970. *Bombing/incendiary.* Revolutionary leftist. Oakland, California. The Selective Service office is bombed, causing an estimated $200 in damage.

May 6, 1970. *Bombing/explosive.* Revolutionary leftist. Longview, Washington. An explosion occurs at the Longview National Guard Armory.

May 6, 1970. *Bombing/incendiary.* Revolutionary leftist. Kent, Ohio. The Army Reserve building is firebombed, causing an estimated damage of $5000.

May 6, 1970. *Bombing/incendiary.* Revolutionary leftist. Reading, Pennsylvania. An explosion causes a fire at the U.S. Army Reserve building.

May 6, 1970. *Bombing/incendiary.* Revolutionary leftist. Portland, Oregon. Government offices are firebombed, causing an estimated damage of $1000.

May 6, 1970. *Arson.* Revolutionary leftist. Berkeley, California. The Asian studies building at the University of California is set on fire.

May 6, 1970. *Arson.* Revolutionary leftist. Brooklyn, New York. Three buildings at State University of New York are set on fire.

May 7, 1970. *Arson.* Revolutionary leftist. Shaker Heights, Ohio. The ROTC building at John Carroll University is set on fire.

May 7, 1970. *Bombing/incendiary.* Revolutionary leftist. Reno, Nevada. The ROTC building at the University of Nevada is firebombed.

May 7, 1970. *Bombing/incendiary.* Revolutionary leftist. Athens, Ohio. The ROTC building on the campus of Ohio University is firebombed.

May 7, 1970. *Bombing/incendiary.* Revolutionary leftist. Colorado Springs, Colorado. The ROTC building at the College of Colorado is firebombed.

May 7, 1970. *Bombing/incendiary.* Revolutionary leftist. Mankato, Minnesota. The local National Guard Armory is firebombed.

May 7, 1970. *Bombing/incendiary.* Revolutionary leftist. Buffalo, New York. The ROTC building at the state university campus is firebombed.

May 7, 1970. *Bombing/incendiary.* Revolutionary leftist. Cleveland, Ohio. The ROTC building at Case Western Reserve University is firebombed.

May 7, 1970. *Arson.* Revolutionary leftist. Charlottesville, Virginia. A fire is set at the ROTC building at the University of Virginia.

May 7, 1970. *Bombing/incendiary.* Revolutionary leftist. Tuscaloosa, Alabama. Two buildings at the University of Alabama are hit by firebombs; one building is completely destroyed.

May 7, 1970. *Bombing/incendiary.* Revolutionary leftist. Valparaiso, Indiana. The administration building at Valparaiso University is destroyed by a firebomb.

May 7, 1970. *Arson.* Revolutionary leftist. Carbondale, Illinois. Two buildings at Southern Illinois University are destroyed by fire.

May 7, 1970. *Bombing/incendiary.* Revolutionary leftist. San Francisco, California. The ROTC building at the University of San Francisco is firebombed.

May 7, 1970. *Arson.* Revolutionary leftist. Marietta, Ohio. The Marietta College bookstore is destroyed by fire.

May 7, 1970. *Arson.* Revolutionary leftist. Middlebury, Connecticut. A Middlebury College building is destroyed by fire.

May 7, 1970. *Arson.* Revolutionary leftist. New York City, New York. Arson at the campus center of Fordham University causes damage of $1000. Two Molotov cocktails are found in the bushes near the administration building.

May 8, 1970. *Bombing/incendiary.* Revolutionary leftist. Boston, Massachusetts. The Boston City National Guard Armory is firebombed.

May 8, 1970. *Bombing/incendiary.* Revolutionary leftist. New London, Connecticut. The National Guard Armory is firebombed.

May 8, 1970. *Attempted bombing.* Revolutionary leftist. New York City, New York. The attempted bombing of a computer at New York University results in $100,000 in damage. The computer is owned by the Atomic Energy Commission.

May 8, 1970. *Arson.* Revolutionary leftist. Ann Arbor, Michigan. A fire is set at the ROTC building at the University of Michigan.

May 8, 1970. *Arson.* Revolutionary leftist. Duluth, Minnesota. Several fires are set on the University of Michigan campus.

May 9, 1970. *Shooting.* Black militant. Sacramento, California. Police officer Bernard Bennett is critically wounded by sniper fire; he dies four days later.

May 9, 1970. *Bombing/explosive.* Revolutionary leftist. Hollywood, California. A time bomb is set off at the Selective Service office, causing damage estimated at $10,000.

May 9, 1970. *Arson.* Revolutionary leftist. Brooklyn, New York. A fire set at the humanities building of Long Island University causes $100,000 worth of damage.

May 9, 1970. *Bombing/incendiary.* Revolutionary leftist. Boston, Massachusetts. The Arthur D. Little Company is firebombed.

May 9, 1970. *Arson.* Revolutionary leftist. Carbondale, Illinois. Several fires are set on the campus of Southern Illinois University.

May 9, 1970. *Arson.* Revolutionary leftist. Fort Collins, Colorado. A fire destroys Colorado State University's administration building.

May 10, 1970. *Bombing/explosive.* Revolutionary leftist, Weather Underground. Washington, D.C. The National Guard Association building is bombed, causing minor structural damage. The bombing was said to be a response by the Weather Underground to the killing of four students at Kent State by the National Guard on May 4, 1970.

May 10, 1970. *Bombing.* Revolutionary leftist. Hollywood, California. A bomb explodes at the Selective Service office, causing heavy damage.

May 11, 1970. *Bombing/incendiary.* Revolutionary leftist. Chicago, Illinois. The Loyola University ROTC building is firebombed, causing only minor damage.

May 11, 1970. *Bombing/explosive.* Revolutionary leftist. Rocky Flats, Colorado. The Atomic Energy Commission is bombed, causing an estimated damage of $45 million.

May 11, 1970. *Arson.* Revolutionary leftist. Trenton, New Jersey. A fire set in a portable classroom building causes damage estimated at $150,000.

May 11, 1970. *Bombing/incendiary.* Revolutionary leftist. Athens, Ohio. The dormitory dining hall complex at Ohio University is firebombed, causing $125,000 in damage.

May 11, 1970. *Bombing/incendiary.* Revolutionary leftist. Rutgers, New Jersey. Livingston College's police science building is destroyed by a firebomb.

May 11, 1970. *Arson.* Revolutionary leftist. Bloomington, Indiana. The music building at Illinois Wesleyan University is set on fire.

May 12, 1970. *Arson.* Revolutionary leftist. Detroit, Michigan. A fire is set at the Selective Service office.

May 13, 1970. *Bombing/explosive.* Revolutionary leftist. Des Moines, Iowa. A massive explosion at Des Moines Police Station causes $200,000 in damage.

May 13, 1970. *Bombing/explosive.* Revolutionary leftist. Salt Lake City, Utah. The National Guard building is bombed, causing an estimated damage of $8000–$10,000.

May 14, 1970. *Bombing/incendiary.* Revolutionary leftist. New York City, New York. The ROTC building at Brooklyn Polytechnic Institute is firebombed, causing $50,000 in damage.

May 14, 1970. *Bombing/explosive.* Revolutionary leftist. Melrose, Massachusetts. An explosion occurs at the National Guard Armory.

May 14, 1970. *Shooting.* Black militant. Florida. Two white women, Donna Fink and Marlene Mahnke, are killed after their car was stolen by three black males.

May 15, 1970. *Shooting.* Black militant. South Carolina. During an attempted robbery, John Bazemore and one of the robbers are killed. The two other robbers are arrested at a police roadblock later in the day. The robbers are linked to a series of shootings of whites in Florida, South Carolina, and North Carolina. One of the three robbers is Ben Chaney, the brother of James Chaney, a murdered civil rights worker.

May 15, 1970. *Arson.* Revolutionary leftist. Bloomington, Indiana. A fire set in the ROTC annex at the University of Indiana causes heavy damage.

May 15, 1970. *Bombing/incendiary.* Revolutionary leftist. Springfield, Missouri. Molotov cocktails cause damage of $10,000 to the industrial education building at Southwest Missouri State College.

May 15, 1970. *Arson.* Revolutionary leftist. Berkeley, California. Three buildings on the University of California campus are set on fire; the estimated damage is $1000.

May 16, 1970. *Bombing/incendiary.* Revolutionary leftist. Bronx, New York. A U.S. Army truck is firebombed.

May 16, 1970. *Arson.* Revolutionary leftist. Richmond, Virginia. A fire is set in the Coburn Hall Chapel at Virginia Union University.

May 17, 1970. *Attempted bombing.* Puerto Rican nationalist, Armed Independence Movement. Puerto Rico. An attempted bombing of an Army recruiting station occurs.

May 18, 1970. *Arson.* Revolutionary leftist. Nashville, Tennessee. A fire destroys Livingston Hall at Fisk University.

May 18, 1970. *Bombing/incendiary.* Revolutionary leftist. Peoria, Illinois. A Molotov cocktail damages the dean of admissions' office at Bradley University, causing $1000 worth of damage.

May 19, 1970. *Bombing/incendiary.* Revolutionary leftist. Afton, Missouri. The Selective Service office is firebombed, causing an estimated damage of $1600.

May 20, 1970. *Bombing/explosive.* Revolutionary leftist. Quincy, Florida. An explosion and the resulting fire at a power substation cause an estimated $600,000 in damage.

May 20, 1970. *Shooting.* Black militant. Muncie, Indiana. A police car is struck by gunshots.

May 20, 1970. *Bombing/incendiary.* Revolutionary leftist. Fresno, California. The computer center at Fresno State College is firebombed, causing an estimated damage of $1 million.

May 22, 1970. *Shooting.* Black militant. St. Paul, Minnesota. Police officer James Sackett is slain by sniper fire.

May 23, 1970. *Bombing/explosive.* Revolutionary leftist. Ames, Iowa. The bombing of the Ames police headquarters in city hall leaves 10 persons injured. In addition, two police cars are destroyed and the building and a nearby hotel are damaged.

May 24, 1970. *Bombing/incendiary.* Revolutionary leftist. Council Bluffs, Iowa. The police station is firebombed.

May 25, 1970. *Arson.* Revolutionary leftist. Los Angeles, California. A fire occurs at Los Angeles City College, causing an estimated damage of $1500.

May 26, 1970. *Bombing/incendiary.* Black militant. Oxford, North Carolina. A tobacco warehouse is firebombed, causing $1 million in damage.

May 27, 1970. *Bombing/explosive.* Revolutionary leftist. Los Angeles, California. The Selective Service office is bombed.

May 27, 1970. *Bombing/explosive.* Revolutionary leftist. Los Angeles, California. The Los Angeles induction center is pipe bombed.

May 28, 1970. *Shooting.* Black militant, Black Panthers. Sacramento, California. A policeman in his car is wounded by a sniper.

May 28, 1970. *Bombing.* Revolutionary leftist. Fullerton, California. A building at Fullerton State College is bombed, causing an estimated damage of $27,000.

May 28, 1970. *Bombing.* Revolutionary leftist. New York City, New York. A lecture hall at Rockefeller University is pipe bombed.

May 29, 1970. *Shooting.* Black militant. Cleveland, Ohio. A police officer is wounded by sniper fire.

May 29, 1970. *Bombing.* Black militant. Oakland, California. The family home of the deceased Oakland Chief of Police is pipe bombed.

May 30, 1970. *Bombing/explosive.* Revolutionary leftist. San Francisco, California. A bomb explodes at the ROTC building at the University of San Francisco.

May 31, 1970. *Bombing/explosive.* Revolutionary leftist. New York City, New York. An explosion at the World Trade Center causes only minor damage and no injuries.

May 31, 1970. *Assault.* Jewish, Jewish Defense League. New York City, New York. JDL members beat up Nazis.

June 2, 1970. *Bombing/explosive.* Revolutionary leftist. Baton Rouge, Louisiana. A power transformer is bombed, causing an estimated damage of $40,000.

June 2, 1970. *Bombing.* Revolutionary leftist. Joliet, Illinois. A bomb explodes in State Representative William G. Barr's car; Barr is badly injured.

June 4, 1970. *Bombing.* Black militant. Oakland, California. A pipe bomb explodes under a police car.

June 5, 1970. *Bombing/incendiary.* Revolutionary leftist. Isla Vista, California. A bank is firebombed.

June 5, 1970. *Bombing/explosive.* Revolutionary leftist. Los Angeles, California. An explosion at the ROTC building at the University of California causes an estimated damage of $10,000.

June 5, 1970. *Arson.* Revolutionary leftist. Los Angeles, California. A fire is set at a Bank of America branch in East Los Angeles.

June 7, 1970. *Bombing.* Black militant. Los Angeles, California. A grenade is thrown at a police car parked outside a police station.

June 8, 1970. *Bombing.* Black militant. Oakland, California. A pipe bomb destroys a police car.

June 8, 1970. *Bombing.* Revolutionary leftist. Isla Vista, California. A Bank of America branch is bombed.

June 8, 1970. *Bombing/explosive.* Revolutionary leftist. Chicago, Illinois. There is an explosion at the National Socialist White Peoples Party headquarters. Members of the Students for a Democratic Society (SDS) are suspected.

June 9, 1970. *Bombing/incendiary.* Black militant. Stratford, New Jersey. A Molotov cocktail causes a fire at the Stratford Police Station; the estimated damage is $35,000.

June 9, 1970. *Arson.* Revolutionary leftist. Galesburg, Illinois. The Selective Service office is damaged by arson.

June 9, 1970. *Bombing/explosive.* Revolutionary leftist, Weather Underground. New York City, New York. A bomb explodes on the 2nd floor of New York Police headquarters.

June 10, 1970. *Arson.* Revolutionary leftist. Lincoln, Nebraska. Fires are set in the Military and Naval Science building at the University of Nebraska.

June 11, 1970. *Bombing/explosive.* Black militant. Omaha, Nebraska. A bomb explodes at the Omaha Police Department building; no injuries are reported.

June 12, 1970. *Shooting.* Black militant. Cairo, Illinois. Shots are fired at an Illinois State Police patrol; one officer receives minor injuries.

June 13, 1970. *Bombing/explosive.* Revolutionary leftist. Des Moines, Iowa. A bomb explosion at the Greater Des Moines Chamber of Commerce building causes $75,000 in estimated damage. The surrounding property damage is estimated at $25,000.

June 13, 1970. *Bombing/explosive.* Revolutionary leftist. Kansas City, Kansas. A bomb explodes at Mid-Continental National Bank.

June 15, 1970. *Bombing.* Black militant. Manhattan Beach, California. The police station and the fire station are bombed.

June 15, 1970. *Bombing/incendiary.* Revolutionary leftist. San Diego, California. A firebomb causes $200,000 worth of damage to U.S. Navy destroyer *Richard B. Anderson,* which was bound for Vietnam.

June 19, 1970. *Shooting.* Black militant. El Monte, California. A police officer, Richard Radetich, is shot and killed.

June 19, 1970. *Shooting.* Black militant. Chicago, Illinois. Police officer Kenneth Kaner is shot and killed while sitting in his patrol car.

June 19, 1970. *Bombing/explosive.* Revolutionary leftist. Berkeley, California. Two branches of Bank of America are bombed.

June 20, 1970. *Bombing/explosive.* Jewish, Jewish Defense League. New York City, New York. Amtorg Trading offices are bombed as a protest against Soviet treatment of Jews.

June 29, 1970. *Shooting.* Black militant, National Coalition to Combat Fascism. Detroit, Michigan. Three police officers are ambushed and wounded.

June 29, 1970. *Bombing/explosive.* Revolutionary leftist. Des Moines, Iowa. The bombing of Harvey Ingham Hall of Science at Drake University causes damage of $200,000.

June 29, 1970. *Shoot-out.* Black militant. Cleveland, Ohio. Police are wounded by gunfire from Black Nationalist headquarters.

June 30, 1970. *Shooting.* Black militant. Plainfield, New York. Two police officers are hit by sniper fire. Officer Robert Perry dies the next day.

July 1, 1970. *Bombing/incendiary.* Revolutionary leftist. Walnut Creek, Colorado. A bank is firebombed.

July 1, 1970. *Bombing/explosive.* Revolutionary leftist. Berkeley, California. The UCLA library is bombed, and the University of California's Center for East Asian Studies is damaged by fire.

July 1, 1970. *Bombing/explosive.* Revolutionary leftist, Revolutionary Force 7. Washington, D.C. The Inter-American Defense Board headquarters is bombed by Revolutionary Force Group 7.

July 2, 1970. *Bombing/explosive.* Revolutionary leftist, Revolutionary Force 7. Washington, D.C. Three South American embassies are bombed. The attack is claimed by Revolutionary Force Group 7.

July 2, 1970. *Bombing/explosive.* Black militant. Compton, California. Tom Harper, a black militant, blows himself up outside police headquarters.

July 2, 1970. *Bombing/explosive.* White racist. Omaha, Nebraska. A black-owned business is bombed.

July 3, 1970. *Bombing/explosive.* Revolutionary leftist. Seattle, Washington. An explosion occurs outside a bank.

July 4, 1970. *Bombing/explosive.* Revolutionary leftist. Long Beach, New York. Democratic Party headquarters is bombed.

July 4, 1970. *Bombing/explosive.* Irish Republican Army? New York City, New York. A bombing occurs outside a British Overseas Airways Corporation (BOAC) office; it is presumed to be in protest over Northern Ireland.

July 4, 1970. *Bombing/incendiary.* Revolutionary leftist. Fort Hamilton, New York. An Army truck is firebombed.

July 6, 1970. *Bombing/explosive.* Revolutionary leftist. Boston, Massachusetts. A bank is bombed.

July 7, 1970. *Attempted bombing.* Revolutionary leftist. New York City, New York. An attempted bombing of the South African Consulate occurs.

July 7, 1970. *Bombing/explosive.* Revolutionary leftist. New York City, New York. A model of a missile on display at the World's Fair is bombed. A Viet Cong flag is left at the scene.

July 7, 1970. *Bombing/explosive.* Revolutionary leftist. New York City, New York. Three people are wounded in a pipe bombing of the Haitian Consulate.

July 7, 1970. *Bombing/explosive.* Revolutionary leftist. New York City, New York. A Portuguese travel agency is bombed.

July 8, 1970. *Shooting.* White racist. New Bedford, Massachusetts. One black is killed and three others are wounded in a series of drive-by shootings.

July 8, 1970. *Bombing/explosive.* Revolutionary leftist. Flushing, New York. The Hall of Science is bombed. A Viet Cong flag is found nearby.

July 12, 1970. *Attempted bombing.* Revolutionary leftist. Palo Alto, California. An attempted bombing of a bank occurs.

July 14, 1970. *Bombing/explosive.* Revolutionary leftist. New York City, New York. A Marine recruiting booth is bombed.

July 14, 1970. *Bombing/incendiary.* White racist. Chicago, Illinois. The city civil rights office is firebombed.

July 15, 1970. *Bombing/explosive.* Revolutionary leftist. New York City, New York. The Chase Manhattan Bank is bombed.

July 16, 1970. *Bombing/incendiary.* White racist. Chicago, Illinois. Southeast Community Organization offices are firebombed.

July 16, 1970. *Bombing/explosive.* Revolutionary leftist. New York City, New York. A Marine recruiting office is bombed.

July 16, 1970. *Bombing/incendiary.* Revolutionary leftist. St. Paul, Minnesota. The Selective Service office is firebombed.

July 17, 1970. *Shooting.* Black militant. Chicago, Illinois. Police officers James Severin and Tony Rizzato are killed by a sniper.

July 17, 1970. *Shooting.* Black militant. Lawrence, Kansas. A police officer is seriously wounded by sniper fire.

July 18, 1970. *Bombing/incendiary.* Revolutionary leftist. Des Plaines, Illinois. The Selective Service office is firebombed.

July 21, 1970. *Bombing/explosive.* Revolutionary leftist. San Diego, California. A pipe bomb explodes at the Bank of America, causing an estimated damage of $1000.

July 22, 1970. *Bombing/explosive.* Revolutionary leftist. New York City, New York. Police vehicles are bombed.

July 22, 1970. *Bombing/incendiary.* Revolutionary leftist. Camden, New Jersey. The Army recruiting office is firebombed.

July 23, 1970. *Bombing/explosive.* Revolutionary leftist. Oakland, California.

Oakland Highway Patrol headquarters is bombed. The bomb made a two-foot crater in the building.

July 23, 1970. *Bombing/explosive.* Revolutionary leftist. Wellesley, Massachusetts. The police station is bombed.

July 24, 1970. *Bombing/incendiary.* Jewish, Jewish Defense League. New York City, New York. A black community center is firebombed.

July 25, 1970. *Bombing/explosive.* Revolutionary leftist. St. Ignace, Michigan. The CIA office is bombed, causing moderate damage.

July 26, 1970. *Bombing/explosive.* Revolutionary leftist. Sparta, Wisconsin. There are three explosions at Camp McCoy Army Base.

July 26, 1970. *Shoot-out.* Revolutionary leftist. Houston, Texas. Carl Hampton is shot and killed in a gun battle with police. The shoot-out followed a rally by the Peoples Party.

July 27, 1970. *Bombing/explosive.* Revolutionary leftist, Weather Underground. New York City, New York. Bank of America is pipe bombed. Viet Cong flags are found nearby.

July 28, 1970. *Bombing/explosive.* Revolutionary leftist. San Francisco, California. Armed Forces Police headquarters is bombed.

July 30, 1970. *Bombing/explosive.* Revolutionary leftist, Weather Underground. Oakland, California. Alameda County Courthouse is bombed; a Weather Underground faction claims responsibility.

July 30, 1970. *Shooting*. Black militant. New Brunswick, New Jersey. Police are shot at by snipers.

July 30, 1970. *Attempted bombing*. Black militant, Black Panthers. Chicago, Illinois. Explosive devices found on power lines are defused.

August 1, 1970. *Bombing/explosive*. Revolutionary leftist. New York City, New York. The Bank of Brazil is pipe bombed.

August 2, 1970. *Bombing/explosive*. Black militant. Berkeley, California. A police car is bombed.

August 6, 1970. *Shooting*. Black militant. San Jose, California. Police officer Richard Huerte is shot dead while writing a traffic ticket.

August 6, 1970. *Bombing/incendiary*. Revolutionary leftist. Placentia, California. A bank is firebombed.

August 7, 1970. *Bombing/incendiary*. Revolutionary leftist. Dundalk, Maryland. The Selective Service office is bombed for the fourth time in six months.

August 7, 1970. *Shoot-out*. Black militant. San Rafael, California. In an attempt by black militants to free prisoners at Marin County Courthouse, four people are killed and two others are seriously wounded. Those killed include Judge Harold Haley, who was taken hostage, Jonathan Jackson, and two prisoners.

August 10, 1970. *Bombing/incendiary*. Revolutionary leftist. Portland, Oregon. The Selective Service building is firebombed, causing an estimated damage of $1000.

August 11, 1970. *Shoot-out*. Black militant. San Bernadino, California. One black male is wounded by police gunfire after snipers fired at them from a black housing project.

August 13, 1970. *Shooting*. Black militant. Chicago, Illinois. Police detective James Alfano is shot and killed by a sniper while sitting in his unmarked car.

August 15, 1970. *Shooting*. White racist. West Point, Mississippi. John Thomas, a black civil rights activist, is shot and killed.

August 17, 1970. *Bombing/explosive*. Black militant, Black Panthers. Omaha, Nebraska. A booby-trap bomb kills police office Larry Minard and wounds seven others.

August 18, 1970. *Bombing/explosive*. Revolutionary leftist. Minneapolis, Minnesota. The Selective Service office is bombed, causing $500,000 in estimated damage.

August 20, 1970. *Shooting*. Black militant. Berkeley, California. Police officer Ronald Tsukamoto is shot dead.

August 21, 1970. *Bombing/incendiary*. Revolutionary leftist. Eugene, Oregon. A university building is firebombed.

August 22, 1970. *Bombing/incendiary*. Revolutionary leftist. Baltimore, Maryland. A National Guard truck is firebombed.

August 24, 1970. *Bombing/explosive*. Revolutionary leftist, New Years Gang. Madison, Wisconsin. A massive explosion at the Army math building at the University of Wisconsin kills Robert Fassnacht, a graduate student who was working in the building. Four people are injured and property damage is estimated at $1.5

million. Three of the four members of the New Years Gang were eventually captured.

August 25, 1970. *Bombing/incendiary.* Revolutionary leftist. Burlington, Mississippi. The police headquarters is firebombed.

August 27, 1970. *Bombing/incendiary.* Revolutionary leftist. Athens, Georgia. A bomb is thrown at the ROTC building at the University of Georgia.

August 27, 1970. *Shoot-out.* Black militant. New York City, New York. Harvey Nobles, a black militant, is killed in a gun battle with police.

August 28, 1970. *Attempted bombing.* Revolutionary leftist. Boston, Massachusetts. An attempted bombing of the John F. Kennedy School of Government building occurs.

August 28, 1970. *Bombing/explosive.* White racist. Rocky Mount, North Carolina. An explosion occurs at a desegregated school.

August 28, 1970. *Bombing/incendiary.* Revolutionary leftist. Walnut Creek, California. The National Guard Armory is firebombed.

August 29, 1970. *Shooting.* Black militant, Black Panthers. Philadelphia, Pennsylvania. Police sergeant Frank Von Colln is shot to death in the Cobbs Creek police station.

August 29, 1970. *Bombing/explosive.* Revolutionary leftist. Washington, D.C. The Portuguese Embassy and the Rhodesian Information Office are bombed. Responsibility for the attack is claimed by the Revolutionary Action Party.

August 29, 1970. *Bombing/incendiary.* Revolutionary leftist. Walnut Creek, California. The courthouse is firebombed.

August 30, 1970. *Shooting.* Black militant. Bronx, New York. A police officer is shot and wounded.

August 30, 1970. *Shooting.* Black militant. Philadelphia, Pennsylvania. Two police officers are wounded by two gunmen.

August 31, 1970. *Shoot-out.* Black militant, Black Panthers. Philadelphia, Pennsylvania. Three police officers are wounded in a dawn raid on a Black Panther office.

August 31, 1970. *Bombing.* Revolutionary leftist. Crescent City, California. A sheriff's car is bombed.

September 1, 1970. *Shooting.* Black militant. New York City, New York. A police officer is shot and wounded.

September 1, 1970. *Robbery.* Revolutionary leftist. Philadelphia, Pennsylvania. A bank is robbed. The group led by Susan Saxe is believed to be responsible. Later in the month, a policeman is killed during a second bank robbery by the group.

September 4, 1970. *Bombing/explosive.* Revolutionary leftist. St. Paul, Minnesota. An explosion occurs at an oil storage tank.

September 5, 1970. *Bombing/explosive.* Revolutionary leftist. Los Angeles, California. The Hall of Justice is bombed, causing an estimated damage of $10,000.

September 5, 1970. *Attempted bombing.* Revolutionary leftist. Santa Ana, California. The courthouse is the target of an attempted bombing.

September 5, 1970. *Bombing/explosive.* Revolutionary leftist. Dewitt, Iowa. The police station is bombed.

September 6, 1970. *Bombing/incendiary.* Revolutionary leftist. Berkeley, California. A bank is firebombed.

September 6, 1970. *Attempted bombing.* Revolutionary leftist. Fitchburg, Mississippi. An attempted bombing of a police station occurs.

September 10, 1970. *Bombing/incendiary.* Revolutionary leftist. Gainesville, Florida. The ROTC building is firebombed, causing $2000 in damage.

September 13, 1970. *Escape.* Revolutionary leftist, Weather Underground. St. Luis, California. The Weather Underground helps Timothy Leary escape from a minimal security prison.

September 15, 1970. *Shoot-out.* Black militant, Black Panthers. New Orleans, Louisiana. In a shoot-out with Black Panthers, police kill one black militant and wound 21. The Panthers are accused of attempted murder but are acquitted a year later in the first Panther trial before a black judge and a black jury.

September 18, 1970. *Shooting.* Black militant. Toledo, Ohio. Police officer William Miscannon is killed in his patrol car by a black man who walks up to the car and starts shooting.

September 19, 1970. *Shooting.* White racist, Ku Klux Klan. Sumter, South Carolina. A black man, Walter Odom, is killed by security guards at a Klan rally.

September 20, 1970. *Robbery.* Revolutionary leftist. Newburyport, Massachusetts.

The National Guard Armory is raided by a group led by two Brandeis students, Susan Saxe and Katherine Power. Explosives and ammunition are stolen.

September 23, 1970. *Robbery.* Revolutionary leftist. Brighton, Massachusetts. A group led by two Brandeis students, Susan Saxe and Katherine Power, robs State Street Bank and Trust Company. A police officer, Walter Schroeder, is killed during the robbery.

September 24, 1970. *Bombing/explosive.* Unknown. New York City, New York. A bomb explodes near the Kuwaiti consul's office.

September 25, 1970. *Attempted bombing.* Revolutionary leftist. Berkeley, California. An attempted bombing of a university gym occurs.

September 25, 1970. *Bombing/explosive.* Revolutionary leftist, Weather Underground. New York City, New York. An Army recruiting station is bombed.

September 26, 1970. *Bombing/explosive.* Unknown. New York City, New York. The Ivory Coast Mission to the UN is bombed.

September 28, 1970. *Shooting.* Black militant. Cleveland, Ohio. Joseph Tracz is killed and another police officer is wounded by a black gunman.

September 30, 1970. *Shoot-out.* Black militant. Atlantic City, New Jersey. Police officer John Burke is killed in a shoot-out.

October 1970. *Shooting.* Black militant, Black Muslims. New York City, New York. A Black Muslim official is wounded by a shotgun blast. A Black Muslim dissident is shot to death in revenge a week later.

October 1, 1970. *Bombing/explosive.* Revolutionary leftist. Kearney, New Jersey. The police headquarters is bombed.

October 2, 1970. *Bombing/explosive.* Revolutionary leftist. Eugene, Oregon. A bomb explodes on the University of Oregon campus, causing $50,000 in damage.

October 5, 1970. *Bombing/explosive.* Revolutionary leftist. Bluefield, West Virginia. An explosion occurs on the campus of Bluefield State College.

October 5, 1970. *Bombing/explosive.* Revolutionary leftist, Weather Underground. Chicago, Illinois. The Haymarket Square statue is bombed again, causing $1000 in damage.

October 6, 1970. *Bombing/explosive.* Revolutionary leftist. Annapolis, Maryland. An explosion occurs outside state offices.

October 6, 1970. *Bombing/explosive.* Jewish, Jewish Defense League. New York City, New York. ThePalestine Liberation Organization (PLO) office is bombed.

October 8, 1970. *Bombing/explosive.* Revolutionary leftist. Santa Barbara, California. The National Guard facility is bombed, causing $400 in damage.

October 8, 1970. *Bombing/explosive.* Revolutionary leftist. Seattle, Washington. The ROTC building is bombed, causing $150,000 in damage.

October 8, 1970. *Bombing/explosive.* Revolutionary leftist, Weather Underground. San Rafael, California. A bomb explodes in Marin County Courthouse, causing $100,000 in damage.

October 10, 1970. *Bombing/explosive.* Revolutionary leftist. New York City, New York. A courthouse is bombed, causing $50,000 in damage.

October 14, 1970. *Bombing/explosive.* Revolutionary leftist, Weather Underground. Cambridge, Massachusetts. The bombing of the Harvard University library is claimed by a Weather Underground faction, the Proud Eagle Tribe.

October 15, 1970. *Bombing/explosive.* Revolutionary leftist. Jersey City, New Jersey. A bank is bombed.

October 15, 1970. *Bombing/explosive.* Revolutionary leftist. Kansas City, Missouri. A police station is bombed.

October 15, 1970. *Bombing/explosive.* Revolutionary leftist, Weather Underground. Cambridge, Massachusetts. The bombing of Massachusetts Institute of Technology is claimed by a Weather Underground faction, the Proud Eagle Tribe.

October 17, 1970. *Bombing/explosive.* Revolutionary leftist. Worcester, Massachusetts. A courthouse is bombed.

October 17, 1970. *Bombing/explosive.* Puerto Rican nationalist, Macheteros. Puerto Rico. The Macheteros, along with other revolutionary groups, participate in a series of eight bomb attacks against United States government facilities located in Puerto Rico.

October 18, 1970. *Shooting.* Black militant, Black Muslims. Cordele, Georgia. Police Sergeant Carl Watson is killed while trying to arrest a Black Muslim.

October 18, 1970. *Bombing/explosive.* Revolutionary leftist. Irvine, California. Stanford University Research Institute is bombed.

October 22, 1970. *Bombing/explosive.* Black militant, Black Liberation Army. San Francisco, California. A church is bombed during the funeral of a policeman killed during a bank robbery.

October 22, 1970. *Bombing/incendiary.* Revolutionary leftist. Racine, Wisconsin. A Molotov cocktail is thrown at city hall.

October 24, 1970. *Bombing/incendiary.* Black militant. Norfolk, Virginia. A post office is firebombed.

October 24, 1970. *Shoot-out.* Black militant. Cairo, Illinois. A police station is attacked by large numbers of blacks dressed in Army fatigues.

October 24, 1970. *Shooting.* Black militant, National Coalition to Combat Fascism. Detroit, Michigan. Police officer Glenn Smith is killed by a shotgun blast.

October 25, 1970. *Bombing/explosive.* Revolutionary leftist. Washington, D.C. A post office is bombed.

October 25, 1970. *Attempted bombing.* Revolutionary leftist. Berkeley, California. An attempted bombing of a University of California gymnasium occurs.

October 26, 1970. *Arson.* Revolutionary leftist. Berkeley, California. A bank near the University of California Irvine Campus is gutted by fire.

October 28, 1970. *Bombing/explosive.* Revolutionary leftist. Stuart, Florida. A courthouse is bombed.

October 29, 1970. *Bombing/incendiary.* Revolutionary leftist. El Toro, California. A Marine base is firebombed.

October 30, 1970. *Bombing/explosive.* Revolutionary leftist. New York City, New York. Two explosions occur at a National Guard Armory.

November 1, 1970. *Bombing/incendiary.* Revolutionary leftist. Ann Arbor, Michigan. A ROTC vehicle is firebombed.

November 1, 1970. *Bombing/explosive.* Revolutionary leftist. Fresno, California. A newspaper office is bombed.

November 1, 1970. *Bombing/explosive.* Revolutionary leftist. Fresno, California. A military induction center is bombed.

November 1, 1970. *Shooting.* White racist. Newcastle, Pennsylvania. A black man is killed in a drive-by shooting.

November 8, 1970. *Arson.* Black militant. Cairo, Illinois. A lumberyard owned by a white vigilante is set on fire.

November 8, 1970. *Shooting.* White racist. Cairo, Illinois. A black man is wounded by sniper fire from a white neighborhood shot into a black neighborhood.

November 12, 1970. *Shoot-out.* Black militant, Black Panthers. Carbondale, Illinois. In a shoot-out, six police and four Black Panthers are wounded.

November 12, 1970. *Bombing/incendiary.* Revolutionary leftist. Chicago, Illinois. The Selective Service board office is firebombed.

November 14, 1970. *Bombing/explosive.* Puerto Rican nationalist. San Juan, Puerto Rico. Five hotels are bombed.

November 18, 1970. *Bombing/incendiary.* Revolutionary leftist. St. Petersburg, Florida. A police car is firebombed.

November 21, 1970. *Attempted bombing.* Revolutionary leftist. Portland, Oregon. An attempted bombing of city hall occurs.

November 22, 1970. *Bombing/explosive.* Revolutionary leftist. Whitefish Bay, Wisconsin. A National Guard truck is bombed.

November 23, 1970. *Bombing/explosive.* Puerto Rican nationalist. San Juan, Puerto Rico. The Dominican Embassy is bombed.

November 25, 1970. *Bombing/explosive.* Jewish, Jewish Defense League. New York City, New York. Pipe bombs explode in Soviet Aeroflot Airlines and Intourist offices.

November 26, 1970. *Shoot-out.* Black militant. New Orleans, Louisiana. One Panther is wounded when police raid Black Panther Party headquarters.

December 1, 1970. *Bombing/explosive.* Revolutionary leftist. Eugene, Oregon. The University of Oregon is bombed, causing $9000 in damage.

December 5, 1970. *Shooting.* Black militant. Cairo, Illinois. A deputy sheriff is shot and wounded.

December 11, 1970. *Bombing/explosive.* Revolutionary leftist. Lawrence, Kansas. The university computer center is bombed.

December 14, 1970. *Bombing/explosive.* Puerto Rican nationalist, Armed Independence Movement. New York City, New York. General Electric headquarters is bombed.

December 14, 1970. *Bombing/incendiary.* Puerto Rican nationalist, Armed Independence Movement. Bridgeport, Connecticut. The Antipoverty Agency is firebombed.

December 14, 1970. *Bombing/incendiary.* Puerto Rican nationalist, Armed Independence Movement. Havana, Illinois. A state senator's office is firebombed.

December 15, 1970. *Bombing/explosive.* Revolutionary leftist. Isla Vista, California. A bank is bombed.

December 15, 1970. *Bombing/incendiary.* Revolutionary leftist. Storrs, Connecticut. A Molotov cocktail is thrown into the ROTC office.

December 16, 1970. *Bombing/explosive.* Revolutionary leftist. Hollywood, Florida. The draft board is bombed.

December 18, 1970. *Bombing/explosive.* Revolutionary leftist. San Mateo, California. The draft board is bombed.

December 19, 1970. *Bombing/explosive.* Revolutionary leftist. San Francisco, California. A police station is bombed.

December 22, 1970. *Bombing/explosive.* Revolutionary leftist. Whitefish, Wisconsin. A National Guard truck is destroyed.

December 31, 1970. *Bombing/explosive.* Revolutionary leftist. El Monte, California. An explosion occurs outside a courthouse.

January 1971. *Shoot-out.* Black militant, Black Liberation Army. Tampa, Florida. A member of the Black Liberation Army (BLA) is killed in a shoot-out with police.

January 4, 1971. *Bombing/explosive.* Revolutionary leftist. Oakland, California. A military induction center is bombed.

January 5, 1971. *Bombing/explosive.* Revolutionary leftist. Claremont, California. The ROTC building is bombed.

January 5, 1971. *Bombing/explosive.* Revolutionary leftist. Oxnard, California. A military induction center is bombed.

January 6, 1971. *Shooting.* Black militant, Black Panthers. San Francisco, California. Fred Bennett is murdered in a feud between Black Panther factions.

January 7, 1971. *Bombing/explosive.* Unknown. Pomona, California. Campfire Girls headquarters is bombed, causing $50,000 in damage.

January 8, 1971. *Bombing/explosive.* Jewish, Jewish Defense League. Washington, D.C. An explosion occurs in the Soviet cultural affairs office.

January 12, 1971. *Bombing/explosive.* Revolutionary leftist. Rolling Hills, California. The Chamber of Commerce is bombed.

January 13, 1971. *Shooting.* Black militant, Black Liberation Army. San Francisco, California. A policeman is shot and wounded by BLA members.

January 15, 1971. *Bombing/explosive.* Revolutionary leftist. New York City, New York. Military recruiting stations are bombed.

January 17, 1971. *Bombing/incendiary.* Jewish, Jewish Defense League. New York City, New York. The United Arab Republic Mission to the UN is firebombed.

January 19, 1971. *Shooting.* Black militant, Black Liberation Army. San Francisco, California. Two police officers are wounded by BLA members.

January 24, 1971. *Assault.* Black militant, Black Liberation Army. New York City, Brooklyn. A policeman is stabbed as he sits in his patrol car in Brooklyn. A phone call from the BLA to the *New York Times* had said that a policeman would be killed at 8 a.m.—the time of the attack.

January 26, 1971. *Shooting.* Black militant, Black Liberation Army. Brooklyn, New York. A policeman is shot after he stops a stolen car in Brooklyn.

January 29, 1971. *Bombing/explosive.* Chicano Liberation Front. Los Angeles, California. Tomas Ortiz, a young Chicano employee, is killed when a federal building is bombed by the Chicano Liberation Front.

February 1971. *Shooting.* Black militant, Black Panthers. High Point, North Carolina. A police lieutenant is shot and wounded after stopping a car driven by a Black Panther.

February 4, 1971. *Arson.* White racist. Charlotte, North Carolina. A desegregationist lawyer's office is set on fire.

February 4, 1971. *Bombing/explosive.* Revolutionary leftist. Oakland, California. A military induction center is bombed.

February 5, 1971. *Arson.* Revolutionary leftist. Santa Barbara, California. The ROTC building is set on fire.

February 6, 1971. *Shoot-out.* White racist. Wilmington, North Carolina. In a shoot-out between black and white gunmen around a black church, a white man is killed.

February 10, 1971. *Arson.* Jewish, Jewish Defense League. Washington, D.C. Three cars belonging to the Soviet Embassy are set on fire.

February 12, 1971. *Bombing/incendiary.* Revolutionary leftist. Santa Cruz, California. A military recruiting office is fire-bombed, causing $4000 in damage.

February 13, 1971. *Bombing/explosive.* Revolutionary leftist. Atlanta, Georgia. A military induction center is bombed.

February 14, 1971. *Bombing/incendiary.* Revolutionary leftist. Bristol, Pennsylvania. The draft board is bombed.

February 17, 1971. *Bombing/explosive.* Revolutionary leftist. Milwaukee, Wisconsin. A bomb explodes on the campus of the University of Wisconsin.

February 22, 1971. *Bombing/explosive.* Chicano Liberation Front. Los Angeles, California. A realty office building is bombed by the Chicano Liberation Front.

February 27, 1971. *Bombing/explosive.* Revolutionary leftist. Berkeley, California. A courthouse and a bank are bombed.

March 1, 1971. *Bombing/explosive.* Puerto Rican nationalist. New York City, New York. The new school for Social Research is bombed.

March 1, 1971. *Bombing/explosive.* Revolutionary leftist, Weather Underground. Washington, D.C. Responsibility for the bombing of the Capitol Building is claimed by the Weather Underground as a protest over the invasion of Laos.

March 1, 1971. *Attempted bombing.* Chicano Liberation Front. Vernon, California. A bank is the target of an attempted bombing.

March 1, 1971. *Arson.* Revolutionary leftist. Honolulu, Hawaii. The ROTC building is set on fire.

March 2, 1971. *Bombing/incendiary.* Jewish, Jewish Defense League. New York City, New York. The Iraqi Mission to the UN is firebombed.

March 3, 1971. *Bombing/explosive.* Revolutionary leftist. Berkeley, California. A bank is bombed.

March 3, 1971. *Bombing/explosive.* Revolutionary leftist. Santa Barbara, California. An electric transformer is bombed.

March 5, 1971. *Arson.* Revolutionary leftist. Honolulu, Hawaii. A building on the University of Hawaii campus is set on fire.

March 6, 1971. *Arson.* White racist. Texarkana, Texas. Arsonists set fire to four black churches.

March 8, 1971. *Bombing/explosive.* Revolutionary leftist. St. Louis, Missouri. The ROTC building at the University of Washington is bombed.

March 9, 1971. *Shooting.* Black militant, Black Panthers. New York City, New York. Robert Webb is killed while selling papers. He is a member of the Newton faction and is another victim of the feud within the Black Panther Party.

March 9, 1971. *Bombing/explosive.* Revolutionary leftist. Fort Lupton, California. The police headquarters is bombed.

March 11, 1971. *Shoot-out.* Puerto Rican nationalist. Rio Piedras, Puerto Rico. Two police officers and a student at the University of Puerto Rico are shot to death.

March 12, 1971. *Bombing/explosive.* White racist, Ku Klux Klan. Houston, Texas. The Socialist Workers Party office is bombed.

March 12, 1971. *Bombing/explosive.* Revolutionary leftist. Portland, Oregon. The police community relations office is bombed, causing $10,000 in damage.

March 15, 1971. *Bombing/incendiary.* Revolutionary leftist. San Mateo, California. The draft board is firebombed.

March 16, 1971. *Attempted bombing.* Revolutionary leftist, Weather Underground. San Francisco, California. A courthouse is the target of an attempted bombing.

March 17, 1971. *Arson.* Revolutionary leftist. Ithaca, New York. The ROTC building at Cornell University is set on fire.

March 18, 1971. *Bombing/incendiary.* Revolutionary leftist. Jacksonville, Florida. A military recruiting office is bombed.

March 19, 1971. *Bombing/incendiary.* Revolutionary leftist. Detroit, Michigan. Oakland Community College lab is bombed.

March 20, 1971. *Bombing/explosive.* Puerto Rican nationalist, Armed Independence

Movement. New York City, New York. The B. Altman Department Store is bombed.

March 21, 1971. *Arson.* Revolutionary leftist. Medford, Massachusetts. The Fletcher School of Law and Diplomacy at Tufts is set on fire, causing $75,000 in damage.

March 23, 1971. *Bombing/explosive.* Revolutionary leftist, Weather Underground. Mill Valley, California. A Bank of America branch is bombed.

March 23, 1971. *Bombing/explosive.* Revolutionary leftist. Los Angeles, California. A bank is bombed.

March 23, 1971. *Bombing/explosive.* Revolutionary leftist. Detroit, Michigan. A bomb explodes on the campus of Wayne State University, causing $3000–$5000 in damage.

March 26, 1971. *Bombing/explosive.* Revolutionary leftist. New York City, New York. A bomb explodes on the campus of Brooklyn Community College

March 27, 1971. *Arson.* Revolutionary leftist. Baltimore, Maryland. An electric box for Baltimore Gas & Electric is set on fire, causing $75,000 in damage.

March 27, 1971. *Bombing/explosive.* Revolutionary leftist. Riverview, Michigan. The Firestone plant is bombed.

March 28, 1971. *Bombing/explosive.* Revolutionary leftist. Dundalk, Maryland. An electric facility is bombed.

March 30, 1971. *Attempted bombing.* Black militant, Black Liberation Army. San Francisco, California. A police station is the target of an attempted bombing.

March 30, 1971. *Bombing/explosive.* Revolutionary leftist. Bradford, Pennsylvania. City hall and the police headquarters are bombed.

March 30, 1971. *Bombing/explosive.* Cuban, Secret Cuban Government. New York City, New York. The Cuban diplomatic office is bombed.

March 30, 1971. *Bombing/explosive.* Jewish, Jewish Defense League. New York City, New York. A bomb explodes outside Communist Party headquarters.

March 31, 1971. *Bombing/incendiary.* Revolutionary leftist. Boston, Massachusetts. A letter bomb is sent to government offices.

March 31, 1971. *Bombing/incendiary.* Revolutionary leftist. Denver, Colorado. A recruiting center is firebombed.

April 1, 1971. *Bombing/explosive.* Revolutionary leftist. Los Angeles, California. City hall is bombed, causing $5000 in damage.

April 2, 1971. *Shooting.* Black militant, Black Panthers. Riverside, California. Police officer Leonard Christiansen is shot and killed.

April 3, 1971. *Bombing/explosive.* Revolutionary leftist. Norman, Oklahoma. The police headquarters is bombed.

April 3, 1971. *Assault.* White racist, Ku Klux Klan. Ypsilanti, Michigan. A black school principal is abducted at gunpoint; he is then tarred and feathered.

April 3, 1971. *Bombing/incendiary.* Revolutionary leftist. Los Angeles, California. A Bank of America branch is firebombed.

April 6, 1971. *Bombing/incendiary.* Revolutionary leftist. San Jose, California. A Bank of America branch is firebombed.

April 8, 1971. *Bombing/explosive.* Revolutionary leftist. Fresno, California. A courthouse is bombed.

April 8, 1971. *Arson.* Revolutionary leftist. Santa Cruz, California. A university building is set on fire.

April 10, 1971. *Bombing/incendiary.* Revolutionary leftist. Stanford, California. Pacific Gas and Electric is firebombed.

April 12, 1971. *Bombing/explosive.* Black militant, Black Revolutionary Assault Team. New York City, New York. The South African Consulate is bombed.

April 14, 1971. *Bombing/incendiary.* Revolutionary leftist. Stanford, California. Campus police headquarters at Stanford University is firebombed.

April 15, 1971. *Bombing/explosive.* Revolutionary leftist. Los Angeles, California. The Selective Service office is bombed.

April 17, 1971. *Shooting.* Black militant, Black Panthers. Queens, New York. The burned and tortured body of Samuel Napier, a Black Panther member belonging to the Newton faction, is found shot in the burned ruins of the Black Panther office in Queens. Six members of the Eldridge Cleaver faction are indicted for his murder.

April 19, 1971. *Shoot-out.* Black militant, Black Liberation Army. New York City, New York. A shoot-out between police and three BLA gunmen leaves two policemen wounded. One gunman, Howard Russell, is killed, one escapes, and the other is arrested.

April 19, 1971. *Bombing/explosive.* Black militant, Black Revolutionary Assault Team. New York City, New York. The South African tourist office is bombed.

April 20, 1971. *Bombing/incendiary.* Revolutionary leftist. Richfield, Minnesota. The Selective Service board is firebombed.

April 21, 1971. *Bombing/explosive.* Revolutionary leftist. Fresno, California. An induction center is bombed.

April 22, 1971. *Bombing/explosive.* Jewish, Jewish Defense League. New York City, New York. The Soviet trade mission is bombed.

April 23, 1971. *Bombing/explosive.* Revolutionary leftist. Stanford, California. A Stanford University office is bombed, causing $25,000 in damage.

April 23, 1971. *Bombing/explosive.* Chicano Liberation Front. Fresno, California. A state office building is bombed.

April 24, 1971. *Bombing/explosive.* Revolutionary leftist. Youngstown, Ohio. The National Guard Armory is bombed.

April 25, 1971. *Bombing/incendiary.* Revolutionary leftist. Claremont, California. The ROTC buildings at Claremont Men's College and Pomona College are bombed.

April 25, 1971. *Assault.* Jewish, Jewish Defense League. New York City, New York. JDL demonstrators beat up Nazis.

April 26, 1971. *Bombing/incendiary.* Revolutionary leftist. Claremont, California.

The office of the president of Claremont University is firebombed.

April 30, 1971. *Attempted bombing.* Revolutionary leftist. Braintree, Massachusetts. The Selective Service board is the target of an attempted bombing.

May 1, 1971. *Bombing/explosive.* Revolutionary leftist. Santa Cruz, California. Bank of America is bombed, causing $12,000 in damage.

May 4, 1971. *Bombing/incendiary.* Revolutionary leftist. Los Angeles, California. A Molotov cocktail is thrown into a post office.

May 4, 1971. *Attempted bombing.* Revolutionary leftist. San Bruno, California. Bank of America is the target of an attempted bombing.

May 5, 1971. *Bombing/explosive.* Revolutionary leftist. Chico, California. Bank of America is bombed.

May 5, 1971. *Bombing/incendiary.* Revolutionary leftist. Kansas City, Kansas. The Selective Service board is firebombed.

May 5, 1971. *Attempted bombing.* Revolutionary leftist. Boulder, Colorado. A bank is the target of an attempted bombing.

May 6, 1971. *Bombing/incendiary.* Revolutionary leftist. Burlingame, California. A Molotov cocktail is thrown into the Army recruiting center.

May 6, 1971. *Bombing/explosive.* Revolutionary leftist. Hawthorne, Nevada. An explosion at a military base kills one person.

May 6, 1971. *Bombing/explosive.* Revolutionary leftist. Monte Vista, California. A power substation is bombed, killing one person.

May 8, 1971. *Bombing/explosive.* Revolutionary leftist. Los Angeles, California. A county social service office is bombed.

May 9, 1971. *Bombing/explosive.* Revolutionary leftist. Berkeley, California. Bank of America is bombed.

May 11, 1971. *Bombing/incendiary.* Revolutionary leftist. Baltimore, Maryland. Army Reserve jeeps are bombed.

May 11, 1971. *Bombing/explosive.* Revolutionary leftist. Los Angeles, California. Three banks are bombed.

May 13, 1971. *Shooting.* Black militant, Black Panthers. Chicago, Illinois. Three police officers are wounded by snipers.

May 19, 1971. *Shooting.* Black militant, Black Liberation Army. New York City, New York. Two policemen guarding the home of the district attorney who is prosecuting Black Panthers are shot and wounded in machine-gun attack. The BLA sends a communiqué to newspapers claiming responsibility.

May 20, 1971. *Attempted bombing.* Revolutionary leftist. Washington, D.C. A police station is the target of an attempted bombing.

May 20, 1971. *Bombing/incendiary.* Revolutionary leftist. San Jose, California. The IBM office is bombed.

May 21, 1971. *Shooting.* Black militant, Black Liberation Army. New York City, New York. Two policemen, Waverly

Jones and Joseph Piagentini, are shot in their backs and killed in an ambush at a Harlem housing project. The BLA sends a communiqué to newspapers claiming responsibility. Jones was black, Piagentini white.

May 22, 1971. *Bombing/incendiary.* Revolutionary leftist. Kent, Ohio. The National Guard Armory is bombed.

May 23, 1971. *Bombing/explosive.* Revolutionary leftist. Oakland, California. Bank of America is bombed, causing $15,000 in damage.

May 25, 1971. *Bombing/explosive.* Revolutionary leftist. Walnut Creek, California. A Pacific Gas and Electric installation is bombed.

May 26, 1971. *Shooting.* White racist. Drew, Mississippi. Joetta Collier, a black teenager, is killed in a drive-by shooting.

May 29, 1971. *Bombing/explosive.* Revolutionary leftist. Tucson, Arizona. Two banks are bombed.

May 30, 1971. *Shoot-out.* Black militant. Cairo, Illinois. In a shoot-out with black militants, three police are wounded.

June 3, 1971. *Bombing/explosive.* Revolutionary leftist. El Sereno, California. A bank is bombed, causing $10,000 in damage.

June 5, 1971. *Robbery.* Black militant, Black Liberation Armyy. New York City, New York. Four BLA members hold up the Triple O Social Club in the Bronx, but they are captured by police. The submachine gun used in the holdup is identified as that used in the attack on police on May 19, 1971.

June 6, 1971. *Bombing/explosive.* Revolutionary leftist. Menlo Park, California. Wells Fargo Bank is bombed.

June 8, 1971. *Shoot-out.* Black militant. Houston, Texas. A police raid on the headquarters of the Peoples Party leads to a shoot-out.

June 10, 1971. *Bombing/explosive.* Revolutionary leftist. Petaluma, California. Bank of America is bombed, causing slight damage.

June 13, 1971. *Bombing/explosive.* Revolutionary leftist. Los Angeles, California. The Mexican tourist office is bombed.

June 16, 1971. *Attempted bombing.* Revolutionary leftist. Santa Cruz, California. A county office is the target of an attempted bombing.

June 18, 1971. *Robbery.* Black militant, Black Liberation Army. New York City, New York. A bank is robbed by the BLA.

June 21, 1971. *Attempted bombing.* Revolutionary leftist. San Jose, California. City council offices are the target of an attempted bombing.

June 22, 1971. *Attempted bombing.* Jewish, Jewish Defense League. Glen Cove, New York. A Soviet residential estate is the target of an attempted bombing.

June 24, 1971. *Bombing/explosive.* Revolutionary leftist. Caldwell, New Jersey. One person is injured when a correctional facility is bombed.

June 24, 1971. *Bombing/explosive.* Revolutionary leftist. Oakland, California. Bank of America is bombed, causing $2000 in damage.

June 25, 1971. *Attempted bombing.* Revolutionary leftist. Freeport, New York. The Selective Service board is the target of an attempted firebombing.

June 26, 1971. *Bombing/explosive.* Revolutionary leftist. Los Angeles, California. The Security Pacific National Bank is bombed.

June 27, 1971. *Bombing/explosive.* Revolutionary leftist. Detroit, Michigan. The National Bank of Detroit is bombed.

July 1971. *Bombing/explosive.* Cuban, Secret Cuban Government. New York City, New York. A theater is bombed to protest a performance by a Cuban dance group.

July 3, 1971. *Bombing/explosive.* Revolutionary leftist. Beverly Hills, California. The Army Reserve training center is bombed.

July 4, 1971. *Bombing/explosive.* Revolutionary leftist. San Jose, California. Federal offices are bombed, causing $500,000 in damage.

July 8, 1971. *Bombing/explosive.* Chicano Liberation Front. Los Angeles, California. The Pan American National Bank is bombed.

July 9, 1971. *Bombing/explosive.* Revolutionary leftist. San Diego, California. The Selective Service headquarters is bombed.

July 9, 1971. *Bombing/explosive.* Revolutionary leftist. Providence, Rhode Island. City hall is bombed.

July 21, 1971. *Robbery.* Black militant, Black Liberation Army. San Francisco, California. A bank is robbed by the BLA; $9400 is taken.

July 24, 1971. *Bombing/explosive.* Revolutionary leftist. Santa Cruz, California. The National Guard building is bombed.

July 25, 1971. *Bombing/incendiary.* Jewish, Jewish Defense League. New York City, New York. A Soviet diplomat's car is firebombed.

July 28, 1971. *Bombing/explosive.* Revolutionary leftist. Torrance, California. The courthouse is bombed.

July 28, 1971. *Bombing/explosive.* Revolutionary leftist. Ben Lomond, California. A Bank of America branch is bombed.

July 30, 1971. *Bombing/explosive.* Jewish, Jewish Defense League. Beverley Hills, California. A travel agency is bombed, causing $3000 in damage.

August 10, 1971. *Bombing/incendiary.* Revolutionary leftist. Berkeley, California. A University of California building is firebombed.

August 11, 1971. *Bombing/explosive.* Jewish, Jewish Defense League. New York City, New York. A trucking firm is bombed.

August 16, 1971. *Bombing/explosive.* Revolutionary leftist. Pittsburg, California. A Bank of America branch is bombed.

August 18, 1971. *Shoot-out.* Black militant, Republic of New Africa. Jackson, Mississippi. A police raid on the Republic of New Africa headquarters results in a gun battle in which three police officers are wounded. Lieutenant William Skinner dies of his wounds a few days later.

August 19, 1971. *Shooting.* Unknown. Corpus Christi, Texas. A policeman is wounded by a sniper.

August 20, 1971. *Robbery.* Black militant, Black Liberation Army. San Francisco, California. A bank is robbed; $15,000 is taken.

August 22, 1971. *Bombing/incendiary.* Puerto Rican nationalist, Armed Independence Movement. New York City, New York. Nine supermarkets are bombed.

August 23, 1971. *Robbery.* Black militant, Black Liberation Army. Fayetteville, Georgia. The BLA robs a bank and kills a policeman, Michael Kaylor.

August 23, 1971. *Robbery.* Black militant, Black Liberation Army. New York City, New York. The BLA robs a bank in Queens.

August 24, 1971. *Bombing/incendiary.* Revolutionary leftist. Hammond, Indiana. A federal office building is firebombed.

August 27, 1971. *Bombing/incendiary.* Chicano Liberation Front. Los Angeles, California. A real estate office is firebombed.

August 27, 1971. *Shoot-out.* Black militant, Black Liberation Army. San Francisco, California. Two BLA members in a car are arrested after attempting to machine-gun a police car when both cars were stopped at a traffic light. The machine gun jammed and the police car pursued the suspects' car until it crashed. The gun found in the car was that taken from slain New York policeman Joseph Piagentini killed on May 21, 1971.

August 28, 1971. *Bombing/explosive.* Revolutionary leftist, Weather Underground. Sacramento, California. The Office of California Prisons is bombed by the Weather Underground as a protest over the death of George Jackson.

August 28, 1971. *Bombing/explosive.* Revolutionary leftist, Weather Underground. Sacramento, California. The Department of Corrections is bombed by the Weather Underground as a protest over the death of George Jackson.

August 29, 1971. *Shooting.* Black militant, Black Liberation Army. San Francisco, California. Sergeant John Young is killed in an attack on Ingleside Police Station; he was the desk sergeant. The gunmen fired a shotgun through an opening in the bulletproof glass partition. The attackers had planned to place a bomb in the police station.

August 29, 1971. *Bombing/explosive.* Revolutionary leftist, Weather Underground. San Francisco, California. A bank is bombed, causing $5000 in damage.

August 29, 1971. *Bombing/explosive.* Chicano Liberation Front. Vernon, California. Bank of America is bombed.

August 30, 1971. *Bombing/incendiary.* White racist, Ku Klux Klan. Pontiac, Michigan. Ten schoolbuses are destroyed by a firebomb.

September 1, 1971. *Bombing/explosive.* White racist. Columbus, Georgia. Two classrooms in a vacant school are bombed.

September 2, 1971. *Attempted bombing.* Revolutionary leftist. Fort Bragg, North Carolina. Fort Bragg Army Base is the target of an attempted bombing.

September 4, 1971. *Bombing/incendiary.* White racist. Kannapolis, North Carolina. An elementary school is firebombed.

September 7, 1971. *Bombing/explosive.* Revolutionary leftist. San Francisco, California. A Bank of America branch is bombed.

September 17, 1971. *Bombing/explosive.* Revolutionary leftist, Weather Underground. Albany, New York. The Department of Corrections is bombed in protest over prison riot deaths at Attica.

September 18, 1971. *Shooting.* Black militant. Plainfield, New Jersey. Patrolmen Frank Buczek is killed in an ambush.

September 18, 1971. *Robbery.* Black militant, Black Liberation Army. San Francisco, California. A bank is robbed; $20,000 is taken.

September 20, 1971. *Bombing/explosive.* Black militant, Black Revolutionary Assault Team. New York City, New York. The Zaire Mission to the UN is bombed.

September 24, 1971. *Bombing/explosive.* Revolutionary leftist. Portland, Oregon. A recruiting center is bombed, causing $400 in damage.

September 24, 1971. *Bombing/explosive.* Revolutionary leftist, Weather Underground. Los Angeles, California. Chase Manhattan Bank is bombed.

September 24, 1971. *Hijacking.* Revolutionary leftist, White Panthers. Detroit, Michigan. Two White Panthers attempt to hijack a Boeing 727.

September 24, 1971. *Bombing/explosive.* Revolutionary leftist, Weather Underground. New York City, New York. Chase Manhattan Bank is bombed.

October 3, 1971. *Bombing/incendiary.* Revolutionary leftist. Tampa, Florida. The ROTC building at Tampa University is firebombed.

October 7, 1971. *Robbery.* Black militant, Black Liberation Army. Fulton, Georgia. A bank is robbed; $25,000 is taken.

October 11, 1971. *Bombing/explosive.* Revolutionary leftist. Santa Cruz, California. Wells Fargo Bank is bombed.

October 14, 1971. *Bombing/explosive.* Unknown. San Francisco, California. The Iranian consul's house is bombed, causing $1 million in damage, and four people are injured.

October 18, 1971. *Bombing/explosive.* Jewish, Jewish Defense League. Los Angeles, California. A travel agency is bombed.

October 20, 1971. *Shooting.* Jewish, Jewish Defense League. New York City, New York. Shots are fired at the Russian Mission to the UN.

October 31, 1971. *Bombing/incendiary.* Revolutionary leftist. Nassau, New York. A college building is bombed by members of the SDS.

November 1971. *Shooting.* Black militant, Black Panthers. California. Sandra Pratt is tortured and murdered in a feud between Panther factions.

November 2, 1971. *Bombing/incendiary.* Revolutionary leftist, Weather Underground. Los Angeles, California. A Bank of America branch is firebombed.

November 3, 1971. *Shooting.* Black militant, Black Liberation Army. Atlanta, Georgia. A police officer, James Greene, is killed by the BLA, who take his badge and his gun.

November 8, 1971. *Shooting.* Black militant, Republic of New Africa. New Mexico. New Mexico State Trooper Robert Rosenbloom is shot and killed by members of the Republic of New Africa.

November 10, 1971. *Attempted bombing.* Revolutionary leftist. New York City, New York. The National Guard Armory is the target of an attempted bombing.

November 11, 1971. *Shooting.* Black militant, Black Liberation Army. North Carolina. A sheriff's deputy is shot and wounded when he stops a car driven by two BLA members. Both men are later captured by police.

November 15, 1971. *Attempted bombing.* Revolutionary leftist. Cambridge, Mississippi. A bank is the target of an attempted bombing.

November 17, 1971. *Bombing/explosive.* Revolutionary leftist. Boise, Idaho. An induction center is bombed.

November 17, 1971. *Bombing/explosive.* Revolutionary leftist. San Francisco, California. Bank of America is bombed.

November 18, 1971. *Bombing/explosive.* Revolutionary leftist. Wellesley, Massachusetts. The Honeywell Corporation office is bombed, causing $15,000 in damage.

November 18, 1971. *Bombing/incendiary.* Revolutionary leftist. Norman, Oklahoma. A college is firebombed, causing $25,000 in damage.

November 18, 1971. *Bombing/explosive.* Revolutionary leftist. Deer Park, New York. A bank is bombed.

November 22, 1971. *Bombing/explosive.* Revolutionary leftist. San Bernadino, California. The district attorney's office is bombed.

November 22, 1971. *Bombing/incendiary.* Puerto Rican nationalist. Camden, New Jersey. A bank and an office building are firebombed.

November 27, 1971. *Hijacking.* Black militant, Republic of New Africa. Albuquerque, New Mexico. Three members of the Republic of New Africa successfully hijack a plane to Cuba.

November 30, 1971. *Bombing/explosive.* Revolutionary leftist. Nassau, New York. A community college is bombed.

November 30, 1971. *Bombing/incendiary.* Revolutionary leftist. Akron, Ohio. The Army Reserve center is firebombed.

December 5, 1971. *Bombing/explosive.* Jewish, Jewish Armed Resistance. New York City, New York. A Russian gift shop is bombed.

December 6, 1971. *Bombing/explosive.* Jewish, Jewish Armed Resistance. Shakopee, Minnesota. A Russian gift shop is bombed.

December 7, 1971. *Bombing/explosive.* Revolutionary leftist. Stanford, California.

Stanford Linear Accelerator Center is bombed, causing $100,000 in damage.

December 12, 1971. *Escape.* Black militant, Black Liberation Army. DeKalb County, Georgia. Three BLA members escape from jail.

December 20, 1971. *Bombing/explosive.* Revolutionary leftist. Cambridge, Massachusetts. The police headquarters is bombed.

December 20, 1971. *Bombing/explosive.* Black militant, Black Liberation Army. New York City, New York. A police patrol car is chasing a stolen car when a grenade is thrown at the police car. The occupants of the stolen car are identified as members of the BLA by photos shown to witnesses.

December 22, 1971. *Bombing/incendiary.* Puerto Rican nationalist. New York City, New York. A bank is firebombed.

December 31, 1971. *Shoot-out.* Black militant, Black Liberation Army. New York City, New York. There is a shoot-out between the BLA and a rival black group.

December 31, 1971. *Shoot-out.* Black militant, Black Liberation Army. Odessa, Florida. A BLA member, Frank Fields, is killed in a shoot-out with the FBI (Federal Bureau of Investigation).

1972. *Bombing/explosive.* Jewish, Jewish Defense League. Hollywood, California. The home of a Palestinian activist is bombed.

January 1972. *Shooting.* Black militant, Black Muslims. Chicago, Illinois. Two Black Muslim dissidents are found shot dead.

January 5, 1972. *Bombing/explosive.* Revolutionary leftist. Buffalo, New York. A correctional services office is bombed.

January 6, 1972. *Shooting.* Rightist, Secret Army Organization. San Diego, California. A left-wing activist is wounded by a shot through his window.

January 7, 1972. *Attempted bombing.* Revolutionary leftist. Chicago, Illinois. The bomb placed in a bank safety deposit box by Ronald Kaufman is defused.

January 7, 1972. *Attempted bombing.* Revolutionary leftist. New York City, New York. The bomb placed in a bank safety deposit box by Ronald Kaufman is defused.

January 7, 1972. *Attempted bombing.* Revolutionary leftist. San Francisco, California. The bomb placed in a bank safety deposit box by Ronald Kaufman is defused.

January 10, 1972. *Shoot-out.* Black militant, Black Muslims. Baton Rouge, Louisiana. In a shoot-out between Black Muslims and police, four people are killed, two sheriffs and two Black Muslims; another 31 people are wounded.

January 12, 1972. *Shooting.* Black militant, Black Liberation Army. Houston, Texas. Two off-duty housing detectives are shot.

January 17, 1972. *Bombing/explosive.* Revolutionary leftist. Stanford, California. Stanford University offices are bombed.

January 22, 1972. *Bombing/explosive.* Revolutionary leftist. New York City, New York. Portuguese airline offices are bombed.

January 26, 1972. *Bombing/explosive.* Jewish, Jewish Defense League. New York City, New York. Sol Hurok's booking office is bombed, killing Iris Kones, a secretary. Hurok was targeted by the JDL because he booked Soviet performers.

January 27, 1972. *Shooting.* Black militant, Black Liberation Army. New York City, New York. A policeman is wounded by a gunshot.

January 27, 1972. *Shooting.* Black militant, Black Liberation Army. New York City, New York. Two policemen, Gregory Foster and Rocco Laurie, are ambushed and killed as they leave a restaurant after enquiring about an illegally parked car. One of the three attackers does a victory dance after the shooting.

February 14, 1972. *Shoot-out.* Black militant, Black Liberation Army. St. Louis, Missouri. A shoot-out with police results in the death of a BLA member, Ronald Carter, and the arrest of two other BLA members. The gun found was later identified as the one taken from one of the policemen killed in New York in January 1972.

February 16, 1972. *Bombing/explosive.* Revolutionary leftist. Manchester, New Hampshire. The police department is bombed, causing $5000 in damage. The People's Liberation Army claims responsibility for the attack.

March 1972. *Bombing/explosive.* Cuban, Secret Cuban Government. San Juan, Puerto Rico. Two drugstores are bombed.

March 1972. *Bombing/explosive.* Cuban, Secret Cuban Government. New York City, New York. A theater is bombed.

March 1, 1972. *Shooting.* White racist. San Jose, California. James Carr, a black militant, is shot to death by two whites in his front yard.

March 11, 1972. *Bombing/explosive.* Jewish, Jewish Armed Resistance. New York City, New York. Jewish Armed Resistance intends to bomb the house of a Nazi concentration camp guard but bombs the wrong house.

March 16, 1972. *Robbery and shoot-out.* Black militant, Black Liberation Army. New York City, New York. The BLA robs a bank, getting away with $188,000. A policeman is wounded in a shoot-out following the robbery.

March 29, 1972. *Bombing/explosive.* Cuban. Biscayne, Florida. A Soviet ship is bombed.

April 6, 1972. *Shooting.* Black militant, Black Panthers. San Francisco, California. Jimmy Carr, a suspected police informer, is murdered.

April 14, 1972. *Shoot-out.* Black militant, Black Muslims. New York City, New York. A shoot-out at a Muslim temple leaves eight wounded. Policeman Phillip Cardillo is killed.

May 3, 1972. *Shooting.* Black militant, de Mau Mau. Highland Park, Illinois. Michael Gerschenson, a white man, is murdered by de Mau Mau.

May 9, 1972. *Arson.* Revolutionary leftist. San Jose, California. The Navy Reserve Armory is set on fire, causing $200,000 in damage.

May 9, 1972. *Assault.* Jewish, Jewish Defense League. Washington, D.C. JDL members break into the Austrian Consulate and beat the Austrian ambassador to the UN.

May 14, 1972. *Bombing/explosive.* Revolutionary leftist. Jamaica, New York. The Army Reserve center is bombed.

May 15, 1972. *Shooting.* Quasi-terrorist. Laurel, Maryland. George Wallace, a presidential candidate in the Democratic primaries, is shot by Arthur Bremer while giving a speech at a shopping mall. In his diary, Bremer also describes stalking Richard M. Nixon; he was apparently motivated by a desire to become famous rather than by political ideology.

May 19, 1972. *Bombing/explosive.* Revolutionary leftist, Weather Underground. Arlington, Virginia. The Pentagon is bombed, causing $800,000 in damage.

May 20, 1972. *Bombing/explosive.* Puerto Rican nationalist. Dorado, Puerto Rico. A beauty pageant at a hotel is bombed.

May 24, 1972. *Bombing/explosive.* Jewish, Jewish Defense League. New York City, New York. The Soviet Mission to the UN residence is bombed.

May 27, 1972. *Shooting.* Black militant, Black Panthers. Jersey City, New Jersey. Isaiah Rowley, BPP defense minister, is killed by a shotgun blast.

May 27, 1972. *Bombing/incendiary.* Revolutionary leftist. New York City, New York. Molotov cocktails are thrown into Columbia University offices.

May 31, 1972. *Bombing/incendiary.* Revolutionary leftist. Denver, Colorado. A police station is firebombed.

June 14, 1972. *Bombing/explosive.* Cuban, Frente de Liberacion Nacional de Cuba. San Juan, Puerto Rico. A store that sends packages to Cuba is bombed.

June 19, 1972. *Bombing/explosive.* Rightist, Secret Army Organization. San Diego, California. A pornographic theater is bombed.

June 20, 1972. *Shooting.* Black militant, de Mau Mau. Chicago, Illinois. Kathleen Fiene, a white woman, is murdered by de Mau Mau.

July 21, 1972. *Bombing/incendiary.* Black militant. Washington, D.C. A Molotov cocktail is thrown into a police car.

July 30, 1972. *Attempted bombing.* Black militant. St. Louis, Illinois. A police station is the target of an attempted bombing.

July 31, 1972. *Shooting.* White racist, Neal Long. Dayton, Ohio. Five blacks are wounded by a shotgun blast from a car. This is the first attack by Neal Long.

August 4, 1972. *Shooting.* Black militant, de Mau Mau. Barrington Hills, Illinois. Four whites are found murdered: Paul Corbett, his wife Marion, her sister Dorothy Derry, and her daughter, Barbara Boand. This is the first murder attributed to "de Mau Mau" by law enforcement.

August 5, 1972. *Shooting.* Black militant, Black Liberation Army. Newark, New Jersey. A policeman is shot and wounded. The gunman is captured hours later and is identified as a suspect in the murders of two policemen, Foster and Laurie, killed on January 27, 1972.

August 21, 1972. *Shooting.* White racist, Neal Long. Dayton, Ohio. Two blacks are wounded by a shotgun blast from a car.

August 28, 1972. *Shooting.* Black militant. Columbus, Ohio. Police officer Joseph Edwards is killed in an ambush.

September 2, 1972. *Shooting.* Black militant, de Mau Mau. Highland Park, Illinois. William Richter, a white man, is murdered by de Mau Mau.

September 3, 1972. *Shooting.* Black militant, de Mau Mau. Chicago, Illinois. Three whites, Stephen Hawtree, his wife, and his son, are murdered by de Mau Mau.

September 9, 1972. *Shooting.* Black militant, de Mau Mau. Grand Island, Nebraska. Two whites are murdered in their home by de Mau Mau.

September 14, 1972. *Bombing/explosive.* Jewish. Hollywood, California. The apartment of a Palestinian Arab is bombed.

October 1, 1972. *Bombing/explosive.* Black militant, Black Liberation Army. Los Angeles, California. A police car is bombed.

October 6, 1972. *Escape.* Revolutionary leftist. Chino, California. A member of Venceramos, a leftist revolutionary group, escapes while he is being transported from prison. During the escape, a prison guard, Jesus Sanchez, is killed.

October 7, 1972. *Bombing/explosive.* Black militant, Black Liberation Army. Los Angeles, California. A police car is bombed.

October 26, 1972. *Shooting.* Black militant. Houston, Texas. Jerry Spruill, a police officer, is shot in the back and killed as he leaves a restaurant.

October 28, 1972. *Robbery and hijacking.* Revolutionary leftist. Arlington, Virginia. Four leftists rob a bank, killing the bank manager, Henry Candee, and a policeman, Israel Gonzalez. A few days later, they hijack a jet plane and escape to Cuba.

November 15, 1972. *Shooting.* Black militant. Kennett Square, Pennsylvania. Two police officers, William Davis and Richard Posey, are killed by a sniper.

November 27, 1972. *Shooting.* Black militant. Pontiac, Michigan. Five white students are shot and wounded by blacks.

December 1972. *Bombing/explosive.* Cuban, Frente de Liberacion Nacional de Cuba. New York City, New York. A travel agency is bombed.

December 11, 1972. *Bombing/explosive.* Cuban, Frente de Liberacion Nacional de Cuba. New York City, New York. A business trading with Cuba is bombed.

December 12, 1972. *Bombing/explosive.* Cuban, Secret Cuban Government. Miami, Florida. A travel agency is bombed.

December 26, 1972. *Bombing/explosive.* Puerto Rican nationalist. New York City, New York. Three department stores are bombed.

December 27, 1972. *Shooting.* Black militant, Black Liberation Army. Detroit, Michigan. Police officer Robert Bradford is shot and killed by the BLA.

December 28, 1972. *Kidnapping.* Black militant, Black Liberation Army. New York City, New York. A bar owner is held for a $20,000 ransom.

December 31, 1972. *Shooting.* Black militant, Republic of New Africa. New Orleans, Louisiana. A police cadet, Alfred Harrell, is killed and two other police officers are wounded in sniper attack. Bullets are later matched to the rifle used by Mark Essex in a motel shooting a week later.

January 2, 1973. *Robbery.* Black militant, Black Liberation Army. New York City, New York. During the robbery of a social club, one man is shot and killed.

January 7, 1973. *Shooting.* Black militant, Republic of New Africa. New Orleans, Louisiana. Mark Essex, a black male with links to the Republic of New Africa, shoots 6 and wounds 21 during an attack in a motel. The dead include two hotel guests, Robert and Elizabeth Steagall, the hotel manager, Frank Schneider, and three police officers, Louis Sirgo, Phil Coleman, and Paul Persigo. All the victims were white. Mark Essex is killed by police at the end of a day-long shoot-out.

January 10, 1973. *Shooting.* Black militant, Black Liberation Army. New York City, New York. Shots are fired at police.

January 12, 1973. *Shooting.* Black militant, Black Liberation Army. New York City, New York. Two housing police are shot in front of a bar.

January 15, 1973. *Shooting.* Black militant, Black Liberation Army. Brooklyn, New York. In Brooklyn a black man opens fire with an automatic weapon on a police car, wounding two policemen.

January 18, 1973. *Shooting.* Black militant, Black Muslims. Washington, D.C. Two adults and five children are murdered by Black Muslims. They were the family of Hamaas Abdul Khaalis, a Hanafi Muslim leader who had denounced the Black Muslim leader Elijah Muhammad, calling him a "lying deceiver."

January 18, 1973. *Bombing/incendiary.* Revolutionary leftist. Pueblo, Colorado. A Molotov cocktail is thrown at a police station.

January 19, 1973. *Robbery.* Black militant, Black Muslims. Brooklyn, New York. The robbery of a gunshop leads to a shoot-out between police and Black Muslims in which patrolman Stephen Gilroy is killed and two others are wounded.

January 20, 1973. *Shooting.* Black militant, Black Muslims. Los Angeles, California. A Black Muslim is killed in a feud between rival factions.

January 22, 1973. *Bombing/incendiary.* Revolutionary leftist. Alton, Illinois. A Molotov cocktail is thrown at a police station.

January 23, 1973. *Shoot-out.* Black militant, Black Liberation Army. New York City, New York. Two BLA members, Woodie Green and Al White, are killed by police and two police officers are wounded.

January 27, 1973. *Shooting.* Armenian. Los Angeles, California. Gourgen Yanikian invites two Turkish diplomats, Mehmet Baydar and Bahadir Demir, to lunch and then murders them. He was taking revenge for the murder of his family by Turks in 1915.

January 28, 1973. *Shooting.* Black militant, Black Liberation Army. New York City, New York. In Queens three black men

open fire with automatic weapons on a police car, wounding two policemen.

February 9, 1973. *Robbery.* Black militant, Black Liberation Army. New York City, New York. A bank is robbed by the BLA.

February 16, 1973. *Attempted bombing.* Puerto Rican nationalist, Armed Independence Movement. New York City, New York. An incendiary device is discovered at Alexander's Department Store.

February 27, 1973. *Occupation.* American Indian Movement. Wounded Knee, South Dakota. Members of the American Indian Movement (AIM) take over the village of Wounded Knee. The occupation lasts for 71 days and is followed by sporadic violence on the Pine Ridge reservation between supporters of the tribal authorities and the AIM.

February 28, 1973. *Shoot-out.* American Indian Movement. Wounded Knee, South Dakota. An AIM militant is killed in a shoot-out with police.

March 1, 1973. *Arson.* American Indian Movement. Wounded Knee, South Dakota. An AIM supporter's house is set on fire.

March 2, 1973. *Shoot-out.* Black militant, Black Liberation Army. New York City, New York. A gun battle occurs between police and BLA members.

March 4, 1973. *Attempted bombing.* Black September. New York City, New York. Bombs are set to go off outside two Israeli banks and an El Al Airlines warehouse on the day that the Israeli Prime Minister is due to arrive in New York, but the fuses are faulty. The Palestinian group, Black September, is believed to be responsible.

March 6, 1973. *Shoot-out.* Black militant, Black Liberation Army. New York City, New York. A gun battle occurs between police and BLA members.

March 14, 1973. *Bombing/explosive.* Puerto Rican nationalist. Rio Piedras, Puerto Rico. University offices are bombed.

March 17, 1973. *Shoot-out.* Chicano Liberation Front. Denver, Colorado. Eight police are wounded in a gun battle with militants of the Chicano Liberation Front.

March 26, 1973. *Shooting.* American Indian Movement. Wounded Knee, South Dakota. A U.S. Marshall is wounded by a rifle shot.

March 27, 1973. *Robbery.* Black militant, Black Liberation Army. New York City, New York. A supermarket is robbed by the BLA.

March 27, 1973. *Arson.* American Indian Movement. Wounded Knee, South Dakota. A trading post is burned to the ground by AIM militants.

March 28, 1973. *Bombing/explosive.* Cuban, Secret Cuban Government. New York City, New York. The Center for Cuban Studies is bombed.

March 29, 1973. *Attempted bombing.* Cuban, Frente de Liberacion Nacional de Cuba. Union, New Jersey. A bookstore is the target of an attempted bombing.

April 10, 1973. *Robbery.* Black militant, Black Liberation Army. New York City, New York. A bank is robbed by the BLA.

April 10, 1973. *Robbery.* Black militant, Black Liberation Army. New York City, New York. Telephone company men are held at gunpoint.

April 13, 1973. *Shooting.* American Indian Movement. Pine Ridge, South Dakota. Frank Clearwater, an AIM member, is shot by the FBI; he dies a few days later.

April 16, 1973. *Shooting.* Black September. Washington, D.C. Shots are fired at what had been the home of a Jordanian diplomat. Responsibility for the attack is claimed by Black September.

April 27, 1973. *Shooting.* American Indian Movement. Wounded Knee, South Dakota. Lawrence Lamonte, an AIM member, is shot and killed in a gunfight with U.S. Marshalls.

May 1, 1973. *Shooting.* Black militant, Black Muslims. New York City, New York. H. A. Jamal, a Malcolm X supporter, is shot and killed by a black gunman.

May 2, 1973. *Shoot-out.* Revolutionary leftist, May 19th Communist Organization. Turnpike, New Jersey. Joanne Chesimard, also known as Assata Shakur, is captured after a shoot-out with police. One state trooper is wounded and another trooper, Werner Foerster, is killed.

May 8, 1973. *Bombing/explosive.* Revolutionary leftist, Weather Underground. New York City, New York. A corporation headquarters is bombed.

May 18, 1973. *Bombing/incendiary.* Revolutionary leftist, Weather Underground. New York City, New York. Two police cars are firebombed.

May 19, 1973. *Robbery.* Black militant, Black Liberation Army. Mount Vernon, New York. Two police officers are wounded during a robbery by the BLA.

June 5, 1973. *Shoot-out.* Black militant, Black Liberation Army. New York City, New York. Transit detective Sidney Thompson is killed in a shoot-out with the BLA. He wounds two BLA members.

June 19, 1973. *Shooting.* Black militant. Atlanta, Georgia. A policeman, Larry Barkwell, is killed with his own gun in a dispute with black militants who are selling literature on the street.

June 19, 1973. *Shooting.* American Indian Movement. Pine Ridge, South Dakota. Clarence Cross, an AIM member, is killed by reservation police.

June 20, 1973. *Bombing/incendiary.* Jewish, Jewish Defense League. New York City, New York. A Soviet car is set on fire.

July 1, 1973. *Shooting.* Palestine Liberation Organization. Bethesda, Maryland. Yosef Alon, Israeli military attaché, is gunned down outside his home. "Voice of Palestine" radio station says it was in retaliation for the killing of a Black September member, Mohammed Boudia, in Paris the week before.

July 18, 1973. *Robbery.* Black militant, Black Liberation Army. New York City, New York. A bank is robbed by the BLA.

July 24, 1973. *Bombing/explosive.* Cuban, Secret Cuban Government. New York City, New York. A Cuban exhibition is bombed.

July 30, 1973. *Shooting.* American Indian Movement. Pine Ridge, South Dakota.

Julius Bad Heart Bull, a member of the AIM, is murdered by supporters of the traditional chiefs.

August 27, 1973. *Bombing/explosive.* Irish Republican Army. Washington, D.C. A secretary at the British Embassy is severely injured when a letter bomb explodes as she is opening it. The IRA is suspected.

August 27, 1973. *Shooting.* American Indian Movement. Pine Ridge, South Dakota. Donald Crow, an AIM member, is murdered.

September 4, 1973. *Shooting.* Black militant, Black Muslims. Newark, New Jersey. James Shabazz, a Black Muslim leader, is murdered by members of a rival faction, the New World of Islam.

September 17, 1973. *Shoot-out.* Black militant, Black Liberation Army. New York City, New York. Three police are wounded in a shoot-out with the BLA.

September 18, 1973. *Assault.* Black militant, Black Muslims. New Jersey. Two brothers are found beheaded; they were Black Muslim dissidents.

September 26, 1973. *Shooting.* White racist, Neal Long. Dayton, Ohio. Edward Tillman, a black male, is killed by a shotgun blast from a car. Another black man is shot and wounded the same night.

September 26, 1973. *Attempted bombing.* White racist. Louisiana. Byron de la Beckwith is arrested with a bomb in his car. He was allegedly planning to kill the regional director of the ADL.

September 28, 1973. *Bombing/explosive.* Revolutionary leftist, Weather Underground. New York City, New York. ITT Corporation headquarters is bombed to protest its involvement in Chile, causing $80,000 in damage.

October 2, 1973. *Shooting.* Revolutionary leftist. Oakland, California. A sniper shoots the pilot of a police helicopter, which then crashes. Two police officers, Wendell Troyer and David Guider, are killed. The August 7th Guerrilla Movement claims responsibility for the attack.

October 17, 1973. *Shooting.* American Indian Movement. Pine Ridge, South Dakota. AIM member Pedro Bisonette is killed by reservation police.

October 18, 1973. *Shooting.* Black militant, Black Muslims. New Jersey. Two Black Muslims are murdered; they are victims of a feud between Black Muslim factions.

October 20, 1973. *Assault.* Black militant, Death Angels. San Francisco, California. A white couple is kidnapped by three black males. The woman, Quita Hague, is hacked to death, while her husband survives but with his face mutilated. This is the first officially acknowledged attack carried out by the Death Angels, a group of Black Muslims.

October 22, 1973. *Assault.* Black militant, Death Angels. San Francisco, California. A white woman is raped by an individual linked to the Death Angels.

October 26, 1973. *Attempted bombing.* Armenian. New York City, New York. The Turkish Information Office is the target of an attempted bombing by Yanikian Commandos.

October 30, 1973. *Shooting.* Black militant, Death Angels. San Francisco, California.

A white female student, Frances Rose, is shot at the entrance to the University of California. A suspect is arrested leaving the scene of the murder but is later released.

November 1, 1973. *Bombing/incendiary.* Puerto Rican nationalist. Hato Rey, Puerto Rico. The FBI office is firebombed.

November 4, 1973. *Bombing/incendiary.* Revolutionary leftist. Madison, Wisconsin. A police car is firebombed.

November 6, 1973. *Shooting.* Revolutionary leftist, Symbionese Liberation Army. Oakland, California. Marcus Foster is killed and his deputy, Robert Blackburn, is seriously wounded when they are shot by three gunmen. Foster was the first black school superintendent of Oakland. This was the first attack by the Symbionese Liberation Army (SLA).

November 14, 1973. *Shoot-out.* Black militant, Black Liberation Army. New York City, New York. Twymon Myers, a wanted BLA member, is shot and killed by police.

November 14, 1973. *Shooting.* American Indian Movement. Pine Ridge, South Dakota. Philip Little Crow, an AIM member, is murdered.

November 26, 1973. *Shooting.* White racist, Ku Klux Klan. Gadsden, Alabama. Rev. Edward Pace, a black minister, is murdered by a Klansman.

December 6, 1973. *Shooting.* Black militant, Death Angels. San Francisco, California. An Arab immigrant grocer, Saleem Erakat, is tied up and killed in his store by a single shot. The reward offered for information eventually leads to the capture of Death Angels.

December 12, 1973. *Shooting.* Black militant, Death Angels. San Francisco, California. Paul Dancik, a white male, is shot and killed while using a public telephone.

December 13, 1973. *Shooting.* Black militant, Death Angels. San Francisco, California. Marietta DiGirolamo, a white woman, is shot on the street and dies on the way to the hospital.

December 13, 1973. *Shooting.* Black militant, Death Angels. San Francisco, California. Arthur Agnos, a white male, is shot and wounded while talking to friends on the street.

December 18, 1973. *Shooting.* White racist, Neal Long. Dayton, Ohio. A black male is wounded by a shotgun blast from a car.

December 20, 1973. *Shooting.* Black militant, Death Angels. San Francisco, California. Angela Roselli, a white woman, is shot and wounded on the street.

December 20, 1973. *Shooting.* Black militant, Death Angels. San Francisco, California. Ilario Bertuccio, an elderly white man, is shot to death on the street.

December 23, 1973. *Shooting.* Black militant, Death Angels. San Francisco, California. Neal Moynihan is shot to death on the street.

December 23, 1973. *Shooting.* Black militant, Death Angels. San Francisco, California. Mildred Hosler, an elderly white woman, is shot to death on the street 10 minutes after the murder of Neal Moynihan.

December 24, 1973. *Assault.* Black militant, Death Angels. San Francisco, California. An unidentified white male is kidnapped, tortured, and mutilated. His body is found on the beach.

December 27, 1973. *Attempted escape.* Black militant, Black Liberation Army. New York City, New York. Three men attempt to free BLA members from prison but are arrested themselves.

December 30, 1973. *Bombing/explosive.* Cuban, Frente de Liberacion Nacional de Cuba. Miami, Florida. A British ship is bombed.

January 10, 1974. *Shoot-out.* Revolutionary leftist, Symbionese Liberation Army. Concord, California. After a policeman stops a van, the men in the van start shooting but are later captured. They are Russell Little and Joseph Remiro, members of the SLA; a gun in their possession is the one used to kill Marcus Foster on November 6, 1973.

January 12, 1974. *Bombing/explosive.* Unknown. San Jose, California. A high school is bombed.

January 23, 1974. *Bombing/explosive.* Unknown. Lancaster, California. A high school is bombed.

January 28, 1974. *Shooting.* Black militant, Death Angels. San Francisco, California. Tana Smith, a white woman, is shot and killed on the street.

January 28, 1974. *Shooting.* Black militant, Death Angels. San Francisco, California. John Bambic, an elderly white man, is shot and killed while rummaging in a dumpster.

January 28, 1974. *Shooting.* Black militant, Death Angels. San Francisco, California. Jane Holly, a white woman, is shot and killed in a public laundromat. She was the only white person in the establishment.

January 28, 1974. *Shooting.* Black militant, Death Angels. San Francisco, California. Vincent Wollin, an elderly white man, is shot and killed on the street.

January 28, 1974. *Shooting.* Black militant, Death Angels. San Francisco, California. A white woman is shot and wounded while moving her belongings into her new apartment. She is paralyzed from the waist down. All five victims on this night are shot with the same weapon, and witnesses identify two black males as the shooters.

January 29, 1974. *Bombing/explosive.* Black militant, Black Liberation Army. Lawrence, Kansas. A University of Kansas dormitory is bombed.

February 3, 1974. *Attempted bombing.* Revolutionary leftist. Laurel, Maryland. A police vehicle is the target of an attempted bombing.

February 4, 1974. *Kidnapping.* Revolutionary leftist, Symbionese Liberation Army. Berkeley, California. Patricia Hearst is kidnapped from her apartment. She is the youngest daughter of the chairman of the Hearst Corporation. A "Declaration of Revolutionary War" by the SLA a week later calls for Randolph Hearst to donate free food to welfare recipients and other poor people.

February 4, 1974. *Shoot-out.* Black militant, Black Muslims. New York City, New York. Minister Abdullah Rahman and four other Sunni Muslims are killed in the Yasin Mosque by suspected Black Muslim gunmen.

February 17, 1974. *Shoot-out.* Black militant, Black Muslims. Tampa, Florida. In a gunfight between police and Black Muslims, a Black Muslim is killed.

February 18, 1974. *Shooting.* American Indian Movement. Pine Ridge, South Dakota. Two AIM members, Verlyn Bad Heart Bull and Edward Standing Soldier, are murdered.

February 20, 1974. *Kidnapping.* Rightist. Atlanta, Georgia. The editor of the *Atlanta Constitution* is kidnapped by the American Revolutionary Army. They demand a $700,000 ransom, which is paid by the newspaper.

February 24, 1974. *Bombing/explosive.* Unknown. Boulder, Colorado. An elementary school is bombed.

March 3, 1974. *Bombing/explosive.* Revolutionary leftist. San Francisco, California. Americans for Justice claim credit for a bombing.

March 7, 1974. *Bombing/explosive.* Revolutionary leftist. Portland, Oregon. A state office building is bombed.

March 7, 1974. *Bombing/explosive.* Revolutionary leftist, Weather Underground. San Francisco, California. The Health, Education and Welfare building is bombed. A Weather Underground communiqué denounces the agency's role in oppressing women.

March 16, 1974. *Bombing/explosive.* Revolutionary leftist. Pasadena, California. The police headquarters is bombed.

March 16, 1974. *Bombing/explosive.* Revolutionary leftist. Boulder, Colorado. The courthouse is bombed, causing $500 in damage.

March 21, 1974. *Bombing/explosive.* Revolutionary leftist. Stockton, California. Two supermarkets are bombed.

March 21, 1974. *Bombing/explosive.* Revolutionary leftist. Folcroft, Pennsylvania. The police department is bombed, causing $5000 in damage.

March 26, 1974. *Bombing/explosive.* Revolutionary leftist. Arlington, Illinois. An explosion in what appears to be a bomb factory injures one person.

April 1, 1974. *Shooting.* Black militant, Death Angels. San Francisco, California. Two young Salvation Army cadets are gunned down on the street as they walk together. The man, Thomas Rainwater, is killed, while the woman survives.

April 13, 1974. *Shooting.* Cuban. Coral Gables, Florida. Jose Torrientes, anti-Castro leader and former Cuban government official, is shot in his house by a sniper. Allegations claim that the Cuban government is responsible.

April 14, 1974. *Shooting.* Black militant, Death Angels. San Francisco, California. Two young white males are shot and wounded while waiting at a bus stop.

April 15, 1974. *Robbery.* Revolutionary leftist, Symbionese Liberation Army. San Francisco, California. A bank is robbed by the Symbionese Liberation Army.

April 16, 1974. *Shooting.* Black militant, Death Angels. San Francisco, California.

Nelson Shields, a white male, is shot and killed as he is unloading his station wagon.

April 17, 1974. *Attempted escape.* Black militant, Black Liberation Army. New York City, New York. An attempt to free BLA prisoners fails.

April 18, 1974. *Bombing/explosive.* Revolutionary leftist. Prosser, Washington. An explosion destroys a police car.

April 24, 1974. *Bombing/incendiary.* Revolutionary leftist. Cecil, Maryland. A police car is firebombed.

May 1974. *Assault and arson.* Jewish, Jewish Defense League. Manhattan, New York. JDL members beat an Arab-American activist with a lead pipe, breaking his back. A few days later his offices are the target of an arson attack.

May 1, 1974. *Bombing/explosive.* Unknown. New York City, New York. A bomb explodes in an airport locker, injuring two people.

May 3, 1974. *Robbery.* Black militant, Black Liberation Army. New Haven, Connecticut. A policeman is wounded during a bank robbery by the BLA.

May 4, 1974. *Bombing/explosive.* Revolutionary leftist. New York City, New York. An explosion destroys a military simulator.

May 12, 1974. *Shooting.* White racist, Neal Long. Dayton, Ohio. Rev. William Wright, a black minister, is killed by a shotgun blast as he leaves his church.

May 16, 1974. *Robbery.* Revolutionary leftist, Symbionese Liberation Army. Los Angeles, California. A sporting goods store is robbed. The robbers flee and force a car driver to help them escape.

May 17, 1974. *Shoot-out.* Revolutionary leftist, Symbionese Liberation Army. Los Angeles, California. Six members of the SLA are killed in a gun battle with the police. In the shoot-out, the house is set on fire.

May 20, 1974. *Bombing/incendiary.* Revolutionary leftist. Yuba City, California. An unoccupied police car is firebombed.

May 21, 1974. *Bombing/incendiary.* Revolutionary leftist. Yuba City, California. A state motor vehicle office is firebombed, causing extensive damage.

May 31, 1974. *Bombing/explosive.* Revolutionary leftist, Weather Underground. Los Angeles, California. The state attorney general's office is bombed.

May 31, 1974. *Bombing/explosive.* Revolutionary leftist. Chicago, Illinois. The police department is bombed.

June 1974. *Attempted bombing.* Unknown. New York City, New York. Gift-wrapped bombs are placed in nine department stores. All the devices are disarmed successfully.

June 2, 1974. *Shooting.* Black militant, Black Liberation Army. New York City, New York. Policemen are shot at by BLA members on the Delaware Memorial Bridge.

June 11, 1974. *Shooting.* Chicano Liberation Front. Union City, California. Police Chief William Cann is shot and fatally wounded by a sniper at a meeting in a Catholic church to discuss Latino grievances.

June 11, 1974. *Bombing/explosive.* Revolutionary leftist. St. Louis, Missouri. An explosion destroys a policeman's private car.

June 11, 1974. *Bombing/explosive.* Revolutionary leftist. San Pedro, California. A courthouse is bombed.

June 13, 1974. *Bombing/explosive.* Revolutionary leftist, Weather Underground. Pittsburgh, Pennsylvania. Gulf Oil offices are bombed, causing $450,000 in damage.

June 14, 1974. *Bombing/explosive.* Puerto Rican nationalist, Armed Forces of National Liberation. Chicago, Illinois. Two dynamite bombs are set off.

July 1974. *Shooting.* White racist, Neal Long. Dayton, Ohio. A black male is wounded by a shotgun blast from a car.

July 3, 1974. *Shooting.* White racist, Neal Long. Dayton, Ohio. James McKinney, a black male, is killed by a shotgun blast from a car.

July 12, 1974. *Shoot-out.* Revolutionary leftist, White Panthers. San Francisco, California. A shoot-out occurs between police and White Panthers.

July 22, 1974. *Shooting.* White racist, Neal Long. Dayton, Ohio. Willie Buford, a black male, is killed in front of his home by a shotgun blast from a car.

July 23, 1974. *Bombing/explosive.* Unknown. Washington, D.C. A foreign mission is damaged by a pipe bomb.

August 5, 1974. *Attempted bombing.* Revolutionary leftist, New World Liberation

Front. Burlingame, California. An insurance agency is the target of an attempted bombing.

August 6, 1974. *Bombing/explosive.* Quasiterrorist. Los Angeles, California. Muharem Kurbegovic, known as the "alphabet bomber" because he supposedly picks his targets in alphabetical order, bombs the Los Angeles International Airport, killing 3 people and injuring 35. His manifesto was signed "Aliens of America," and he made a series of bizarre demands.

August 7, 1974. *Attempted bombing.* Unknown. New York City, New York. A dynamite bomb planted at the UN General Assembly Building is disarmed by police.

August 8, 1974. *Attempted bombing.* Revolutionary leftist, New World Liberation Front. San Francisco, California. An automobile agency is the target of an attempted bombing.

August 15, 1974. *Attempted escape.* Black militant, Black Liberation Army. Brooklyn, New York. Three BLA members attempt to break out of prison; one escapes but is quickly recaptured, and one is shot by police during the attempt.

August 31, 1974. *Bombing/explosive.* Puerto Rican nationalist, Armed Forces of National Liberation. New York City, New York. A bomb explodes in Lincoln Center.

September 3, 1974. *Bombing/explosive.* Revolutionary leftist, New World Liberation Front. San Francisco, California. A stock brokerage firm is bombed.

September 7, 1974. *Shooting.* American Indian Movement. Pine Ridge, South Dakota. An AIM member, Dennis LeCompte, is murdered.

September 10, 1974. *Bombing/explosive.* Revolutionary leftist, Weather Underground. San Leandro, California. The Anaconda Corporation office is bombed.

September 16, 1974. *Shooting.* American Indian Movement. Pine Ridge, South Dakota. An AIM member, Robert Reddy, is murdered.

September 28, 1974. *Bombing/explosive.* Puerto Rican nationalist. Newark, New Jersey. Two people are wounded when a police station is bombed.

September 28, 1974. *Bombing/explosive.* Puerto Rican nationalist. Newark, New Jersey. City hall is bombed.

October 2, 1974. *Bombing/explosive.* Revolutionary leftist, New World Liberation Front. San Francisco, California. A hotel receives a warning call and then is bombed.

October 5, 1974. *Bombing/explosive.* Revolutionary leftist, New World Liberation Front. Los Angeles, California. A hotel re-ceives a warning call and then is bombed.

October 9, 1974. *Bombing/explosive.* Cuban, Frente de Liberacion Nacional de Cuba. Puerto Rico. A theater is bombed.

October 24, 1974. *Shooting.* Black militant, Black Muslims. Montgomery, Alabama. A police officer is killed when Black Muslims open fire.

October 26, 1974. *Bombing/explosive.* Puerto Rican nationalist, Armed Forces of National Liberation. New York City, New York. The Federal Reserve Bank Building is bombed.

October 26, 1974. *Bombing/explosive.* Puerto Rican nationalist, Armed Forces of National Liberation. New York City, New York. The Marine Midland Bank Building is bombed.

October 26, 1974. *Bombing/explosive.* Puerto Rican nationalist, Armed Forces of National Liberation. New York City, New York. Exxon and Chemical Bank are bombed.

October 26, 1974. *Bombing/explosive.* Puerto Rican nationalist, Armed Forces of National Liberation. New York City, New York. A bomb explodes at Rockefeller Plaza, the home of Banco de Ponce.

October 26, 1974. *Bombing/explosive.* Puerto Rican nationalist, Armed Forces of National Liberation. New York City, New York. Lever Brothers House is bombed.

October 26, 1974. *Bombing/explosive.* Puerto Rican nationalist, Armed Forces of National Liberation. New York City, New York. Union Carbide is bombed.

October 28, 1974. *Bombing/incendiary.* Revolutionary leftist. El Paso, Texas. A Molotov cocktail is thrown at a police car.

October 30, 1974. *Bombing/explosive.* Revolutionary leftist, New World Liberation Front. Los Altos, California. An ITT executive's home is bombed.

November 2, 1974. *Bombing/incendiary.* Revolutionary leftist. El Paso, Texas. A Molotov cocktail is thrown at a police car.

November 9, 1974. *Bombing/explosive.* Cuban, Frente de Liberacion Nacional de Cuba. New York City, New York. The Organization of American States Building is bombed.

November 10, 1974. *Bombing/explosive.* Jewish, Jewish Defense League. Los Angeles, California. A UN office is bombed, causing $20,000 in damage.

November 11, 1974. *Bombing/explosive.* Cuban, Frente de Liberacion Nacional de Cuba. New York City, New York. The hotel where Cuban officials are staying is bombed.

November 17, 1974. *Shooting.* American Indian Movement. Pine Ridge, South Dakota. An AIM member, Jesse Trueblood, is murdered.

December 1974. *Assault.* Black militant, Black Muslims. A Washington, D.C. jail. A Black Muslim prisoner is murdered by other Black Muslims. He was a potential witness in the Hanafi murder case of January 1973.

December 1974. *Bombing/explosive.* Cuban. Puerto Rico. A grenade attack on a Soviet ship wounds one person.

December 1, 1974. *Bombing/explosive.* Puerto Rican nationalist. Puerto Rico. Army Reserve vehicles are destroyed.

December 1, 1974. *Bombing/explosive.* Puerto Rican nationalist, Armed Forces of National Liberation. Puerto Rico. Burger King is bombed; this may be a strike-related incident in support of striking Puerto Rican workers.

December 1, 1974. *Bombing/explosive.* Puerto Rican nationalist, Armed Forces of National Liberation. Puerto Rico. The ITT building is bombed.

December 2, 1974. *Bombing/explosive.* Puerto Rican nationalist. Puerto Rico. An oil refinery is bombed.

December 11, 1974. *Bombing/explosive.* Puerto Rican nationalist, Armed Forces of National Liberation. New York City, New York. A policeman is injured by a booby-trap bomb. He is permanently disabled. The Armed Forces of National Liberation (FALN) claims responsibility for the attack.

December 13, 1974. *Bombing/explosive.* Puerto Rican nationalist, Armed Forces of National Liberation. Puerto Rico. An electric transformer is bombed.

December 13, 1974. *Shooting.* Black militant, Black Panthers. Berkeley, California. Betty Van Patter, a white woman who was auditing the books of a Black Panther affiliated organization, is murdered. It is generally believed that she had unearthed evidence of corruption.

December 19, 1974. *Bombing/explosive.* Revolutionary leftist, New World Liberation Front. San Francisco, California. General Motors offices are bombed.

December 31, 1974. *Attempted bombing.* Puerto Rican nationalist, Armed Forces of National Liberation. Puerto Rico. An unexploded bomb is found.

December 31, 1974. *Bombing/explosive.* Puerto Rican nationalist, Armed Forces of National Liberation. Puerto Rico. A Chase Manhattan Bank branch is bombed.

December 31, 1974. *Bombing/explosive.* Puerto Rican nationalist, Armed Forces of National Liberation. Puerto Rico. The bombing of an electrical transformer leads to a power outage.

1975. *Assault.* American Indian Movement. Pine Ridge, South Dakota. Anna Mae Aquash is murdered by members of the AIM because she is suspected of being a police informant. She disappeared in late 1975, and her body was not found until February 1976.

1975. *Hijacking.* Jewish, Jewish Defense League. New York City, New York. A JDL member hijacks a helicopter and demands a $2 million ransom to buy guns for the JDL. The pilot is shot in the attack.

January 4, 1975. *Bombing/explosive.* Revolutionary leftist. Columbus, Ohio. The police department is bombed.

January 11, 1975. *Bombing/explosive.* Cuban. Mayaguez, Puerto Rico. A bomb explodes in a restaurant near a pro-independence rally, killing Angel Chavonnier and Eddie Ramos and injuring 11.

January 23, 1975. *Robbery.* Jewish, Jewish Defense League. Philadelphia, Pennsylvania. The printing presses of an Arabic language newspaper are stolen.

January 24, 1975. *Bombing/explosive.* Puerto Rican nationalist, Armed Forces of National Liberation. New York City, New York. The bombing of Fraunces Tavern Restaurant in Lower Manhattan leaves 4 dead and 53 injured. The dead are Harold Sherburne, Alejandro Berger, Frank Conor, and James Gezork. In a typed message, the FALN claims responsibility for the bombing saying it was in retaliation for the bombing of a rally in Puerto Rico 13 days earlier.

January 29, 1975. *Bombing/explosive.* Revolutionary leftist, Weather Underground. Washington, D.C. The State Department is bombed.

January 29, 1975. *Attempted bombing.* Revolutionary leftist, Weather Underground. Oakland, California. A bomb placed in a federal building fails to detonate.

February 1, 1975. *Bombing/explosive.* Cuban, Omega7. New York City, New York. The Venezuelan Consulate is bombed.

February 2, 1975. *Bombing.* White racist/rightist, National Socialist Liberation Front. Santa Monica, California. A left-wing rally is teargassed, allegedly by the National Socialist Liberation Front.

February 3, 1975. *Bombing/explosive.* Revolutionary leftist, New World Liberation Front. San Jose, California. General Motors and Pacific Telephone Company offices are bombed.

February 3, 1975. *Bombing/explosive.* Revolutionary leftist, Continental Revolutionary Army. Denver, Colorado. The U.S. Securities and Exchange Commission is bombed by the Continental Revolutionary Army.

February 4, 1975. *Bombing/explosive.* Revolutionary leftist, New World Liberation Front. El Granada, California. A bomb explodes on an Air Force Station near a fuel tank.

February 4, 1975. *Bombing/explosive.* White racist/rightist, National Socialist Liberation Front. Los Angeles, California. The Socialist Workers Party office is bombed.

February 5, 1975. *Bombing/explosive.* Revolutionary leftist, New World Liberation Front. Oakland, California. Vulcan Foundry is bombed.

February 6, 1975. *Bombing/explosive.* Cuban, Accion Cubana/Cuban Action Commandos. Los Angeles, California. A Socialist bookstore is bombed.

February 6, 1975. *Bombing/explosive.* Revolutionary leftist, New World Liberation Front. San Francisco, California. A TV station is bombed.

February 11, 1975. *Bombing/explosive.* Cuban, Accion Cubana/Cuban Action Commandos. Elizabeth, New Jersey. A bombing is attributed to an anti-Castro group.

February 16, 1975. *Attempted escape.* Black militant, Black Liberation Army. New York. An attempted prison escape by BLA members is foiled.

February 21, 1975. *Shooting.* Cuban. Miami, Florida. Luciano Nieves, a Cuban who advocated dialogue with the Castro regime, is murdered.

February 26, 1975. *Bombing/explosive.* Cuban, Accion Cubana/Cuban Action Commandos. San Francisco, California. KCET radio station is bombed.

March 2, 1975. *Bombing/explosive.* Revolutionary leftist, Weather Underground. Shelton, Connecticut. A factory is destroyed by bombs and a resulting fire, causing $2 million in damage. The Weather Underground claims responsibility.

March 10, 1975. *Bombing/explosive.* Chicano Liberation Front. San Jose, California. Three pipe bombs explode: one at a bank, one at a corporation headquarters, and one at a Safeway store.

March 12, 1975. *Bombing/explosive.* Revolutionary leftist, New World Liberation Front. Bruno Hills, California. An electric line is bombed.

March 20, 1975. *Bombing/explosive.* Revolutionary leftist, New World Liberation Front. San Bruno, California. Six electrical transmission towers are bombed.

March 27, 1975. *Bombing/explosive.* Revolutionary leftist, New World Liberation Front. San Jose, California. Five bombings occur at electric corporation offices.

March 27, 1975. *Bombing/explosive.* Cuban, Accion Cubana/Cuban Action Commandos. Los Angeles, California. The Panamian tourist office is bombed.

March 27, 1975. *Bombing/explosive.* Revolutionary leftist, Red Guerrilla Force. Berkeley, California. The FBI office is bombed.

March 27, 1975. *Bombing/explosive.* Cuban, Accion Cubana/Cuban Action Commandos. Los Angeles, California. The Costa Rican Consulate is bombed.

March 29, 1975. *Bombing/explosive.* Revolutionary leftist, New World Liberation Front. Sacramento, California. A Pacific Gas and Electric transformer is bombed.

April 2, 1975. *Bombing/explosive.* Puerto Rican nationalist, Armed Forces of National Liberation. New York City, New York. The N.Y. Life Insurance Building is bombed.

April 2, 1975. *Bombing/explosive.* Puerto Rican nationalist, Armed Forces of National Liberation. New York City, New York. The Metropolitan Life Insurance Building is bombed.

April 2, 1975. *Bombing/explosive.* Puerto Rican nationalist, Armed Forces of National Liberation. New York City, New York. American Bank and Trust is bombed.

April 2, 1975. *Bombing/explosive.* Puerto Rican nationalist, Armed Forces of National Liberation. New York City, New York. A Blimpies sub shop is bombed.

April 3, 1975. *Bombing/explosive.* Cuban, Accion Cubana/Cuban Action Commandos. Los Angeles, California. The Communist Party office is bombed.

April 4, 1975. *Bombing/explosive.* Revolutionary leftist. San Francisco, California. Corporation offices are bombed.

April 4, 1975. *Bombing/explosive.* Puerto Rican nationalist, Armed Forces of National Liberation. New York City, New York. Commercial buildings are bombed, injuring four.

April 5, 1975. *Bombing.* Jewish, Jewish Defense League. Los Angeles, California. The Iraqi Airways office is bombed.

April 5, 1975. *Attempted bombing.* Jewish, Jewish Defense League. Los Angeles, California. A dynamite bomb is found in a tourist office.

April 8, 1975. *Bombing/explosive.* Revolutionary leftist, New World Liberation Front. San Jose, California. An electric substation is bombed.

April 13, 1975. *Bombing/explosive.* Cuban, Accion Cubana/Cuban Action Commandos. Los Angeles, California. A Socialist bookstore is bombed.

April 21, 1975. *Robbery.* Revolutionary leftist, Symbionese Liberation Army. Sacramento, California. Carmichael Crocker

Bank is robbed. During the robbery, Myra Opsahl, a bank customer, is shot and killed.

April 28, 1975. *Bombing/explosive.* Revolutionary leftist. Denver, Colorado. A bank is bombed.

April 28, 1975. *Bombing/explosive.* Revolutionary leftist. Denver, Colorado. A CIA officer's house is bombed.

May 1, 1975. *Bombing/explosive.* Revolutionary leftist, New World Liberation Front. Sacramento, California. A corrections office is bombed.

May 2, 1975. *Bombing/explosive.* Cuban, Accion Cubana/Cuban Action Commandos. Santa Monica, California. A Socialist bookstore is bombed.

May 7, 1975. *Bombing/explosive.* Cuban, Accion Cubana/Cuban Action Commandos. Los Angeles, California. A Socialist bookstore is bombed.

May 9, 1975. *Bombing/explosive.* Revolutionary leftist, New World Liberation Front. Berkeley, California. An electric company office is bombed.

May 23, 1975. *Bombing/explosive.* Puerto Rican nationalist, Armed Forces of National Liberation. Puerto Rico. Two banks and a McDonald's fast-food restaurant are bombed.

May 23, 1975. *Shooting.* White racist, Neal Long. Dayton, Ohio. A black male is wounded by a shotgun blast from a car.

May 25, 1975. *Attempted escape.* Black militant, Black Liberation Army. Brooklyn, New York. Melvin Kearney, a BLA member, falls to his death in an escape attempt.

May 31, 1975. *Bombing/explosive.* Revolutionary leftist, George Jackson Brigade. Olympia, Washington. The bombing of a corrections office causes $100,000 in damage.

June 8, 1975. *Shooting.* Revolutionary leftist, New World Liberation Front? San Francisco, California. Wilbert Jackson, the head of the United Prisoners Union, and his companion, Sally Voye, are shot and killed while sitting in his car. A phone caller allegedly from the New World Liberation Front (NWLF) says he was killed because he was a police informer.

June 14, 1975. *Bombing/explosive.* Puerto Rican nationalist, Armed Forces of National Liberation. Chicago, Illinois. First National Bank is bombed.

June 15, 1975. *Attempted bombing.* Puerto Rican nationalist, Armed Forces of National Liberation. Chicago, Illinois. The United Bank Federal Building is the target of an attempted bombing; the bomb does not detonate.

June 16, 1975. *Bombing/explosive.* Revolutionary leftist, Weather Underground. New York City, New York. A Puerto Rican bank branch is bombed by the Weather Underground in solidarity with striking Puerto Rican workers.

June 16, 1975. *Bombing/explosive.* Puerto Rican nationalist, Armed Forces of National Liberation. New York City, New York. Four trucks belonging to Puerto Rico Telephone Company are bombed; this may be a strike-related incident in support of striking Puerto Rican workers.

June 16, 1975. *Bombing/explosive.* Revolutionary leftist, Weather Underground.

New York City, New York. The Rockefeller Center branch of Banco de Ponce is bombed.

June 26, 1975. *Shoot-out.* American Indian Movement. Pine Ridge, South Dakota. Two FBI agents, Jack Coler and Ronald Williams, and an AIM member, Joseph Stunz, are killed in a gunfight.

June 27, 1975. *Bombing/explosive.* Unknown. Mount Rushmore, South Dakota. A bomb explodes at the Mount Rushmore tourist office. A warning was phoned in before the explosion.

June 27, 1975. *Bombing/explosive.* Revolutionary leftist, New World Liberation Front. Almeda, California. An explosion at the Bureau of Indian Affairs office causes $74,000 in damage.

July 1975. *Shooting.* Cuban. New York City, New York. Shots are fired at the home of a Cuban diplomat.

July 2, 1975. *Shooting.* White racist. Chattanooga, Tennessee. Four Black Muslims are wounded by a shotgun fired from a passing car.

July 5, 1975. *Shooting.* American Indian Movement. Pine Ridge, South Dakota. An FBI helicopter crashes after shots are fired at it.

July 14, 1975. *Bombing/explosive.* White racist. Cleveland, Ohio. The headquarters of a black militant organization is bombed, causing $5000 in damage.

July 15, 1975. *Bombing/explosive.* Cuban, Accion Cubana/Cuban Action Commandos. Los Angeles, California. Four people are injured when a bomb explodes at the Mexican Consulate.

July 15, 1975. *Shooting.* White racist, Neal Long. Dayton, Ohio. In separate incidents two black men are killed, and a black woman is wounded when fired at from a car. The two dead men are Robert Hoard and Larry Romine.

July 18, 1975. *Bombing/explosive.* Cuban, Frente de Liberacion Nacional de Cuba. Washington, D.C. The Costa Rican Embassy is bombed.

July 21, 1975. *Bombing/explosive.* Revolutionary leftist, Red Guerrilla Force. San Francisco, California. A bomb explodes in a women's restroom at the building housing the Bureau of Alcohol, Tobacco and Firearms (BATF).

August 5, 1975. *Bombing/explosive.* Revolutionary leftist, George Jackson Brigade. Tacoma, Washington. A courthouse is bombed.

August 6, 1975. *Bombing/explosive.* Revolutionary leftist, George Jackson Brigade. Tacoma, Washington. The Bureau of Indian Affairs office is bombed.

August 8, 1975. *Bombing/explosive.* Revolutionary leftist. Denver, Colorado. A courthouse is bombed.

August 8, 1975. *Bombing/explosive.* Revolutionary leftist, New World Liberation Front. California. The home of an executive of Safeway's board of directors is bombed.

August 16, 1975. *Shooting.* Rightist, Nazis. El Monte, California. Joseph Tommassi, who had set up a new Nazi party, is killed by members of the American Nazi Party.

August 16, 1975. *Bombing/explosive.* White racist, Ku Klux Klan. Greenville,

Alabama. A car bomb explodes and injures the judge who indicted three Klansmen for murder.

August 20, 1975. *Bombing/incendiary.* Revolutionary leftist, New World Liberation Front. San Rafael, California. Sheriffs' cars are firebombed.

September 5, 1975. *Bombing/explosive.* Revolutionary leftist, Weather Underground. Salt Lake, Utah. Kennecott Corporation is bombed for its involvement in the overthrow of the Chilean government, causing $50,000 in damage.

September 5, 1975. *Shooting.* Quasi-terrorist. Sacramento, California. Lynette "Squeaky" Fromme, a member of the Charles Manson cult, attempts to assassinate President Ford.

September 12, 1975. *Attempted bombing.* Revolutionary leftist, New World Liberation Front. Phoenix, Arizona. A federal building is the target of an attempted bombing.

September 12, 1975. *Attempted bombing.* Revolutionary leftist, New World Liberation Front. Seattle, Washington. The Veterans Administration building is the target of an attempted bombing.

September 15, 1975. *Bombing/explosive.* Revolutionary leftist. Seattle, Washington. Ralph Ford is killed by his own bomb, which explodes prematurely outside a supermarket.

September 16, 1975. *Shooting.* White racist. Redwood City, California. Darylle Knowles, a black teenager, is killed in a drive-by shooting by a member of the

Aryan Brotherhood. The murderer converts to Christianity and confesses to the crime six years later.

September 18, 1975. *Bombing/explosive.* Revolutionary leftist, George Jackson Brigade. Seattle, Washington. A Safeway store is bombed.

September 19, 1975. *Shooting.* White racist, Neal Long. Dayton, Ohio. Charles Glatt, a desegregation expert who was designing a plan to integrate Dayton schools, is shot and killed by Neal Long. When arrested Long confessed to a series of drive-by shootings of blacks over a three-year period.

September 22, 1975. *Shooting.* Quasi-terrorist. San Francisco, California. Sara Jane Moore, a former radical and an FBI informer, fires a single shot at President Ford as he leaves his hotel.

September 27, 1975. *Bombing/explosive.* Puerto Rican nationalist, Armed Forces of National Liberation. New York City, New York. Pipe bombs explode at six banks and at the U.S. Mission to the UN, causing minor damage.

September 27, 1975. *Bombing/explosive.* Puerto Rican nationalist, Armed Forces of National Liberation. Washington, D.C. A pipe bomb causes minor damage to the State Department building.

September 27, 1975. *Bombing/explosive.* Puerto Rican nationalist, Armed Forces of National Liberation. Chicago, Illinois. Pipe bombs explode at banks and office buildings.

October 1, 1975. *Bombing/explosive.* Revolutionary leftist, New World Liberation Front. Fort Ord, California. A military base is bombed.

October 4, 1975. *Robbery.* Revolutionary leftist, United Freedom Front. Portland, Maine. North East Bank is robbed.

October 6, 1975. *Bombing/explosive.* Cuban, Frente de Liberacion Nacional de Cuba. Miami, Florida. The Dominican Consulate is bombed.

October 10, 1975. *Bombing/explosive.* Cuban, Frente de Liberacion Nacional de Cuba. Fort Lauderdale, Florida. A courthouse is bombed.

October 13, 1975. *Bombing/explosive.* Revolutionary leftist, Emiliano Zapata Unit. Belmont, California. An electric tower is bombed.

October 17, 1975. *Bombing/explosive.* Cuban, Frente de Liberacion Nacional de Cuba. Miami, Florida. A Dominican Republic airline office is bombed.

October 21, 1975. *Bombing/explosive.* Revolutionary leftist. Oakland, California. A Safeway store is bombed.

October 24, 1975. *Bombing/explosive.* Revolutionary leftist. Oakland, California. A Safeway store is bombed.

October 27, 1975. *Bombing/explosive.* Puerto Rican nationalist, Armed Forces of National Liberation. Washington, D.C. The State Department and the Bureau of Indian Affairs are bombed.

October 27, 1975. *Bombing/explosive.* Puerto Rican nationalist, Armed Forces of National Liberation. Chicago, Illinois. Continental National Bank, IBM Plaza, Sears Tower, and the Standard Oil Building are bombed.

October 27, 1975. *Bombing/explosive.* Puerto Rican nationalist, Armed Forces of National Liberation. New York City, New York. National Westminister Bank, First National Bank, and Chase Manhattan Bank are bombed.

October 27, 1975. *Bombing/explosive.* Puerto Rican nationalist, Armed Forces of National Liberation. New York City, New York. The U.S. Mission to the UN is bombed.

October 31, 1975. *Bombing/explosive.* Revolutionary leftist, Emiliano Zapata Unit. Oakland, California. A Safeway store is bombed.

October 31, 1975. *Bombing/explosive.* Cuban. Miami, Florida. A car bomb kills Rolando Masferrer, an anti-Castro activist. The assassination was possibly by Cuban government agents.

November 9, 1975. *Bombing/explosive.* Puerto Rican nationalist, Armed Forces of National Liberation. New York City, New York. First National City Bank is bombed.

November 27, 1975. *Bombing/explosive.* Cuban. Miami, Florida. A Bahamas Airlines airplane is bombed.

November 27, 1975. *Bombing/explosive.* Revolutionary leftist, Emiliano Zapata Unit. San Francisco, California. A Safeway store is bombed.

November 30, 1975. *Bombing/explosive.* Revolutionary leftist, Emiliano Zapata Unit. San Francisco, California. A car belonging to an executive of a hospital equipment firm is bombed.

December 3, 1975. *Bombing/explosive.* Cuban. Miami, Florida. Two post office buildings and the FBI headquarters are bombed.

December 4, 1975. *Bombing/explosive.* Cuban. Miami, Florida. The Miami Police Department and the justice building are bombed.

December 9, 1975. *Bombing/explosive.* White racist. Boston, Massachusetts. The NAACP office is bombed. The bombing follows a desegregation court decision.

December 12, 1975. *Robbery.* Revolutionary leftist, United Freedom Front. Augusta, Maine. Bank of Maine is robbed.

December 23, 1975. *Bombing/explosive.* Revolutionary leftist, Continental Revolutionary Army. Denver, Colorado. A federal building is bombed by the Continental Revolutionary Army.

December 28, 1975. *Bombing/explosive.* Revolutionary leftist, Emiliano Zapata Unit. Belmont, California. A Safeway store is bombed.

December 29, 1975. *Bombing/explosive.* Unknown. New York City, New York. A bomb placed in a luggage locker at LaGuardia International Airport kills 11 and injures 74. A task force of hundreds of New York Police Department detectives and ATF and FBI agents was unable to determine who was responsible for the bombing. However, investigators think that the timing device may have malfunctioned and suspect that a Croatian nationalist group was responsible, since they planted a similar bomb in a locker at Grand Central Terminal.

December 29, 1975. *Bombing/explosive.* Croatian. Chicago, Illinois. A Yugoslav diplomat's home is bombed.

December 30, 1975. *Bombing/explosive.* Revolutionary leftist, Emiliano Zapata Unit. Berkeley, California. Bank of America is bombed.

December 31, 1975. *Bombing/explosive.* Revolutionary leftist. Seattle, Washington. An electric substation is bombed.

December 31, 1975. *Bombing/explosive.* Revolutionary leftist, George Jackson Brigade. Bellevue, Washington. A Safeway store is bombed.

January 10, 1976. *Attempted bombing.* Revolutionary leftist, New World Liberation Front. San Francisco, California. Letter bombs are sent to the homes of two members of the board of supervisors, the legislative branch of the city and county of San Francisco.

January 12, 1976. *Attempted bombing.* Jewish, Jewish Armed Resistance. New York City, New York. Pipe bombs are found at the Iraqi Mission to the UN. Three other pipe bombs are found near the UN. They were set to explode during the debate over Palestine.

January 13, 1976. *Bombing/explosive.* Revolutionary leftist, Emiliano Zapata Unit. Novato, California. A Safeway store is bombed.

January 14, 1976. *Bombing/explosive.* Revolutionary leftist, Red Guerrilla Force. San Francisco, California. The Iranian Consulate is bombed.

January 16, 1976. *Bombing/explosive.* Jewish, Jewish Armed Resistance. New York

City, New York. A pipe bomb explodes at the Polish Consulate.

January 21, 1976. *Attempted bombing.* White racist. Sacramento, California. A Jewish temple is the target of an attempted bombing.

January 23, 1976. *Shoot-out and robbery.* Revolutionary leftist, George Jackson Brigade. Seattle, Washington. Bruce Sidell, a member of the George Jackson Brigade, is killed in a shoot-out during a bank robbery.

January 28, 1976. *Shooting.* Cuban. Florida. Alberto Pico, a Cuban activist, is assassinated, possibly by Cuban government agents or possibly by other Cuban émigrés.

January 30, 1976. *Bombing/explosive.* Revolutionary leftist, Emiliano Zapata Unit. Santa Clara, California. A Safeway store is bombed.

February 1, 1976. *Bombing/explosive.* Revolutionary leftist, New World Liberation Front. San Francisco, California. A slum landlord's car is bombed.

February 1, 1976. *Attempted bombing.* Revolutionary leftist, New World Liberation Front. San Geronimo, California. A Pacific Gas and Electric installation is the target of an attempted bombing.

February 2, 1976. *Bombing/explosive.* Revolutionary leftist, New World Liberation Front. San Francisco, California. A second slum landlord's car is bombed.

February 4, 1976. *Arson.* White racist. Keyes, California. Arson destroys a black home, the residence of one of only two black families in town.

February 12, 1976. *Bombing/incendiary.* Revolutionary leftist, New World Liberation Front. San Simeon, California. The Hearst mansion is bombed. A message demands that the Hearst family pay $250,000 to the defense fund of members William and Emily Harris.

February 13, 1976. *Shooting and attempted bombing.* Revolutionary leftist, New World Liberation Front. San Mateo, California. The sheriff is shot while approaching two men planting a bomb at a Pacific Gas and Electric utility tower.

February 17, 1976. *Shooting.* Revolutionary leftist, Emiliano Zapata Unit. Marin County, California. Shots are fired at a dope dealer's house.

February 27, 1976. *Shooting.* Jewish, Jewish Defense League. New York City, New York. Shots are fired at Soviet diplomats' homes.

March 5, 1976. *Bombing/explosive.* Revolutionary leftist, New World Liberation Front. Hunters Point, California. The Housing Authority building is bombed.

March 5, 1976. *Bombing/explosive.* Revolutionary leftist, Red Guerrilla Force. Palo Alto, California. The laboratory of Hewlett-Packard is bombed.

March 8, 1976. *Bombing/explosive.* White racist. Louisville, Kentucky. A stick of dynamite explodes outside the only black home in a white neighborhood.

March 8, 1976. *Bombing/explosive.* Jewish, Jewish Defense League. New York City, New York. A bomb damages the Soviet Airlines Aeroflot office.

March 9, 1976. *Bombing/explosive.* Revolutionary leftist, New World Liberation Front. Redding, California. Randolph Hearst's mountain resort is bombed.

March 10, 1976. *Shooting.* Revolutionary leftist, George Jackson Brigade. Seattle, Washington. A police officer is shot and wounded by a jail escapee.

March 25, 1976. *Attempted bombing.* Jewish, Jewish Armed Resistance. New York City, New York. An explosive device is found at the Soviet trade agency.

April 1, 1976. *Shooting.* Jewish, Jewish Armed Resistance. New York City, New York. Shots are fired at the Soviet Mission to the UN.

April 5, 1976. *Bombing/explosive.* Unknown. Miami, Florida. An explosion occurs in a hall before Angela Davis, a left-wing black activist, is due to speak.

April 13, 1976. *Shooting.* Cuban. Miami, Florida. Ramon Donestevez, an anti-Castro leader, is assassinated. It is uncertain whether agents of the Cuban government are responsible or if it is the result of a feud within the émigré community.

April 15, 1976. *Bombing/explosive.* Revolutionary leftist, Red Guerrilla Force. San Francisco, California. An office building is bombed by the Red Guerrilla Force.

April 22, 1976. *Bombing/explosive.* Revolutionary leftist, United Freedom Front. Boston, Massachusetts. Suffolk County Courthouse is bombed.

May 2, 1976. *Bombing/explosive.* Jewish, Jewish Armed Resistance. New York City, New York. Pipe bombs explode outside Communist Party headquarters and a Russian bookstore.

May 13, 1976. *Shooting.* Jewish, Jewish Defense League. Hyattsville, Maryland. Shots are fired at Soviet diplomats' homes.

May 14, 1976. *Bombing/explosive.* Revolutionary leftist, New World Liberation Front. San Francisco, California. A bank is bombed.

May 17, 1976. *Bombing/explosive.* Jewish. New York City, New York. Two banks are bombed by "Save Our Israel Soil."

June 6, 1976. *Bombing/explosive.* Puerto Rican nationalist, Armed Forces of National Liberation. Chicago, Illinois. A police station is bombed.

June 6, 1976. *Bombing/explosive.* Cuban, Omega7. New York City, New York. The Cuban Mission to the UN is bombed.

June 6, 1976. *Bombing/explosive.* Puerto Rican nationalist, Armed Forces of National Liberation. New York City, New York. A police station is bombed.

June 7, 1976. *Bombing/explosive.* Puerto Rican nationalist, Armed Forces of National Liberation. Chicago, Illinois. John Hancock Center, Bank Leumi Le-Israel, and First National Plaza are bombed.

June 19, 1976. *Bombing/explosive.* Puerto Rican nationalist, Armed Forces of National Liberation. Chicago, Illinois. A Marshall Field's department store is bombed.

June 21, 1976. *Bombing/explosive.* Revolutionary leftist, United Freedom Front. Lowell, Massachusetts. Middlesex County Courthouse is bombed.

June 25, 1976. *Bombing/explosive.* Puerto Rican nationalist, Armed Forces of National Liberation. New York City, New York. Pan Am Building, First National City Bank, and Chase Manhattan Bank are bombed.

June 25, 1976. *Bombing/explosive.* Jewish, Jewish Armed Resistance. New York City, New York. Pipe bombs explode outside two banks.

July 2, 1976. *Bombing/explosive.* Revolutionary leftist, United Freedom Front. Newburyport, Massachusetts. Essex County Courthouse is bombed.

July 2, 1976. *Bombing/explosive.* Revolutionary leftist. Boston, Massachusetts. An airliner at Logan International Airport is destroyed; responsibility for the action is claimed by the Fred Hampton People's Force.

July 2, 1976. *Bombing/explosive.* Revolutionary leftist. Boston, Massachusetts. The city armory is bombed.

July 4, 1976. *Bombing/explosive.* Revolutionary leftist, United Freedom Front. Revere, Massachusetts. First National Bank of Boston is bombed.

July 12, 1976. *Bombing/incendiary.* Puerto Rican nationalist, Armed Forces of National Liberation. New York City, New York. Macy's, Gimbel's, Lord & Taylor, B. Altman's, Korvettes, and Ohrbachs department stores are bombed.

September 10, 1976. *Bombing/explosive.* Puerto Rican nationalist, Armed Forces of National Liberation. New York City, New York. A police station is bombed.

September 10, 1976. *Bombing/explosive.* Puerto Rican nationalist, Armed Forces of National Liberation. Chicago, Illinois. A Holiday Inn is bombed.

September 10, 1976. *Hijacking and bombing.* Croatian. New York City, New York. A TWA jet en route from LaGuardia International Airport to Chicago is taken over by five hijackers. The leader of the group, Zvonko Busic, tells police he planted a bomb in a locker at Grand Central Terminal. The bomb explodes when police try to deactivate it, killing one policeman, Brian J. Murray, and seriously injuring another.

September 16, 1976. *Bombing/explosive.* Cuban, Omega7. Elizabeth, New Jersey. A Soviet ship is bombed.

September 19, 1976. *Bombing/explosive.* Puerto Rican nationalist, Armed Forces of National Liberation. Chicago, Illinois. A Marshall Field's department store is bombed.

September 20, 1976. *Bombing/explosive.* Revolutionary leftist. San Francisco, California. The South African Consulate is bombed.

September 21, 1976. *Bombing/explosive.* Puerto Rican nationalist, Armed Forces of National Liberation. New York City, New York. The Hilton Hotel is bombed after a dinner for Puerto Rico Governor Rafael Hernandez Colon, protesting his presence.

September 21, 1976. *Bombing/explosive.* Chilean. Washington, D.C. A car bomb kills a Chilean exile, Orlando Letelier, and his American assistant, Ronni Moffitt. Agents of the Chilean government are responsible.

October 3, 1976. *Shooting.* Jewish, Jewish Armed Resistance. Washington, D.C. A Soviet diplomat is shot and wounded.

October 25, 1976. *Shooting.* Cuban. San Juan, Puerto Rico. Aldo Vera Serafin, an anti-Castro Cuban activist, is assassinated.

December 6, 1976. *Attempted bombing.* Unknown. Washington, D.C. A bomb in the office of President-elect Carter's transition team is defused by police.

December 6, 1976. *Attempted robbery.* Revolutionary leftist, May 19th Communist Organization. Pittsburgh, Pennsylvania. Members of the May 19th Communist Organization (M19) attempt to rob an armored car outside a Mellon Bank branch.

December 12, 1976. *Bombing/explosive.* Revolutionary leftist, United Freedom Front. Needham, Massachusetts. Union Carbide Corporation is bombed.

December 14, 1976. *Attempted bombing.* Unknown. San Francisco, California. A bomb is placed in the mayor's home but fails to explode.

1977. *Robbery.* Revolutionary leftist, George Jackson Brigade. Seattle, Washington. At least six robberies are attributed to the George Jackson Brigade during 1977.

January 3, 1977. *Bombing/explosive.* Puerto Rican nationalist. Puerto Rico. The ROTC building is bombed.

January 7, 1977. *Shooting.* Cuban. Miami, Florida. Juan Peruyero, an anti-Castro leader, is shot by a sniper. Allegations indicate that the Cuban government is responsible.

January 14, 1977. *Bombing/explosive.* Puerto Rican nationalist. Puerto Rico. An electric transmission tower is bombed.

January 19, 1977. *Bombing/explosive.* Puerto Rican nationalist. Puerto Rico. An electric transmission tower is bombed.

January 20, 1977. *Bombing/explosive.* Puerto Rican nationalist. Puerto Rico. An electric transmission tower is bombed.

January 21, 1977. *Attempted bombing.* Puerto Rican nationalist. Washington, D.C. Letter bombs are sent to government officials.

January 27, 1977. *Bombing/explosive.* Revolutionary leftist, New World Liberation Front. California. Five bombs explode in a Pacific Gas and Electric substation.

February 3, 1977. *Bombing/explosive.* Revolutionary leftist, New World Liberation Front. San Francisco, California. A pipe bomb destroys the district attorney's car.

February 8, 1977. *Attempted bombing.* Puerto Rican nationalist, Armed Forces of National Liberation. New York City, New York. An electric transmitter is the target of an attempted bombing.

February 14, 1977. *Shooting.* Quasi-terrorist. New Rochelle, New York. Fred Cowan, a Nazi sympathizer, shoots five co-workers after being suspended from his job; he then kills himself.

February 16, 1977. *Bombing/explosive.* Puerto Rican nationalist. Puerto Rico. An electric transmission tower is bombed.

February 18, 1977. *Bombing/explosive.* Puerto Rican nationalist, Armed Forces of National Liberation. New York City, New York. The Chrysler Building, the Texaco Touring Center, the Gulf and Western Building, and The New York Merchandise Mart are bombed.

February 18, 1977. *Bombing/explosive.* Puerto Rican nationalist, Armed Forces of National Liberation. Chicago, Illinois. The Merchandise Mart and the U.S. Gypsum Building are bombed.

February 23, 1977. *Arson.* Anti-abortion. St. Paul, Minnesota. An administrative floor above the Planned Parenthood clinic is set on fire, causing an estimated damage of $250,000.

February 24, 1977. *Attempted bombing.* Puerto Rican nationalist. New York City, New York. Letter bombs are sent to banks.

March 7, 1977. *Kidnapping.* Quasi-terrorist. Warrensville, Ohio. A black man takes the chief of police hostage and demands that President Carter apologize for the oppression of blacks in America and that all whites leave the planet within seven days. After speaking to the president, he releases his hostage unharmed.

March 9, 1977. *Occupation/hostage taking.* Black militant, Black Muslims. Washington, D.C. A group of Hanafi Muslims storm the District Building, the B'Nai B'rith offices, and the Islamic Center. During the takeover of the three buildings,

Maurice Williams, a reporter for a local radio station, is shot dead and 19 others are shot, stabbed, or beaten. The Hanafis, led by Hamaas Khaalis, demanded that the government turn over five Black Muslims convicted of murdering seven of Khaalis's family four years earlier. Khaalis also wanted United Artists to stop showing the movie *Mohammad, Messenger of God.* The 134 hostages were released two days later after negotiations involving the ambassadors of Egypt, Iran, and Pakistan.

March 12, 1977. *Bombing/explosive.* Revolutionary leftist, United Freedom Front. Marlboro, Massachusetts. The Ideal Roller and Graphics factory is bombed. Responsibility for the action is claimed by the Sam Melville–Jonathan Jackson Unit of the NWLF.

March 20, 1977. *Bombing/explosive.* Puerto Rican nationalist, Armed Forces of National Liberation. New York City, New York. Whelan Drug Store is bombed.

March 20, 1977. *Bombing/explosive.* Puerto Rican nationalist, Armed Forces of National Liberation. New York City, New York. American Bank Note Company is bombed.

March 21, 1977. *Bombing/explosive.* Puerto Rican nationalist, Armed Forces of National Liberation. New York City, New York. The FBI office is bombed; a passerby on the street is wounded.

April 9, 1977. *Bombing/explosive.* Puerto Rican nationalist, Armed Forces of National Liberation. New York City, New York. May Company, Bloomingdale's, and Gimbel's department stores are bombed.

April 18, 1977. *Bombing/explosive.* Revolutionary leftist, New World Liberation Front. California. Three electric transformers are destroyed.

May 1, 1977. *Arson.* Anti-abortion. Burlington, Vermont. A fire destroys the Vermont Women's Health Center.

May 12, 1977. *Bombing/explosive.* Revolutionary leftist, George Jackson Brigade. Seattle, Washington. Two banks are bombed.

May 25, 1977. *Bombing/explosive.* Cuban. Fort Lauderdale, Florida. An airline planning to provide flights to Cuba is bombed. The plans were cancelled after the bombing.

May 26, 1977. *Robbery.* Revolutionary leftist, May 19th Communist Organization. New York City, New York. A restaurant, the House O'Weenies, is robbed by M19 members.

May 28, 1977. *Escape.* Revolutionary leftist, May 19th Communist Organization. Alderson, West Virginia. Marilyn Jean Buck escapes from the federal prison while serving a 10-year sentence.

June 4, 1977. *Bombing/explosive.* Puerto Rican nationalist, Armed Forces of National Liberation. Chicago, Illinois. City hall is bombed; FALN claims responsibility.

June 14, 1977. *Shooting.* Croatian. New York City, New York. The Yugoslav Mission to the UN is taken over by Croatian gunmen.

June 19, 1977. *Shooting.* Croatian. New York City, New York. A Serbian editor and a child are shot dead.

July 1977. *Bombing.* White racist, Joseph Paul Franklin. Chattanooga, Tennessee. A synagogue is bombed.

July 29, 1977. *Bombing.* White racist, Joseph Paul Franklin. Rockville, Maryland. A bombing occurs at the home of a Jewish lobbyist. No one is injured. Joseph Paul Franklin later gave details that only a person involved in this bombing could have known.

August 3, 1977. *Bombing/explosive.* Puerto Rican nationalist, Armed Forces of National Liberation. New York City, New York. The Mobil Oil Building is bombed, killing Charles Steinberg and injuring seven. A note says FALN planted the bomb as a warning to multinational corporations that were exploiting Puerto Rican workers.

August 3, 1977. *Bombing/explosive.* Puerto Rican nationalist, Armed Forces of National Liberation. New York City, New York. The Department of Defense Building is bombed; there are no injuries.

August 4, 1977. *Bombing/explosive.* Puerto Rican nationalist, Armed Forces of National Liberation. New York City, New York. The New York Commodity Exchange is bombed.

August 7, 1977. *Shooting.* White racist, Joseph Paul Franklin. Madison, Wisconsin. A black male, Alphonse Manning, and a white female, Toni Schwenn, are shot and killed with a hand gun in a shopping mall parking lot. This is the first in a series of shootings for which Joseph Paul Franklin is a suspect.

August 8, 1977. *Attempted bombing.* Puerto Rican nationalist, Armed Forces of National Liberation. New York City, New

York. The American Metal Climax Building is the target of an attempted bombing.

August 18, 1977. *Arson.* Anti-abortion. Omaha, Nebraska. The Ladies Clinic is set on fire, causing approximately $35,000 in damage.

September 5, 1977. *Shooting.* White racist. Jonesville, North Carolina. A white youth wearing a Nazi armband fires on a party of blacks, killing two and wounding three. He then commits suicide.

September 7, 1977. *Bombing/explosive.* Cuban. Washington, D.C. A Soviet airline office is bombed.

September 19, 1977. *Bombing/explosive.* Cuban. Miami, Florida. Four hotels are bombed.

October 4, 1977. *Bombing/explosive.* Armenian. Los Angeles, California. The home of a UCLA professor is bombed. He teaches Ottoman history and had written a pro-Turkish account of the Armenian genocide of 1915.

October 8, 1977. *Bombing/explosive.* Jewish, Jewish Armed Resistance. Hollywood, California. A liberal Jewish temple is bombed by the Jewish Armed Resistance.

October 8, 1977. *Shooting.* White racist, Joseph Paul Franklin. Richmond Heights, Missouri. A white male, Gerald Gordon, is shot and killed by a sniper, and two others are wounded while they are leaving a bar mitzvah celebration at a Jewish synagogue. Joseph Paul Franklin later admitted this offense and was sentenced to death by lethal injection.

October 10, 1977. *Bombing/explosive.* Revolutionary leftist, New World Liberation

Front. Oregon. A pipe bomb explodes at Trojan Nuclear Power Plant.

October 10, 1977. *Bombing/explosive.* Puerto Rican nationalist. Puerto Rico. The Reserve Officers club is bombed.

October 10, 1977. *Bombing/explosive.* Puerto Rican nationalist. Puerto Rico. A bank is bombed.

October 11, 1977. *Bombing/explosive.* Puerto Rican nationalist, Armed Forces of National Liberation. Chicago, Illinois. A post office is bombed.

October 11, 1977. *Attempted bombing.* Puerto Rican nationalist. New York City, New York. A bank is the target of an attempted bombing.

October 11, 1977. *Bombing/explosive.* Puerto Rican nationalist. Puerto Rico. Corporation offices are bombed.

October 11, 1977. *Bombing/explosive.* Puerto Rican nationalist, Armed Forces of National Liberation. New York City, New York. Gimbel's and Macy's department stores are bombed.

October 12, 1977. *Bombing/explosive.* Puerto Rican nationalist, Armed Forces of National Liberation. New York City, New York. A bomb explodes outside New York Public Library.

October 12, 1977. *Bombing/explosive.* Revolutionary leftist, New World Liberation Front. California. An electric transformer is destroyed, causing damage estimated at $100,000.

October 12, 1977. *Bombing/explosive.* Puerto Rican nationalist, Armed Forces of National Liberation. New York City, New York. A bomb explodes under a police car.

October 15, 1977. *Bombing/explosive.* Puerto Rican nationalist, Armed Forces of National Liberation. New York City, New York. The National Guard Armory is bombed.

October 19, 1977. *Robbery.* Revolutionary leftist, May 19th Communist Organization. Mount Vernon, New York. A Citibank branch is robbed by M19; $13,800 is stolen.

November 1977. *Arson.* Anti-abortion. Cincinnati, Ohio. A fire is set at the Planned Parenthood Abortion Clinic; damage is estimated at $4000.

November 1977. *Attempted bombing.* Anti-abortion. Cincinnati, Ohio. The Margaret Sanger Clinic is the target of an attempted firebombing. A Molotov cocktail hits the outside of the clinic's air conditioner but fails to explode.

November 10, 1977. *Bombing/incendiary.* Revolutionary leftist, New World Liberation Front. California. An oil storage tank is bombed.

November 11, 1977. *Bombing/explosive.* Puerto Rican nationalist. Puerto Rico. A bank is bombed.

November 11, 1977. *Bombing/explosive.* Puerto Rican nationalist. Puerto Rico. An electric substation is bombed.

November 15, 1977. *Attempted bombing.* Puerto Rican nationalist, Armed Forces of National Liberation. New York City, New York. The office of Iran Air is the target of an attempted bombing.

November 28, 1977. *Assault.* Unknown. Washington, D.C. An Indian diplomat is stabbed and seriously wounded. He had received threatening letters from the Universal Proutist Revolutionary Movement.

December 23, 1977. *Bombing/explosive.* Puerto Rican nationalist. Puerto Rico. An electric tower is bombed.

December 23, 1977. *Bombing/explosive.* Cuban. Miami, Florida. The office of Venezuelan Airlines is bombed after Venezuelan Airlines begins flights to Cuba.

December 26, 1977. *Bombing/explosive.* Cuban, Omega7. New York City, New York. The Venezuelan Consulate is bombed.

January 11, 1978. *Attempted bombing.* Puerto Rican nationalist. New York City, New York. A bank is the target of an attempted bombing.

January 14, 1978. *Bombing/explosive.* Puerto Rican nationalist. Puerto Rico. An electric tower is bombed.

January 19, 1978. *Bombing/explosive.* Puerto Rican nationalist. Puerto Rico. Two electric towers are bombed.

January 20, 1978. *Bombing/explosive.* Puerto Rican nationalist. Puerto Rico. An electric tower is bombed.

January 25, 1978. *Bombing/explosive.* Puerto Rican nationalist. Puerto Rico. A bank is bombed.

January 31, 1978. *Bombing/explosive.* Puerto Rican nationalist, Armed Forces of National Liberation. New York City, New York. The Con Edison Building is bombed.

January 31, 1978. *Bombing/explosive.* Puerto Rican nationalist, Armed Forces of National Liberation. New York City, New York. An explosion occurs near a police car.

February 1978. *Bombing/incendiary.* Anti-abortion. Cincinnati, Ohio. A chemical bomb is thrown into the Women for Women Clinic. The chemical in the bomb is on the government's list of chemical warfare agents. The estimated damage is $3000.

February 8, 1978. *Bombing/explosive.* Puerto Rican nationalist. Puerto Rico. A bank is bombed.

February 8, 1978. *Arson.* Anti-abortion. Columbus, Ohio. Arson causes an estimated damage of $200,000 to the Northwest Women's Center.

February 8, 1978. *Attempted bombing.* Puerto Rican nationalist, Armed Forces of National Liberation. New York City, New York. A power transmitter is the target of an attempted bombing.

February 8, 1978. *Bombing/explosive.* Puerto Rican nationalist. San Juan, Puerto Rico. The FBI building is bombed.

February 15, 1978. *Assault and arson.* Anti-abortion. Cleveland, Ohio. The Concerned Women's Abortion Clinic is destroyed when a man enters, blinds a technician with chemicals, and then sets the clinic on fire.

February 16, 1978. *Attempted bombing.* Puerto Rican nationalist, Armed Forces of National Liberation. New York City, New York. Manufacturer's Bank is the target of an attempted bombing.

February 16, 1978. *Bombing/explosive.* Puerto Rican nationalist. Puerto Rico. Seven U.S. corporation offices are bombed.

February 24, 1978. *Arson.* Anti-abortion. Akron, Ohio. The Akron Women's Clinic is set on fire.

March 6, 1978. *Shooting.* White racist, Joseph Paul Franklin. Gwinette County, Georgia. A sniper shooting and wounding of *Hustler* publisher Larry Flynt leaves him paralyzed from the waist down. His lawyer is also wounded, though not seriously. Joseph Paul Franklin later admitted to these shootings.

March 14, 1978. *Bombing/explosive.* Revolutionary leftist, New World Liberation Front. San Francisco, California. Electric transformers are destroyed, cutting power to 75,000 homes.

March 22, 1978. *Bombing/explosive.* Chicano Liberation Front. Denver, Colorado. Carlos Zapata, a Chicano activist, is killed when a bomb explodes prematurely as he places it outside a Veterans of Foreign Wars (VFW) post. A few minutes before, another bomb shatters windows in a two-block radius.

April 7, 1978. *Bombing/explosive.* Puerto Rican nationalist. San Juan, Puerto Rico. The Chilean Consulate is bombed.

April 11, 1978. *Bombing/explosive.* Puerto Rican nationalist. San Juan, Puerto Rico. The Coast Guard Club is bombed.

April 14, 1978. *Bombing/explosive.* Puerto Rican nationalist. Puerto Rico. Coast Guard housing is bombed.

April 14, 1978. *Bombing/explosive.* Puerto Rican nationalist. Puerto Rico. The Army recruiting center is bombed.

April 14, 1978. *Attempted bombing.* Puerto Rican nationalist. Puerto Rico. A bank is the target of an attempted bombing.

April 19, 1978. *Bombing/explosive.* Puerto Rican nationalist. Puerto Rico. A post office is bombed.

May 9, 1978. *Bombing/explosive.* Puerto Rican nationalist. Puerto Rico. Three post offices are bombed.

May 10, 1978. *Bombing/explosive.* Puerto Rican nationalist. Puerto Rico. The Army recruiting center is bombed.

May 14, 1978. *Bombing/explosive.* Jewish, Jewish Armed Resistance. New York City, New York. An explosion at a Russian-language newspaper office causes heavy damage.

May 15, 1978. *Bombing/incendiary.* Anti-abortion. Burlington, Vermont. The front porch and the door of the Vermont Women's Health Center are firebombed.

May 18, 1978. *Bombing/explosive.* Puerto Rican nationalist. Puerto Rico. A bomb destroys a government vehicle.

May 22, 1978. *Bombing/explosive.* Puerto Rican nationalist, Armed Forces of National Liberation. New York City, New York. Bombs explode in John F. Kennedy International Airport.

May 22, 1978. *Bombing/explosive.* Puerto Rican nationalist, Armed Forces of National Liberation. Newark, New Jersey. Bombs explode in Newark International Airport.

May 22, 1978. *Bombing/incendiary.* Puerto Rican nationalist, Armed Forces of National Liberation. Washington, D.C. Bombs explode outside the Justice Department.

May 25, 1978. *Bombing/explosive.* Unabomber. Evanston, Illinois. A package found on the University of Illinois campus is returned to the apparent sender, a professor at Northwestern University. He turns it over to campus security because he had not sent the package. The package explodes when it is opened, injuring a security guard.

June 6, 1978. *Bombing/explosive.* Puerto Rican nationalist. Puerto Rico. A post office is bombed.

June 6, 1978. *Bombing/explosive.* Puerto Rican nationalist. Puerto Rico. A government vehicle is bombed.

June 10, 1978. *Bombing/incendiary.* Anti-abortion. Columbus, Ohio. A firebomb is tossed through the window of Founder's Clinic.

June 13, 1978. *Bombing/incendiary.* Anti-abortion. Iowa City, Iowa. The Emma Goldman Clinic for Women is firebombed.

June 24, 1978. *Bombing/explosive.* Puerto Rican nationalist, Armed Forces of National Liberation. Schaumburg, Illinois. J.C. Penney, Marshall Field's, and Sears department stores are bombed.

July 7, 1978. *Bombing/explosive.* Puerto Rican nationalist. Puerto Rico. A bank is bombed.

July 10, 1978. *Bombing/incendiary.* Jewish, Jewish Armed Resistance. New York City,

New York. A small incendiary bomb explodes outside the Soviet tourist office. Responsibility for the bombing is claimed by the Jewish Armed Resistance; it is said to be a protest against the trials of Jewish dissidents in the Soviet Union.

July 12, 1978. *Bombing/explosive.* Puerto Rican nationalist, Armed Forces of National Liberation. New York City, New York. Macy's Department Store and Korvettes are bombed.

July 19, 1978. *Bombing.* Puerto Rican nationalist. Puerto Rico. A post office is bombed.

July 25, 1978. *Attempted bombing.* Puerto Rican nationalist, Armed Independence Movement. Puerto Rico. Two Puerto Rican nationalists are shot by police during an attempted bombing of an electric tower. This incident, known as the "Cerro Maravilla affair," becomes an election issue when it is alleged that the two youths were entrapped by police.

July 29, 1978. *Shooting.* White racist, Joseph Paul Franklin. Chattanooga, Tennessee. A black male and a white female are shot and killed by a sniper in the Pizza Hut parking lot. Joseph Paul Franklin confessed to these murders and was sentenced to two life sentences, one for murder and one for an unrelated armed robbery offense that occurred in 1977.

July 31, 1978. *Bombing/explosive.* Puerto Rican nationalist. San Juan, Puerto Rico. A bomb destroys a government vehicle.

August 14, 1978. *Attempted bombing.* Croatian. New York City, New York. Bombs are placed in the UN library and in a Grand Central Terminal locker by Croatian Freedom Fighters, but they fail to explode.

August 17, 1978. *Occupation/hostage taking.* Croatian. Chicago, Illinois. The German Consulate is taken over by two Croatian nationalists. Six diplomats were held hostage in an attempt to prevent a Croatian nationalist held in West Germany from being extradited to Yugoslavia.

August 25, 1978. *Shooting and kidnapping.* Puerto Rican nationalist, Macheteros. Puerto Rico. Two Puerto Rican police officers are attacked. Officer Julio Rivera is killed; the other officer is kidnapped but is later released unharmed. The attack is in retaliation for the murder of two independentistas at Cerro Maravilla in July 1978. The Macheteros take credit for this event.

September 9, 1978. *Bombing/explosive.* Cuban, Omega7. New York City, New York. Three people are injured when the Cuban Mission to the UN is bombed.

September 28, 1978. *Shooting.* Croatian. Greenburgh, New York. After refusing to contribute to a Croatian nationalist organization, a Croatian is shot and killed outside his house.

September 29, 1978. *Bombing/explosive.* Puerto Rican nationalist, Armed Forces of National Liberation. New York City, New York. Macy's Department Store is bombed.

October 2, 1978. *Robbery.* Puerto Rican nationalist, Macheteros. Puerto Rico. A storage warehouse is robbed and explosives are taken, including dynamite cartridges, 500 pounds of ammonium nitrate, 988 blasting caps, and 17,500 feet of primacord. The Macheteros claim responsibility along with the Organization of Volunteers for the Puerto Rican Revolution.

October 4, 1978. *Bombing/explosive.* Puerto Rican nationalist. Puerto Rico. A government building is bombed.

October 4, 1978. *Bombing/explosive.* Croatian. Chicago, Illinois. After refusing to contribute to a Croatian nationalist organization, a bomb explodes in the shop of a Croatian businessman.

October 5, 1978. *Bombing/explosive.* Cuban, Omega7. New York City, New York. A bomb explodes outside Madison Square Garden, where Cuban boxers are supposed to fight.

October 6, 1978. *Bombing/explosive.* Cuban, Omega7. Puerto Rico. A tourist agency, the office of the Socialist Party of Puerto Rico, and a Cuban business are bombed.

October 12, 1978. *Robbery.* Revolutionary leftist, May 19th Communist Organization. New York City, New York. A Chase Manhattan branch in New York City is robbed; $8380 is stolen.

October 13, 1978. *Bombing/explosive.* Puerto Rican nationalist, Armed Independence Movement. Puerto Rico. First Federal Savings Bank is bombed.

October 17, 1978. *Bombing/explosive.* Puerto Rican nationalist, Armed Forces of National Liberation. Isabella, Puerto Rico. RCA's radio tower is bombed.

October 23, 1978. *Bombing/explosive.* Cuban, Omega7. New York City, New York. The offices of *La Prensa*, a Cuban newspaper, are bombed.

October 27, 1978. *Bombing/explosive.* Revolutionary leftist, United Freedom Front. Waltham, Massachusetts. Mobil Oil Corporation is bombed.

October 27, 1978. *Bombing/explosive.* Revolutionary leftist, United Freedom Front. Wakefield, Massachusetts. Mobil Oil Corporation is bombed.

October 27, 1978. *Bombing/explosive.* Revolutionary leftist, United Freedom Front. Eastchester, New York. Mobil Oil Corporation is bombed.

November 22, 1978. *Shooting.* Croatian. Glendale, California. After refusing to contribute to a Croatian nationalist organization, Krizan Brkic is gunned down on his way to work.

November 24, 1978. *Bombing/incendiary.* Jewish, Jewish Armed Resistance. New York City, New York. The Egyptian Consulate is firebombed.

November 29, 1978. *Shooting.* Jewish. Baltimore, Maryland. A sniper fires at a Soviet ship with a high-powered rifle.

December 15, 1978. *Assault.* White racist, Ku Klux Klan. Columbus, Georgia. A black preacher is beaten by Klansmen.

December 19, 1978. *Robbery.* Revolutionary leftist, May 19th Communist Organization. Livingston, New Jersey. Bamberger's armored car is robbed; $200,000 is stolen.

December 29, 1978. *Bombing/explosive.* Cuban, Omega7. New York City, New York. The Cuban Mission to the UN is bombed.

December 30, 1978. *Bombing/explosive.* Cuban, Omega7. New York City, New York. Lincoln Center is bombed.

January 4, 1979. *Bombing/explosive.* Cuban. Puerto Rico. A travel office is bombed.

January 13, 1979. *Shooting.* White racist. Chico, California. Jimmy Campbell, a black man, is killed in a drive-by shooting.

January 31, 1979. *Bombing/explosive.* Puerto Rican nationalist, Armed Forces of National Liberation. New York City, New York. The Con Edison Building is bombed.

February 1979. *Bombing/explosive.* Croatian. Milwaukee, Wisconsin. A parcel bomb sent to a Croatian Catholic priest explodes while a police officer is trying to disarm it. The police officer loses his hand.

February 15, 1979. *Arson.* Anti-abortion. Hempstead, New York. Peter Burkin sets fire to the Bill Baird Clinic, injuring himself. The damage is more than $100,000.

February 27, 1979. *Bombing/explosive.* Revolutionary leftist, United Freedom Front. Eastchester, New York. Mobil Oil Corporation is bombed.

February 28, 1979. *Bombing/explosive.* Puerto Rican nationalist, Armed Forces of National Liberation. New York City, New York. A telephone warning is received before the Mobil office is bombed.

March 24, 1979. *Bombing/explosive.* Cuban, Omega7. Weehawken, New Jersey. The business belonging to Eulalio Negrin, a Cuban émigré who advocated negotiations with the Castro regime, is bombed.

March 24, 1979. *Bombing/explosive.* Cuban, Omega7. New York City, New York. Four baggage handlers are injured when a bomb in a suitcase explodes at John F. Kennedy International Airport.

March 26, 1979. *Bombing/explosive.* Cuban, Omega7. Union City, New Jersey. The office of a Cuban favoring "dialogue" with the Castro regime is bombed. Another bomb goes off at a pharmacy that ships medicine to Cuba.

April 1979. *Bombing/explosive.* Croatian. Los Angeles, California. A Croatian nationalist group sends letters demanding money for Croatian immigrants. Two who refuse to pay have their houses and their cars destroyed by pipe bombs.

April 28, 1979. *Shooting.* Cuban, Omega7. Puerto Rico. Carlos Muniz Varela, a Cuban exile leader, is shot and killed.

May 2, 1979. *Bombing/explosive.* Unknown. Bessemer, Alabama. Clifford Hill, a police lieutenant, is killed when a letter bomb explodes.

May 9, 1979. *Bombing/explosive.* Unabomber. Evanston, Illinois. A bomb left in a box at Northwestern University explodes when it is opened, injuring the student who opens it.

May 18, 1979. *Bombing/explosive.* Cuban, Omega7. Washington, D.C. The Cuban Consulate is bombed.

May 26, 1979. *Shoot-out.* White racist, Ku Klux Klan. Decatur, Alabama. During a SCLC parade, shots are exchanged between Klansmen and blacks, leaving four people wounded.

May 27, 1979. *Shooting.* Hawaii for the Hawaiians. Hawaii. A Marine is shot and killed by a group calling itself "Hawaii for the Hawaiians."

June 4, 1979. *Attempted bombing.* Jewish, Jewish Defense League. USA. Three letter bombs are sent to neo-Nazis from the Jewish Action Movement.

June 4, 1979. *Shooting.* White racist, Ku Klux Klan. Birmingham, Alabama. A prosecution witness in the trial of Klansmen is murdered.

June 20, 1979. *Hijacking.* Serbian. Illinois. A Serbian nationalist hijacks an American Airlines jet on a flight from New York to Chicago. He wants the release of another Serbian nationalist who is in jail for bombing a Yugoslav diplomat's home. After freeing the passengers, he forces the plane to fly back to New York. Then he takes over another plane, which flies him to Shannon Airport in Ireland, where he surrenders to authorities.

July 12, 1979. *Shooting.* White racist, Joseph Paul Franklin. Doraville, Georgia. A black male, Harold McIver, manager of a Taco Bell, is shot and killed by a sniper in the parking lot.

August 18, 1979. *Shooting.* White racist, Joseph Paul Franklin. Falls Church, Virginia. A 27-year-old black male, Raymond Turner, is shot and killed in a Burger King restaurant by a sniper. Joseph Paul Franklin later confessed to the murder.

August 31, 1979. *Assault.* Islamic, Al-Fuqra. San Diego, California. An attack occurs at a Hare Krishna temple.

September 11, 1979. *Robbery.* Revolutionary leftist, May 19th Communist Organi-

zation. Paramus, New Jersey. Bamberger's armored car is robbed; $105,000 is stolen.

September 18, 1979. *Bombing/explosive.* Puerto Rican nationalist. Puerto Rico. The National Guard Armory is bombed.

October 17, 1979. *Bombing/explosive.* Puerto Rican nationalist, Armed Forces of National Liberation. Chicago, Illinois. The Great Lakes Naval Station, various federal and local government offices, and the offices of both the Republican Party and the Democratic Party campaign headquarters are bombed.

October 19, 1979. *Bombing/explosive.* Puerto Rican nationalist, Armed Forces of National Liberation. Puerto Rico. Four bombs explode at government offices and statues throughout the island, causing minor property damage.

October 21, 1979. *Shooting.* White racist, Joseph Paul Franklin. Oklahoma City, Oklahoma. A black male, Marion Bressette, and a white female, Jessie Taylor, are shot and killed sniper style while leaving a supermarket. Charges are brought against Joseph Paul Franklin but are later dropped due to a lack of evidence.

October 27, 1979. *Attempted bombing.* Puerto Rican nationalist, Armed Forces of National Liberation. Connecticut. An Amtrack train is the target of a bomb threat.

October 27, 1979. *Bombing/explosive.* Cuban, Omega7. New York City, New York. The Cuban Mission to the UN is bombed.

November 2, 1979. *Escape.* Revolutionary leftist, May 19th Communist Organization. A New Jersey prison. Joanne Chesimard escapes from prison. Two prison guards are briefly held hostage.

November 3, 1979. *Shoot-out.* White racist, Ku Klux Klan. Greensboro, North Carolina. A "Death to the Klan" rally organized by the Communist Workers Party (CWP) is attacked by a nine-car caravan carrying 35 heavily armed Nazis and Klansmen. Five people are killed and 11 are wounded. Those killed include Jim Waller, Sandi Smith, Bill Simpson, Cesar Cauce, and Michael Nathan. All the dead were union activists and members of the CWP. The organizers of the rally claimed that police had colluded with the attackers and failed to protect the demonstrators.

November 15, 1979. *Bombing/explosive.* Unabomber. Airplane in flight from Chicago to Washington, D.C. A bomb mailed from Chicago for delivery to an unknown location explodes aboard a Boeing 727, forcing an emergency landing at Dulles International Airport near Washington, D.C.

November 18, 1979. *Bombing/explosive.* Unknown. New York City, New York. An Israeli bank is bombed.

November 21, 1979. *Bombing/incendiary?* Islamic, Al-Fuqra. Queens, New York. An Iranian (Shi'ite) mosque is attacked.

November 23, 1979. *Bombing/explosive.* Puerto Rican nationalist, Armed Forces of National Liberation. Chicago, Illinois. The Army recruiting center is bombed.

November 24, 1979. *Bombing/explosive.* Puerto Rican nationalist, Armed Forces

of National Liberation. Chicago, Illinois. The Naval Center and recruiting office are bombed.

November 25, 1979. *Shooting.* Cuban, Omega7. Union City, New Jersey. A Cuban exile, Jose Negrin, is assassinated after he called for talks with Castro.

December 3, 1979. *Shooting.* Puerto Rican nationalist, Macheteros. Sabena Seca, Puerto Rico. In retaliation for the murder of Angel Rodriguez in a Tallahassee prison, the Macheteros open fire on a Navy bus in Sebana Seca, Puerto Rico. Two sailors, Emil White and John Ball, are killed and nine are injured.

December 5, 1979. *Bombing/explosive.* Croatian. New York City, New York. A travel agency in Queens is bombed by Croatian Freedom Fighters.

December 7, 1979. *Bombing/explosive.* Cuban, Omega7. New York City, New York. Three people, including two police officers, are injured when the Cuban Mission to the UN is bombed.

December 11, 1979. *Bombing/explosive.* Cuban, Omega7. New York City, New York. The Soviet Mission to the UN is bombed; eight people are injured in the blast.

January 7, 1980. *Bombing/explosive.* Rightist. San Juan, Puerto Rico. The Puerto Rico Bar Association office is bombed. Responsibility for the attack is claimed by the Anti-Communist Alliance.

January 11, 1980. *Shooting.* White racist, Joseph Paul Franklin. Indianapolis, Indiana. A 19-year-old black male, Larry Reese, is shot sniper style and killed in front of Church's Fried Chicken. Joseph Paul Franklin later admitted to this offense.

January 13, 1980. *Bombing/explosive.* Jewish, Jewish Defense League. New York City, New York. An explosion at the office of the Soviet airline Aeroflot injures three. Responsibility for the attack is also claimed by Omega7.

January 14, 1980. *Robbery.* Puerto Rican nationalist, Armed Forces of National Liberation. Wisconsin. A National Guard Armory is raided and weapons are stolen.

January 16, 1980. *Shooting.* White racist, Joseph Paul Franklin. Indianapolis, Indiana. A black male, Lee Watkin, is shot and killed sniper style in front of a fast-food convenience store.

January 22, 1980. *Bombing/explosive.* Taiwanese Independence Movement. Los Angeles, California. A bomb explodes in the baggage area of China Airlines at Los Angeles International Airport, causing $25,000 in damage.

January 26, 1980. *Bombing/incendiary.* Unknown. Arlington, Virginia. A Vietnamese journalist's home is firebombed.

February 17, 1980. *Shooting.* White racist, Ku Klux Klan. Barnegat, New Jersey. A Klansman fires shots into a house.

February 20, 1980. *Attempted robbery.* Revolutionary leftist, May 19th Communist Organization. Greenburgh, New York. M19 attempts to rob an armored car.

February 21, 1980. *Shooting.* Jewish. New York City, New York. Shots are fired at the Soviet Mission to the UN.

March 10, 1980. *Bombing/explosive.* Taiwanese Independence Movement. Los Angeles, California. The home of a Taiwanese general's son is bombed; there are no injuries.

March 13, 1980. *Shooting.* Puerto Rican nationalist, Macheteros. Puerto Rico. A United States Army ROTC vehicle is attacked while transporting three officers to the University of Puerto Rico.

March 13, 1980. *Bombing/incendiary.* Cuban, Omega7. New York City, New York. The Angolan Mission to the UN is firebombed.

March 14, 1980. *Sabotage, vandalism, and property destruction.* Puerto Rican nationalist, Armed Forces of National Liberation. Chicago, Illinois. The Democratic Party and the Republican Party campaign headquarters are both vandalized.

March 17, 1980. *Bombing/explosive.* Croatian. New York City, New York. A Yugoslav bank is bombed by Croatian Freedom Fighters.

April 1980. *Bombing/explosive.* White racist. Jersey City, New Jersey. People United to Serve Humanity headquarters, the organization headed by Jesse Jackson, is bombed.

April 1980. *Bombing/incendiary.* Jewish, Jewish Defense League. Washington, D.C. The office of the Palestine Human Rights Campaign is firebombed. The JDL issues a statement approving the attack.

April 19, 1980. *Shooting.* White racist, Ku Klux Klan. Wrightsville, Georgia. A black child is wounded when Klansmen fire at a black demonstration.

April 19, 1980. *Shooting.* White racist, Ku Klux Klan. Chattanooga, Tennessee. Three Klansmen are arrested after they fire into a crowd, wounding four black women.

April 22, 1980. *Robbery.* Revolutionary leftist, May 19th Communist Organization. Inwood, New York. A Purolator truck outside the European American Bank is robbed; $529,000 is stolen.

May 3, 1980. *Shooting.* White racist, Joseph Paul Franklin. Tomah, Wisconsin. A white female, Rebecca Bergstrom, is found shot in a secluded park near Tomah in central Wisconsin. The Justice Department reported that she was hitchhiking and was picked up by Joseph Paul Franklin. She told him she had dated a Jamaican.

May 12, 1980. *Bombing/incendiary.* Jewish, Jewish Defense League. Mineola, New York. A gasoline firebomb explodes harmlessly outside the home of an accused war criminal. He was convicted by a Soviet court for the slaughter of Jewish children during World War II and was fighting attempts to deport him.

May 22, 1980. *Shooting.* White racist, Ku Klux Klan. Wrightsville, Georgia. A black man is shot and seriously wounded.

May 29, 1980. *Shooting.* White racist, Joseph Paul Franklin. Fort Wayne, Indiana. A black male, Vernon E. Jordan Jr., president of the National Urban League, is shot and wounded by a sniper while in the company of a white woman. Joseph Paul Franklin was acquitted in 1982 of federal charges of violating Mr. Jordan's civil rights. Jurors later said that while they were convinced Mr. Franklin had fired the shots, they were not persuaded that he had violated the civil rights laws.

June 3, 1980. *Bombing/explosive.* Croatian. Washington, D.C. A bomb explodes in a Yugoslav diplomat's home.

June 5, 1980. *Bombing/explosive.* Croatian. New York City, New York. Croatian Freedom Fighters claim responsibility for bombing the Statue of Liberty museum.

June 8, 1980. *Shooting.* White racist, Joseph Paul Franklin. Cincinnati, Ohio. Two young black males, Dante Evans Brown and Darrell Lane, are shot and killed by a sniper on an overpass as they were walking along some railroad tracks.

June 10, 1980. *Bombing/explosive.* Unabomber. Lake Forest, Illinois. A bomb mailed to the home of the president of United Air Lines explodes when he opens it.

June 11, 1980. *Bombing/explosive.* Unknown. Beverly Hills, California. The Iranian Consulate is bombed.

June 15, 1980. *Shooting.* White racist, Joseph Paul Franklin. Johnstown, Pennsylvania. A black male, Arthur Smothers, and a white female, Kathleen Mikula, are killed by a sniper while strolling across a bridge. The male victim was shot once and the female was shot twice with .35 caliber rifle. Joseph Paul Franklin was seen driving a dark green Chevy Nova in the area at the time of the shootings.

June 16, 1980. *Arson.* Unknown. Washington, D.C. Arson at an Iranian newspaper office causes $5000 in damage.

June 21, 1980. *Shooting.* Unknown. New York City, New York. Shots are fired at the home of the Shah of Iran's sister.

July 1980. *Bombing/explosive.* White racist, Ku Klux Klan. Indianapolis, Indiana. A house is bombed, killing eight blacks. A Klansman is arrested for the bombing.

July 4, 1980. *Shooting.* White racist, Ku Klux Klan. Wrightsville, Georgia. Mike Salter, a black civil rights activist, is murdered.

July 14, 1980. *Bombing/explosive.* Puerto Rican nationalist. Dorado, Puerto Rico. A Coast Guard base is bombed.

July 14, 1980. *Bombing/explosive.* Puerto Rican nationalist. San Juan, Puerto Rico. A Coast Guard base is bombed.

July 14, 1980. *Bombing/explosive.* Puerto Rican nationalist. Ponce, Puerto Rico. A Coast Guard base is bombed.

July 14, 1980. *Bombing/explosive.* Puerto Rican nationalist. Mayaguez, Puerto Rico. A Coast Guard base is bombed.

July 17, 1980. *Bombing/explosive.* Jewish, Jewish Defense League. Manhattan Beach, California. A mail bomb delivered to an office kills a secretary, Patricia Wilkerson. Robert Manning, a member of the JDL, is later convicted of the crime.

July 21, 1980. *Bombing/explosive.* Puerto Rican nationalist. Hato Rey, Puerto Rico. A post office is bombed.

July 21, 1980. *Bombing/explosive.* Puerto Rican nationalist. Santurce, Puerto Rico. A post office is bombed.

July 21, 1980. *Bombing/explosive.* Puerto Rican nationalist. Rio Piedras, Puerto Rico. A post office is bombed.

July 21, 1980. *Bombing/explosive.* Puerto Rican nationalist. Sabana Seca, Puerto Rico. A post office is bombed.

July 22, 1980. *Shooting.* Islamic. Bethesda, Maryland. Ali Tabatabai, a former Iranian press attaché, is assassinated outside his house by David Belfield, a black American who converted to Islam. Belfield, who took the name Daoud Salahuddin, was given $4000 by the Iranian government and now lives in exile in Iran.

July 28, 1980. *Bombing/explosive.* Taiwanese Independence Movement. Los Angeles, California. The home of a Taiwanese official is bombed; Li Chian-Lin, the brother of the official, is killed.

August 1980. *Shooting.* White racist, Ku Klux Klan. Detroit, Michigan. A black man is wounded in a drive-by shooting.

August 6, 1980. *Shooting.* Islamic. Los Angeles, California. An Iranian anti-Khomeini activist is assassinated.

August 20, 1980. *Bombing/explosive.* Islamic. Berkeley, California. A pro-Khomeini Iranian student meeting is bombed, injuring one student.

August 20, 1980. *Shooting.* White racist, Joseph Paul Franklin. Salt Lake City, Utah. Two black male joggers, David Martin and Ted Fields, are shot and killed while leaving a park with two white females. The weapon used in the sniper style shooting was a rifle. Joseph Paul Franklin's car, a brown Chevy Camaro, was observed leaving the scene.

September 11, 1980. *Shooting.* Cuban, Omega7. Queens, New York. Felix Garcia-Rodriguez, Cuban attaché to the UN, is shot to death. He was driving home when shots were fired from a nearby car, killing him instantly.

September 14, 1980. *Robbery.* Cuban, Omega7. Belleville, New Jersey. A bank is robbed by members of Omega7.

September 22, 1980. *Shooting.* White racist, Joseph Christopher. Buffalo, New York. Glen Dunn, a black teenager, is shot to death with a .22 caliber gun. This is the first in a series of attacks on black men by a white racist killer. The press calls him "the .22 caliber killer."

September 23, 1980. *Shooting.* White racist, Joseph Christopher. Buffalo, New York. Two black men, Harold Green and Emmanuel Thomas are shot to death with a .22 caliber gun. These two deaths are linked to a similar attack a day earlier.

September 24, 1980. *Shooting.* White racist, Joseph Christopher. Niagara, New York. Joseph McCoy, a black man, is shot to death with a .22 caliber weapon.

September 30, 1980. *Bombing/incendiary.* Jewish, Jewish Defense League. Phoenix, Arizona. A TV station showing a pro-PLO movie is firebombed.

October 1980. *Bombing/incendiary.* White racist. Manchester, Connecticut. A black home is firebombed.

October 6, 1980. *Bombing/incendiary.* Justice Commandos of the Armenian Genocide. Los Angeles, California. The Bel Air home of the Turkish consul general is firebombed.

October 8, 1980. *Attempted bombing.* Jewish, Jewish Defense League. New York City, New York. A pipe bomb is placed in a Slovakian bar.

October 8, 1980. *Assault.* White racist, Joseph Christopher. Buffalo, New York.

Parlor Edwards, a black taxi driver, is found with his heart cut out. The killing is believed to be linked to the .22 caliber killings.

October 9, 1980. *Assault.* White racist, Joseph Christopher. Buffalo, New York. A second black taxi driver, Ernest Jones, is found with his heart cut out. The killing is believed to be linked to the .22 caliber killings.

October 10, 1980. *Assault.* White racist, Joseph Christopher. Buffalo, New York. A white man, believed to be the .22 caliber killer, attempts to strangle a black hospital patient.

October 12, 1980. *Bombing.* Justice Commandos of the Armenian Genocide. New York. A car bomb explodes in front of the Turkish Mission to the UN and injures six people.

October 12, 1980. *Bombing/explosive.* Justice Commandos of the Armenian Genocide. Los Angeles, California. A bomb explodes in a Turkish-owned travel agency, injuring a passerby.

October 15, 1980. *Shooting.* Libyan. Fort Collins, Colorado. A Libyan student who was opposed to Qaddafi is shot and wounded.

October 31, 1980. *Shooting.* White racist. Youngstown, Ohio. White gunmen fire at black pedestrians, killing a woman.

November 1980. *Assault.* White racist, Ku Klux Klan. Pensacola, Florida. Three blacks are beaten with iron pipes by Klansmen.

December 10, 1980. *Shooting.* Quasi-terrorist. Washington, D.C. David Mayer is shot by police after threatening to bomb the Washington Monument.

December 14, 1980. *Arson.* Rightist, Nazis. Los Angeles, California. Arson at a Jewish temple causes $100,000 in damage.

December 22, 1980. *Assault.* White racist, Joseph Christopher. New York City, New York. Six men are stabbed in separate attacks; four are killed and two are wounded. The victims are all blacks or dark-skinned Hispanics.

December 22, 1980. *Bombing/explosive.* Puerto Rican nationalist, Armed Forces of National Liberation. New York City, New York. Penn railway station is bombed.

December 29, 1980. *Assault.* White racist, Joseph Christopher. Rochester, New York. A black man is stabbed and killed. The attack may be linked to the .22 caliber killer.

December 31, 1980. *Assault.* White racist, Joseph Christopher. Buffalo, New York. A black man is stabbed in the heart but survives.

1981. *Assault.* Black militant, Yahweh cult. Miami, Florida. At least eight randomly chosen whites were killed by members of the Yahweh cult. The cult led by Yahweh ben Yahweh believes that whites are devils. Members of the inner circle were required to bring back the ears of their victims as proof of the killings.

January 1981. *Arson.* White racist. Sonora, California. An arson attack on a Jewish restaurant causes $100,000 in damage.

January 1, 1981. *Assault.* White racist, Joseph Christopher. Buffalo, New York.

Two black men are attacked by a white man with a knife.

January 7, 1981. *Bombing/explosive.* Rightist. Puerto Rico. The Puerto Rico Bar Association building is bombed by a Navy officer and two Cubans.

January 8, 1981. *Bombing/explosive.* Puerto Rican nationalist. Puerto Rico. Three post offices are bombed.

January 12, 1981. *Bombing/explosive.* Puerto Rican nationalist, Macheteros. Carolina, Puerto Rico. The Macheteros claim credit for the destruction of nine National Guard planes at the Muniz airport, causing an estimated damage of $50 million.

January 18, 1981. *Assault.* White racist, Joseph Christopher. Fort Benning, Georgia. Joseph Christopher is in the stockade after a knife attack on a black soldier. He is subsequently indicted for the .22 caliber murders.

January 23, 1981. *Bombing/explosive.* Croatian. New York City, New York. A courthouse is bombed by Croatian Freedom Fighters. The pipe bomb causes minor damage.

January 26, 1981. *Bombing/explosive.* Jewish, Jewish Defense League. San Francisco, California. An Iranian bank is bombed to protest the "brutal persecution of Iranian Jewry."

February 1981. *Shooting.* White racist. Tuscaloosa, Alabama. Shots are fired into a black home.

February 1981. *Assault.* White racist, Ku Klux Klan. Tennessee. An informer is tarred and feathered.

February 4, 1981. *Attempted bombing.* Secret Army for the Liberation of Armenia. Los Angeles, California. A bomb placed in the Swiss Consulate is disarmed.

March 18, 1981. *Bombing/explosive.* Unknown. New York City, New York. An incendiary device placed outside the Youth International Party office explodes, injuring the two bomb squad detectives who are examining it.

March 21, 1981. *Assault.* White racist, Ku Klux Klan. Mobile, Alabama. Michael Donald, a black man, is killed and then hung from a tree "to show Klan strength in Alabama." In 1987, a jury awards his mother $7 million in damages against the Klan.

March 23, 1981. *Attempted robbery.* Revolutionary leftist, May 19th Communist Organization. Danbury, Connecticut. M19 attempts to rob a Purolator truck outside a Ramada Inn.

March 30, 1981. *Shooting.* Quasi-terrorist. Washington, D.C. President Reagan is wounded by John Hinkley, who shot him in an attempt to impress actress Jodie Foster. Also injured are a policeman, a secret service agent, and Press Secretary James Brady. Brady was severely paralyzed.

April 9, 1981. *Arson.* Anti-abortion. Saginaw, Michigan. A fire is set in the hallway of the Women's Health Services. Damage is estimated at $30,000.

April 11, 1981. *Shooting.* Jewish. San Francisco, California. Shots are fired at the Soviet Consulate.

April 21, 1981. *Robbery.* Puerto Rican nationalist, Macheteros. Santurce, Puerto

Rico. The Macheteros claim credit for a Wells Fargo robbery in Santurce, Puerto Rico. The amount taken is $348,000.

April 21, 1981. *Shooting.* Black militant, Black Liberation Army. New York City, New York. Two police officers in their patrol car are shot and wounded when they stop a van driven by two black males.

April 24, 1981. *Shooting.* Cuban. Miami, Florida. A Cuban candidate for mayor is murdered outside his home.

April 25, 1981. *Bombing/incendiary.* Jewish, Jewish Defense League. Torrance, California. The Institute for Historical Review (a Holocaust denial organization) is firebombed; responsibility for the firebombing is claimed by the "Jewish Defenders."

April 27, 1981. *Bombing/incendiary.* Iranian. Washington, D.C. An Iranian rug store owned by a supporter of the Khomeini regime is firebombed, causing $1000 in damage.

May 1981. *Attempted robbery.* Revolutionary leftist, May 19th Communist Organization. Mount Vernon, New York. M19 attempts to rob a Brink's truck at the Chase Manhattan Bank branch.

May 1981. *Attempted robbery.* Revolutionary leftist, May 19th Communist Organization. Nanuet, New York. M19 attempts to rob a Brink's truck at the Chemical Bank branch.

May 16, 1981. *Bombing/explosive.* Puerto Rican nationalist, Armed Forces of National Liberation. New York City, New York. A booby-trap bomb left in a restroom at John F. Kennedy International Airport kills Alex McMillan. The

Puerto Rican Armed Resistance claims responsibility.

June 2, 1981. *Robbery.* Revolutionary leftist, May 19th Communist Organization. New York City, New York. A Brink's truck outside the Bronx Chase Manhattan Bank branch is robbed. During the robbery one guard, William Moroney, is killed and another guard is wounded. $292,000 is stolen.

June 3, 1981. *Bombing/explosive.* Justice Commandos of the Armenian Genocide. Anaheim, California. A bombing forces the cancellation of a performance by Turkish folk dancers.

June 25, 1981. *Robbery.* Revolutionary leftist, United Freedom Front. New Britain, Connecticut. New Britain Bank & Trust is robbed.

June 25, 1981. *Bombing/incendiary.* Jewish, Jewish Defense League. Torrance, California. The Institute for Historical Review is firebombed; responsibility for the firebombing is claimed by the Jewish Defenders.

June 27, 1981. *Bombing/explosive.* Taiwanese Independence Movement? College Park, Maryland. A bomb kills a Chinese academic, Cho Ren Wu, and injures four others.

July 1981. *Bombing/incendiary and cross-burning.* White racist, Ku Klux Klan. Suffolk County, New York. A black home is firebombed and a cross is burned.

July 1981. *Shooting.* White racist, Ku Klux Klan. Rodeo, California. Shots are fired at a black home.

July 17, 1981. *Shooting.* Libyan. Ogden, Utah. A Libyan student, Nabil Mansour, is killed and his body is left in the trunk of a car. Mansour was opposed to the Qaddafi regime and had defied orders to return to Libya.

August 7, 1981. *Occupation.* Iranian. Washington, D.C. One man is shot and wounded during an occupation of the Iranian Embassy by anti-Khomeini demonstrators.

August 20, 1981. *Arson.* Liberian. Washington, D.C. The "Black Brigade" claims responsibility for a fire at the Liberian Embassy, which causes $5000 in damage. The fire was a response to the execution of five Liberian politicians.

August 20, 1981. *Bombing/explosive.* Secret Army for the Liberation of Armenia. Hollywood, California. A bomb explodes outside the office of a Swiss firm.

September 3, 1981. *Bombing/explosive.* Jewish, Jewish Defense League. New York City, New York. A small bomb explodes under a Soviet diplomat's car parked near the Soviet Mission to the UN. The bombing is claimed by "Thunder of Zion."

September 6, 1981. *Bombing/explosive.* Jewish, Jewish Defense League. New York City, New York. The Four Continents Book Store is bombed by the Thunder of Zion as a protest against the treatment of Jews in the Soviet Union.

September 11, 1981. *Bombing/explosive.* Cuban, Omega7. Miami, Florida. The *Republica* magazine office is bombed, causing extensive damage.

September 11, 1981. *Bombing/explosive.* Cuban, Omega7. Miami, Florida. The office building housing the Mexican Consulate is bombed, causing $2 million in damage.

September 12, 1981. *Bombing/explosive.* Cuban, Omega7. New York City, New York. A bomb explodes outside the Mexican Mission to the UN.

September 22, 1981. *Bombing/explosive.* Revolutionary leftist, United Freedom Front. Schenectady, New York. The stadium where the South African rugby team was due to play is bombed.

September 25, 1981. *Bombing/explosive.* Revolutionary leftist, United Freedom Front. Evansville, Illinois. The stadium where a South African rugby team was due to play is bombed.

October 1981. *Attempted robbery.* Revolutionary leftist, May 19th Communist Organization. Nanuet, New York. M19 attempts to rob a Brink's truck at the Chemical Bank branch.

October 6, 1981. *Shooting.* Unknown. Langley Park, Maryland. A Sierra Leone political activist is murdered.

October 8, 1981. *Attempted bombing.* Unabomber. Salt Lake City, Utah. A bomb found in a classroom at the University of Utah is defused by a bomb squad.

October 20, 1981. *Robbery.* Revolutionary leftist, May 19th Communist Organization. Nyack, New York. During the robbery of a Brink's armored truck, a Brink's guard, Peter Paige, and two police officers, Waverly Brown and Edward O'Grady, are killed; $1.6 million is taken.

October 23, 1981. *Shoot-out.* Revolutionary leftist, May 19th Communist Organi-

zation. New York City, New York. In a shoot-out with police, Samuel Smith is killed and another member of the May 19th Communist Organization is captured.

October 25, 1981. *Bombing/incendiary.* Jewish, Jewish Defense League. New York City, New York. The Egyptian tourist office is firebombed.

October 28, 1981. *Attempted bombing.* Anti-abortion. Minneapolis, Minnesota. A man enters the Meadowbrook Women's Clinic with a bomb in his briefcase. The bomb did not explode and he was arrested.

November 11, 1981. *Bombing/explosive.* Puerto Rican nationalist, Macheteros. Santurce, Puerto Rico. The Macheteros claim responsibility for bomb attacks at Puerto Rican Electrical Power Authority substations in Santurce, Puerto Rico.

November 12, 1981. *Assault.* Black militant, Yahweh cult. Miami, Florida. An ex-Yahweh member, Aston Green, is beheaded.

November 15, 1981. *Shooting.* Jewish, Jewish Defense League. Glen Cove, New York. Shots are fired at the Soviet ambassador's home.

November 15, 1981. *Assault.* Black militant, Yahweh cult. Miami, Florida. An ex-Yahweh member, Carlton Carey, is murdered in his apartment.

November 21, 1981. *Bombing/explosive.* Justice Commandos of the Armenian Genocide. Beverly Hills, California. The Turkish Consulate is bombed.

November 23, 1981. *Robbery.* Revolutionary leftist, May 19th Communist Organization. Arlington, Virginia. An armored car at the Navy Federal Credit Union is robbed; $1900 is stolen.

November 27, 1981. *Bombing/explosive.* Puerto Rican nationalist, Macheteros. Santurce, Puerto Rico. The Macheteros claim responsibility for bomb attacks at Puerto Rican Electrical Power Authority substations in Santurce, Puerto Rico.

November 27, 1981. *Shooting.* Puerto Rican nationalist, Macheteros. Puerto Rico. Shots are fired at a military base.

November 27, 1981. *Bombing/explosive.* Puerto Rican nationalist, Macheteros. Condado, Puerto Rico. An electric substation is blown up.

December 1981. *Assault.* White racist, Ku Klux Klan. Talladega, Alabama. Three blacks are stabbed by a Klansman.

December 21, 1981. *Shooting.* Revolutionary leftist, United Freedom Front. New Jersey. A New Jersey State Trooper, Philip Lamonaco, is shot and killed after he stops a car driven by Thomas Manning, a member of the United Freedom Front (UFF).

December 21, 1981. *Robbery.* Revolutionary leftist, May 19th Communist Organization. Metter, Georgia. A bank is robbed; $5529 is stolen.

December 24, 1981. *Attempted bombing.* Jewish, Jewish Defense League. New York City, New York. A pipe bomb is placed under a Soviet diplomat's car.

January 16, 1982. *Shooting.* White racist, Ku Klux Klan. Jackson, Mississippi. Shots are fired into a black newspaper office.

January 23, 1982. *Arson.* Anti-abortion. Granite City, Illinois. There is extensive fire damage to the Hope Clinic for Women.

January 23, 1982. *Arson.* Anti-abortion. Boulder, Colorado. The Boulder Valley Clinic is set on fire.

January 28, 1982. *Shooting.* Justice Commandos of the Armenian Genocide. Los Angeles, California. Kemal Arikan, the Turkish consul, is assassinated while his car is stopped at a traffic light. Two men approach his car and begin shooting.

February 1, 1982. *Shooting.* White racist. Cleveland, Ohio. A black minister, Rev. Horace Rickerson, is shot and killed by Frank Spisak, a self-described disciple of Hitler.

February 2, 1982. *Bombing/explosive.* Cuban, Omega7. Miami, Florida. The *Republica* magazine office is bombed for the second time.

February 19, 1982. *Bombing/explosive.* Jewish, Jewish Defense League. Washington, D.C. A Soviet airline office is bombed.

February 19, 1982. *Bombing/explosive.* Cuban, Omega7. Miami, Florida. Trans Cuba, a firm that ships packages to Cuba, is bombed.

February 21, 1982. *Bombing/explosive.* Puerto Rican nationalist. Rio Piedras, Puerto Rico. A bomb explodes at the University of Puerto Rico.

March 1982. *Assault.* White racist, Ku Klux Klan. Baltimore County, Maryland. Two blacks are stabbed by Klansmen.

March 1, 1982. *Bombing/explosive.* Puerto Rican nationalist, Armed Forces of National Liberation. New York City, New York. Bombs explode at the New York Stock Exchange, the American Stock Exchange, Chase Manhattan Bank, and Merrill Lynch.

March 22, 1982. *Bombing/explosive.* Justice Commandos of the Armenian Genocide. Cambridge, Massachusetts. The Turkish consul's store is bombed.

March 25, 1982. *Arson.* Jewish. Tempe, Arizona. An arson attack occurs at an apartment housing Palestinian students. "Death to the PLO" and a Star of David are painted on the car belonging to the students.

March 29, 1982. *Arson.* Anti-abortion. Clearwater, Florida. The Bread and Roses Clinic is set on fire. The Army of God claims responsibility.

April 2, 1982. *Robbery.* Revolutionary leftist, United Freedom Front. Burlington, Vermont. Chittenden Trust Company is robbed.

April 5, 1982. *Bombing/incendiary.* Jewish, Jewish Defense League. Brooklyn, New York. An Arab restaurant is firebombed, killing an elderly woman, Mae Holmes, and injuring eight others. The JDL claims responsibility.

April 28, 1982. *Bombing/explosive.* Jewish, Jewish Defense League. New York City, New York. A pipe bomb damages the Lufthansa airline office.

April 28, 1982. *Bombing/explosive.* Jewish, Jewish Defense League. New York City, New York. The Iraqi Mission to the UN is bombed.

April 29, 1982. *Bombing/explosive.* Puerto Rican nationalist. Bayamon, Puerto Rico. The Department of Natural Resources is bombed.

April 29, 1982. *Bombing/explosive.* Puerto Rican nationalist. San Juan, Puerto Rico. The Communications Authority office is bombed.

May 1982. *Assault.* White racist, Ku Klux Klan. Cobb County, Georgia. Armed Klansmen assault blacks and American Indians.

May 1982. *Assault.* White racist, Ku Klux Klan. Seattle, Washington. A black man is assaulted.

May 4, 1982. *Shooting.* Justice Commandos of the Armenian Genocide. Somerville, Massachusetts. Orhan Gunduz, the Turkish consul, is assassinated in his car by a man dressed in a jogging suit.

May 5, 1982. *Bombing/explosive.* Unabomber. Nashville, Tennessee. A wooden box containing a pipe bomb explodes when it is opened by a secretary.

May 16, 1982. *Shooting.* Puerto Rican nationalist, Macheteros. San Juan, Puerto Rico. The Macheteros attack sailors returning to their ship, the *Pensacola*, in Old San Juan Harbor in retaliation for United States Navy operations on Vieques (the *Ocean Venture*, 1982). One sailor, Daryl Phillips, is killed, and three are wounded.

May 17, 1982. *Bombing/explosive.* Cuban, Omega7. Union City, New Jersey. A Cuban business is bombed.

May 18, 1982. *Bombing/explosive.* Secret Army for the Liberation of Armenia. Los

Angeles, California. A bomb damages the office of a Swiss banking corporation.

May 19, 1982. *Shooting.* Puerto Rican nationalist, Macheteros. Carolina, Puerto Rico. The Macheteros fire on police, killing 1 officer and injuring 12 others in retaliation for forcibly evicting 350 squatter families from Villa Sin Miedo (Village Without Fear) in Carolina, Puerto Rico.

May 20, 1982. *Attempted bombing.* Puerto Rican nationalist, Macheteros. Carolina, Puerto Rico. Caribe Hilton Hotel receives a warning that four bombs have been placed in the hotel. Four plastic containers are found, but the bombs fail to explode.

May 29, 1982. *Bombing/incendiary.* Anti-abortion. St. Petersburg, Florida. The St. Petersburg Women's Health Center is destroyed by a firebomb. The Army of God claims responsibility.

May 30, 1982. *Attempted bombing.* Secret Army for the Liberation of Armenia. Van Nuys, California. A bomb is placed in the freight terminal of Air Canada. Canada had recently sentenced Armenian Secret Army for the Liberation of Armenia (ASALA) members to prison.

May 30, 1982. *Bombing/explosive.* Puerto Rican nationalist. San Juan, Puerto Rico. The bombing of a power station cuts off power to several neighborhoods.

June 1982. *Shooting.* White racist. North Carolina. Gunmen fire on an interracial couple, killing Curtis Anderson and wounding his white girlfriend.

June 1982. *Shooting.* White racist. Cleveland, Ohio. A black man is shot five times by Frank Spisak, but he survives and is able to identify Spisak, a member of the

National Socialist White Peoples Party, who was found guilty of three murders in 1982.

June 6, 1982. *Bombing/explosive.* Anti-abortion. Falls Church, Virginia. Two pipe bombs explode at the Arlington-Fairfax Medical Clinic, causing extensive damage but no injuries. The Army of God claims responsibility.

June 10, 1982. *Bombing/explosive.* Puerto Rican nationalist. Carolina, Puerto Rico. Power substations are bombed.

June 21, 1982. *Bombing/explosive.* Secret Army for the Liberation of Armenia. Los Angeles, California. A bomb explodes in front of the office of a Swiss banking corporation.

June 25, 1982. *Robbery.* Revolutionary leftist, United Freedom Front. Onondaga, New York. Syracuse Savings Bank is robbed.

July 2, 1982. *Bombing/explosive.* Unabomber. Berkeley, California. A small metal pipe bomb in Cory Hall explodes when a computer science professor picks it up.

July 4, 1982. *Bombing/explosive.* Croatian. New York City, New York. A travel agency is bombed.

July 4, 1982. *Attempted bombing.* Croatian. New York City, New York. A Yugoslav airline office is the target of an attempted bombing.

July 5, 1982. *Bombing/explosive.* Jewish, Jewish Defense League. New York City, New York. The Lebanese Consulate is bombed.

July 5, 1982. *Bombing/explosive.* Jewish, Jewish Defense League. New York City, New York. The French Consulate is bombed.

July 8, 1982. *Bombing.* Islamic, Al-Fuqra. Phoenix, Arizona. A pipe bomb damages an Islamic official's car.

August 13, 1982. *Kidnapping.* Anti-abortion. Edwardsville, Illinois. The owner of an abortion clinic, Hector Zevallos, and his wife, Rosalie, are kidnapped by the Army of God. They are released a week later.

August 27, 1982. *Shooting.* White racist. Cleveland, Ohio. Timothy Sheehan is shot to death. His killer, Frank Spisak, thought he was Jewish. This was the second murder attributed to Spisak, a member of the National Socialist White Peoples Party.

August 30, 1982. *Shooting.* White racist. Cleveland, Ohio. Brian Warford is shot and killed by Frank Spisak. Spisak, a Nazi sympathizer, had set out to kill a black person.

September 1982. *Assault.* White racist, Ku Klux Klan. Edinburgh, Indiana. A black man is assaulted and branded with the letters "kkk" on his chest.

September 1, 1982. *Bombing/incendiary?* Islamic, Al-Fuqra. Tempe, Arizona. The Islamic Cultural Center is attacked.

September 1, 1982. *Attempted robbery.* Puerto Rican nationalist, Macheteros. Puerto Rico. A Wells Fargo armored truck en route from San Juan to Naranjito is the target of an attempted robbery, which is attributed to the Macheteros by the FBI.

September 2, 1982. *Bombing/explosive.* Cuban, Omega7. Miami, Florida. The Venezuelan Consulate is bombed to protest the Venezuelan government's imprisonment of accused terrorist Orlando Bosch.

September 5, 1982. *Shooting.* Jewish, Jewish Defense League. Torrance, California. Shots are fired at the Institute for Historical Review; responsibility for the attack is claimed by the Jewish Defenders.

September 8, 1982. *Bombing/explosive.* Cuban, Omega7. Chicago, Illinois. A bookstore is bombed because it was "selling Communist literature."

September 20, 1982. *Bombing/explosive.* Puerto Rican nationalist, Armed Forces of National Liberation. New York City, New York. The Bankers Trust Building is bombed.

September 30, 1982. *Shooting.* Rightist, Nazis. Oroville, California. Nazi Perry Warthan kills his teenage follower, Joseph Hoover, believing him to be a police informer.

October 8, 1982. *Bombing/explosive.* Unknown. New York City, New York. An explosion occurs in the JDL office after a warning call to the police by a man who said, "Long live the Palestinians."

October 26, 1982. *Arson.* Anti-abortion. Cherry Hill, New Jersey. The Cherry Hill Women's Clinic is completely destroyed when gasoline is thrown through the window and ignited.

November 16, 1982. *Robbery.* Puerto Rican nationalist, Macheteros. Carolina, Puerto Rico. One man is killed during a robbery. $300,000 is taken.

December 1982. *Shooting.* White racist, Ku Klux Klan. Dekalb, Georgia. Shots are fired into a black restaurant, wounding one man.

December 8, 1982. *Attempted bombing.* Quasi-terrorist. Washington, D.C. After threatening to blow up the Washington Monument, anti-nuclear weapons demonstrator Norman Mayer is shot and killed by police after a 10-hour siege.

December 14, 1982. *Bombing/incendiary.* Anti-abortion. Portland, Oregon. A Molotov cocktail is thrown through the clinic window of Lovejoy Surgi-Center, causing only minor damage estimated at $500.

December 16, 1982. *Bombing/explosive.* Revolutionary leftist, United Freedom Front. Elmont, New York. The South African Airways office is bombed.

December 16, 1982. *Bombing/explosive.* Revolutionary leftist, United Freedom Front. Harrison, New York. The IBM office is bombed.

December 20, 1982. *Shooting.* Cuban. Key Biscayne, Florida. Ricardo Morales, an anti-Castro Cuban exile, is shot dead in a bar.

December 24, 1982. *Attempted bombing.* Jewish, Jewish Defense League. New York City, New York. A pipe bomb found under a diplomat's car parked near the Soviet Mission to the UN is deactivated by the police. A phone caller said the bomb was a protest to the detention of Anatole Sharansky.

December 31, 1982. *Bombing/explosive.* Puerto Rican nationalist, Armed Forces of National Liberation. New York City, New York. Three police officers are

seriously injured when police headquarters and three other government buildings are bombed on New Year's Eve.

January 11, 1983. *Bombing/explosive.* Cuban, Omega7. Miami, Florida. A cigar company is bombed.

January 28, 1983. *Bombing/explosive.* Revolutionary leftist, Red Guerrilla Force. New York City, New York. The FBI office is bombed.

January 29, 1983. *Shooting.* Unknown. Miami, Florida. The son of Nicaraguan General Perez-Vega is murdered.

February 1983. *Assault.* White racist, Ku Klux Klan. Tallapoosa, Georgia. Klansmen invade the home of an interracial couple and beat the black husband.

February 13, 1983. *Shoot-out.* Rightist, Posse Comitatus. Medina, North Dakota. Two U.S. Marshalls, Kenneth Muir and Robert Cheshire, are killed and three others are wounded when they try to arrest Gordon Kahl, a leader of Posse Comitatus.

February 17, 1983. *Bombing/explosive.* Jewish, Jewish Defense League. Washington, D.C. A Soviet airline office is bombed.

February 23, 1983. *Robbery.* Revolutionary leftist, United Freedom Front. Utica, New York. Marine Midland Bank is robbed.

April 26, 1983. *Bombing/explosive.* Revolutionary leftist, Red Guerrilla Force. Washington, D.C. Fort McNair is bombed.

April 27, 1983. *Attempted bombing.* Haitian. Miami, Florida. Letter bombs are mailed to several Haitian officials and businessmen but are successfully deactivated.

May 12, 1983. *Bombing/explosive.* Revolutionary leftist, United Freedom Front. Uniondale, New York. The Army National Guard is bombed.

May 12, 1983. *Bombing/explosive.* Revolutionary leftist, United Freedom Front. New York City, New York. The Navy National Guard is bombed.

May 26, 1983. *Bombing/incendiary.* Anti-abortion. Norfolk, Virginia. The Hillcrest Clinic is hit by a firebomb thrown by Joseph Grace, which partially destroys two procedure rooms and the waiting area.

May 27, 1983. *Bombing/explosive.* Cuban, Omega7. Miami, Florida. A branch of Continental National Bank is bombed.

June 3, 1983. *Shoot-out.* Rightist, Posse Comitatus. Walnut Ridge, Arkansas. Gordon Kahl and Sheriff Gene Matthews are killed in a shoot-out, when Kahl's farmhouse is surrounded by law enforcement. Kahl was a fugitive who was wanted for killing two U.S. Marshalls on February 13, 1983.

July 1983. *Bombing/incendiary.* Islamic, Al-Fuqra. Portland, Oregon. A hotel owned by Baghwan Shree Rajneesh, an Indian guru, is firebombed by a member of Al-Fuqra. Three pipe bombs were placed in a room on the 4th floor of the hotel by Stephen Paster, who is said to be one of the organizers of Al-Fuqra in the United States.

July 1983. *Bombing/explosive.* White racist. Muscogee, Georgia. Three black churches are bombed.

July 6, 1983. *Robbery.* Revolutionary leftist, United Freedom Front. Rotterdam, New York. Marine Midland Bank is robbed.

July 15, 1983. *Robbery.* Puerto Rican nationalist, Macheteros. Rio Piedras, Puerto Rico. The robbery of a Wells Fargo truck netted $600,000. The driver, Pablo Rivera, is killed during the robbery.

July 23, 1983. *Bombing/incendiary.* Anti-abortion. Boston, Massachusetts. A firebomb attack on the New England Women's Services at 3 a.m. destroys an apartment maintained by the clinic.

July 28, 1983. *Arson.* White racist, Ku Klux Klan. Montgomery, Alabama. Fire damages the Southern Poverty Law Center.

August 8, 1983. *Shooting.* Islamic, Al-Fuqra. Canton, Michigan. The leader of the Muslim Ahmadiyya sect, Dr. Mozaffar Ahmad, is shot to death. The Ahmadiyya Center of Detroit is set on fire shortly afterward. William Cain, an Al-Fuqra follower from Akron, Ohio, was identified as Ahmad's murderer. Both he and an accomplice, Calvin Jones, were killed in the fire.

August 8, 1983. *Bombing/incendiary.* Islamic, Al-Fuqra. Detroit, Michigan. An Islamic leader's house is firebombed.

August 9, 1983. *Arson.* Rightist, Covenant, Sword, and Arm of the Lord. Springfield, Missouri. A gay church is set on fire.

August 16, 1983. *Arson.* Rightist, Covenant, Sword, and Arm of the Lord. Bloomington, Indiana. A Jewish community center is set on fire.

August 18, 1983. *Bombing/explosive.* Puerto Rican nationalist, Armed Forces of National Liberation. Washington, D.C. The U.S. Navy yard is bombed.

August 21, 1983. *Bombing/explosive.* Revolutionary leftist, United Freedom Front. New York City, New York. The Army National Guard is bombed.

August 27, 1983. *Bombing/incendiary.* Unknown. Washington, D.C. The Phillipine Embassy is firebombed.

September 12, 1983. *Robbery.* Puerto Rican nationalist, Macheteros. West Hartford, Connecticut. In the robbery of a Wells Fargo depot in West Hartford, Connecticut, $7.1 million is stolen. The robbery is carried out by Victor Gerena, a guard at the facility. This is the first operation by the Macheteros outside of Puerto Rico.

October 1983. *Robbery.* Rightist, Order/Silent Brotherhood. Seattle, Washington. A bank is robbed; $3000 is stolen.

October 12, 1983. *Bombing/incendiary.* Cuban, Omega7. Miami, Florida. A Cuban store is firebombed.

October 18, 1983. *Robbery.* Revolutionary leftist, United Freedom Front. Dewitt, New York. Onondaga Savings Bank is robbed.

October 28, 1983. *Robbery.* White racist/rightist, Order/Silent Brotherhood. Spokane, Washington. A video store robbery by members of the Order nets only $369.

October 30, 1983. *Rocket fired.* Puerto Rican nationalist, Macheteros. Hato Rey, Puerto Rico. A rocket is fired at the United States Courthouse in Hato Rey, Puerto Rico, by the Macheteros.

November 1983. *Shooting.* White racist, Ku Klux Klan. Pittsboro, North Carolina. Klan leader David Wallace is shot and killed by one of his followers.

November 2, 1983. *Bombing/explosive.* Rightist, Covenant, Sword, and Arm of the Lord. Fulton, Arkansas. A natural gas pipeline is bombed.

November 7, 1983. *Bombing/explosive.* Revolutionary leftist, Red Guerrilla Force. Washington, D.C. The U.S. Capitol Building is bombed.

November 11, 1983. *Robbery.* Rightist, Covenant, Sword, and Arm of the Lord. Arkansas. William Stump, the Jewish owner of a pawn shop, is killed during a robbery by a member of the CSA.

December 1983. *Robbery.* Rightist, Order/Silent Brotherhood. Seattle, Washington. A bank is robbed; $26,000 is stolen.

December 3, 1983. *Bombing/incendiary.* Anti-abortion. Everett, Washington. The firebombing of the Everett Feminist Women's Health Center causes an estimated damage of $40,000.

December 13, 1983. *Bombing/explosive.* Revolutionary leftist, United Freedom Front. East Meadow, New York. The Navy recruiting center is bombed.

December 14, 1983. *Bombing/explosive.* Revolutionary leftist, United Freedom Front. New York City, New York. Honeywell Corporation is bombed.

1984. *Bombing/explosive.* Puerto Rican nationalist, Volunteers for Puerto Rican Revolution. Puerto Rico. Five Army recruiting stations are bombed at different sites throughout Puerto Rico.

January 1984. *Bombing/explosive.* White racist, Ku Klux Klan. Dallas, Texas. An explosion kills Ward Keeton, a police informer.

January 14, 1984. *Arson.* Anti-abortion. Dover, Delaware. A fire destroys the Reproductive Care Center at 7:30 a.m.

January 29, 1984. *Bombing/explosive.* Revolutionary leftist, United Freedom Front. New York City, New York. Motorola Corporation offices are bombed.

January 30, 1984. *Robbery.* Rightist, Order/Silent Brotherhood. Spokane, Washington. A restaurant is robbed of $3600 by members of the Order.

February 17, 1984. *Bombing/explosive.* Anti-abortion. Norfolk, Virginia. A pipe bomb explodes in the Hillcrest Clinic. The attack was claimed by the Army of God.

February 23, 1984. *Bombing/incendiary.* Jewish, Jewish Defense League. New York City, New York. Soviet diplomats' homes are firebombed by Jewish Direct Action.

February 28, 1984. *Bombing/incendiary.* Anti-abortion. College Park, Maryland. At 1:30 a.m. the Prince George's County Reproductive Health Services is firebombed, causing an estimated damage of $70,000. The Army of God claimed responsibility in a phone call to the *Washington Post*.

March 1984. *Bombing/explosive.* White racist. Chicago, Illinois. A black home is bombed; a swastika is painted nearby.

March 4, 1984. *Bombing/explosive.* Anti-abortion. Bellingham, Washington. At 4:30 p.m., the Anonymous Facility Clinic is destroyed by a homemade explosive device, causing an estimated damage of $60,000.

March 16, 1984. *Bombing/explosive.* Anti-abortion. St. Petersburg, Florida. At 4:30 p.m., the Ladies Choice Clinic is destroyed by a homemade explosive, causing an estimated damage of $60,000.

March 16, 1984. *Robbery.* White racist/rightist, Order/Silent Brotherhood. Seattle, Washington. An armored truck is robbed of $43,000.

March 19, 1984. *Bombing/explosive.* Revolutionary leftist, United Freedom Front. Harrison, New York. The IBM office is bombed.

March 26, 1984. *Arson.* Anti-abortion. Everett, Washington. The Everett Feminist Women's Health Center is set on fire at 2:58 a.m., causing an estimated damage of $10,000 to the counseling room.

April 1984. *Bombing/explosive.* White racist. Henderson, North Carolina. A black home is bombed.

April 1984. *Assault.* White racist, Ku Klux Klan. Baltimore County, Maryland. Two blacks are stabbed in a bar by Klansmen.

April 1984. *Bombing/explosive.* White racist. Muscogee, Georgia. A black church is bombed.

April 5, 1984. *Bombing/explosive.* Revolutionary leftist, Red Guerrilla Force. New York City, New York. An Israeli airline building is bombed. The Red Guerrilla Resistance is believed to be a name used by the United Freedom Front.

April 19, 1984. *Arson.* Anti-abortion. Everett, Washington. The Everett Feminist Women's Health Center closes after being attacked for the second time in a month. A gasoline-ignited fire set at 9:40 p.m. causes an estimated damage of $50,000–$75,000.

April 20, 1984. *Bombing/explosive.* Revolutionary leftist, Red Guerrilla Force. Washington, D.C. Fort McNair Officers Club is bombed.

April 22, 1984. *Bombing/explosive and robbery.* Rightist, Order/Silent Brotherhood. Seattle, Washington. A pornographic theater is bombed as a diversion for a robbery.

April 23, 1984. *Robbery.* Rightist, Order/Silent Brotherhood. Seattle, Washington. An armored truck is robbed by the Order; $534,000 is stolen.

April 26, 1984. *Robbery.* Revolutionary leftist, United Freedom Front. Norfolk, Virginia. First VA Bank of Tidewater is robbed.

April 29, 1984. *Bombing/explosive.* White racist/rightist, Order/Silent Brotherhood. Boise, Idaho. A synagogue is bombed.

May 12, 1984. *Attempted arson.* Anti-abortion. Forest Grove, Oregon. An attempted arson at the Bours Birth and Surgery Center results in an estimated damage of $1000. Two devices are attached to the outside of the building but burn themselves out.

May 27, 1984. *Shooting.* Rightist, Order/Silent Brotherhood. Idaho. Walter West, a member of the Order and a suspected informer, is killed.

May 31, 1984. *Sabotage, vandalism, and property destruction.* Animal rights, Animal Liberation Front. Philadelphia, Pennsylvania. The University of Pennsylvania Head Injury Laboratory is raided. Records are stolen and equipment is destroyed; the damage is estimated at $60,000.

June 1984. *Bombing/explosive.* Unknown. Midwest. Eighteen pipe bombs go off or are found in early June throughout the Midwest. The bombs were attached to notes from the "Gay Strike Force Against Public and Police Repression."

June 5, 1984. *Robbery.* Revolutionary leftist, United Freedom Front. Norfolk, Virginia. Sovran Bank is robbed.

June 16, 1984. *Bombing/incendiary.* Islamic, Al-Fuqra. Philadelphia, Pennsylvania. The Hare Krishna temple in Philadelphia is firebombed.

June 17, 1984. *Bombing/explosive.* Islamic, Al-Fuqra. Seattle, Washington. The Vedanta Society (a Hindu organization) is bombed. An Al-Fuqra member is later arrested in connection with the bombing.

June 18, 1984. *Shooting.* Rightist, Order/Silent Brotherhood. Denver, Colorado. Alan Berg, a Jewish talk show host, is gunned down outside his home. On his radio show, Berg had denounced right-wing extremism.

June 25, 1984. *Bombing/explosive.* Anti-abortion. Pensacola, Florida. The Ladies Center is dynamited at 3:50 a.m., destroying the entire building. Twelve sticks of dynamite were used.

June 30, 1984. *Shooting.* White racist. Arkansas. A black state trooper, Louis Bryant, is shot and killed after he stops Richard Snell for a minor traffic violation. Snell is a member of the CSA. He was convicted and later executed on April 19, 1995, the day that Timothy McVeigh blew up the Alfred P. Murrah Federal Building in Oklahoma City.

July 1984. *Arson.* White racist. Lancaster, South Carolina. Three black churches are set on fire.

July 4, 1984. *Bombing/explosive.* Anti-abortion. Washington, D.C. At the National Abortion Federation offices, a propane bomb explodes at 11:50 p.m.

July 4, 1984. *Arson.* Jewish, Jewish Defense League. Torrance, California. Arson totally destroys the offices of the Institute for Historical Review, causing damage estimated at $400,000.

July 7, 1984. *Bombing/explosive.* Anti-abortion. Annapolis, Maryland. A bomb explodes at Planned Parenthood of Maryland at 1 a.m. The blast causes extensive damage. The device is similar to the one used at the National Abortion Federation three days before.

July 19, 1984. *Robbery.* Rightist, Order/Silent Brotherhood. Ukiah, California. The Order robs a Brink's armored truck, escaping with $3.6 million.

August 1, 1984. *Bombing/incendiary.* Islamic, Al-Fuqra. Denver, Colorado. A

Hare Krishna temple is bombed. In March 1993 two Al-Fuqra sect members are charged with conspiracy to commit murder.

August 1, 1984. *Kidnapping.* Islamic, Al-Fuqra. Overland, Kansas. Srinivasu Dasari, a Hindu physician, is kidnapped and presumed murdered.

August 1, 1984. *Assault.* Islamic, Al-Fuqra. Seattle, Washington. A member of the Seattle Vedanta Society is attacked.

August 1, 1984. *Shooting.* Islamic, Al-Fuqra. Tacoma, Washington. Three East Indians are shot to death.

August 20, 1984. *Bombing/explosive.* Anti-abortion. Houston, Texas. There is a bombing at the Cyprus-Fairbanks Family Planning clinic.

August 21, 1984. *Shooting.* Rightist, Order/Silent Brotherhood. Idaho. Ken Shray, a member of the Order, is killed because he is suspected of being an informer.

August 22, 1984. *Bombing/explosive.* Revolutionary leftist, United Freedom Front. Melville, New York. General Electric Company is bombed.

September 1984. *Arson.* White racist. Carroll County, Georgia. The home of an interracial couple is set on fire.

September 7, 1984. *Bombing/incendiary.* Anti-abortion. Houston, Texas. A Molotov cocktail is thrown through the window of the West Loop Clinic, causing an estimated damage of $50,000.

September 7, 1984. *Bombing/incendiary.* Anti-abortion. Houston, Texas. A bomb is thrown through the window of the Women's Outpatient Clinic, completely destroying the front room. There is extensive smoke damage as well.

September 8, 1984. *Arson.* Anti-abortion. Webster, Texas. Arsonists come in through the skylight of Clear Lake Women's Center and set fires. The estimated damage is $120,000.

September 9, 1984. *Bio-terrorism.* Rajneesh. Dalles, Oregon. The followers of Bhagwan Shree Rajneesh poison salad bars in 10 restaurants with salmonella, sickening 751 individuals. This is the first case of bio-terrorism in the U.S. The purpose of the action was to incapacitate so many voters that the Rajneeshi could take over the county in the forthcoming elections.

September 13, 1984. *Bombing/explosive.* Anti-abortion. San Diego, California. The Birth Control Institute is bombed at 4 a.m., causing an estimated damage of $80,000.

September 13, 1984. *Bombing/incendiary.* Anti-abortion. Atlanta, Georgia. A small bomb is thrown through the window of Northside Family Planning in the morning. The resulting fire damages the waiting area.

September 20, 1984. *Bombing/incendiary.* Anti-abortion. Marietta, Georgia. A firebomb is thrown through the window of Planned Parenthood Association, destroying the waiting room and causing extensive smoke damage. This clinic does not perform abortions.

September 26, 1984. *Bombing/explosive.* Revolutionary leftist, Red Guerrilla Force.

New York City, New York. The South African Consulate is bombed.

September 26, 1984. *Bombing/explosive.* Revolutionary leftist, United Freedom Front. Tarrytown, New York. Union Carbide Corporation is bombed.

October 1984. *Shooting.* White racist. Franklin, Tennessee. Four blacks are wounded in a drive-by shooting.

October 15, 1984. *Shooting.* Unknown. Dale City, California. Henry Liu, a Taiwanese journalist who was a critic of the Taiwan regime, is assassinated.

October 15, 1984. *Arson.* Anti-abortion. Eureka, California. There is an arson attempt at Planned Parenthood Association of Humboldt County when a box of debris is pushed against the back of the building and is set on fire. The fire does minimal damage.

October 18, 1984. *Shoot-out.* Rightist, Order/Silent Brotherhood. Sandpoint, Idaho. Gary Yarbrough, a member of the Order, escapes after a shoot-out with the FBI.

October 18, 1984. *Attempted bombing.* Puerto Rican nationalist, Volunteers for Puerto Rican Revolution. Cayey, Puerto Rico. The Army recruiting center is the target of an attempted bombing.

October 23, 1984. *Shoot-out.* Rightist, Posse Comitatus. Cairo, Nebraska. Arthur Kirk's farm is surrounded by police, and he is killed by a SWAT team. Kirk was a member of Posse Comitatus.

October 31, 1984. *Arson.* White racist. New York City, New York. A Hebrew Institute and a synagogue are set on fire.

November 1984. *Shooting.* White racist. Oregon. In what appears to be a racially motivated murder, a black man, Christopher Braithwaite, is killed by a white man who then shoots himself.

November 5, 1984. *Bombing/explosive.* Anti-abortion. Washington, D.C. A small explosion at the American Civil Liberties Union office at 9:55 p.m. destroys the door and damages the wall plaster.

November 11, 1984. *Arson.* Anti-abortion. Houston, Texas. A fire is set in the Colored Women's Center at Alameda Medical Square. The fire burns itself out before firefighters arrive, but there is extensive smoke damage. No one is hurt.

November 19, 1984. *Bombing/explosive.* Anti-abortion. Wheaton, Maryland. The Metro Medical & Women's Center is destroyed by an explosion at 6:15 a.m. Covenant Life Christian Community of Greater Washington picketed the clinic every Saturday.

November 19, 1984. *Bombing/explosive.* Anti-abortion. Rockville, Maryland. The Planned Parenthood clinic is bombed but reopens a short time later.

November 24, 1984. *Shoot-out.* White racist/rightist, Order/Silent Brotherhood. Portland, Oregon. Gary Yarbrough, a member of the Order, is wounded and captured after a shoot-out with the FBI.

December 1984. *Shooting.* White racist, Ku Klux Klan. Rutherford, North Carolina. A Klansman shoots into the house of a black drug dealer.

December 9, 1984. *Shoot-out.* White racist/rightist, Order/Silent Brotherhood. Whidbey Island, Washington. After a two-day gun battle, Robert Matthews, the leader of the Order, is killed. The FBI drops flares on the house from a helicopter, setting it on fire.

December 9, 1984. *Sabotage, vandalism, and property destruction.* Animal rights, Animal Liberation Front. Hope, California. Hope National Medical Center is raided, causing $400,000 in damage.

December 10, 1984. *Bombing/explosive.* Puerto Rican nationalist, Volunteers for Puerto Rican Revolution. Levittown, Puerto Rico. A bomb explodes at the university.

December 10, 1984. *Bombing/explosive.* Puerto Rican nationalist, Volunteers for Puerto Rican Revolution. Rio Piedras, Puerto Rico. The Army recruiting center is bombed.

December 10, 1984. *Bombing/explosive.* Puerto Rican nationalist, Volunteers for Puerto Rican Revolution. Ponce, Puerto Rico. The Army recruiting center is bombed.

December 10, 1984. *Attempted bombing.* Puerto Rican nationalist, Volunteers for Puerto Rican Revolution. Mayaguez, Puerto Rico. The National Guard building is the target of an attempted bombing.

December 23, 1984. *Bombing/explosive.* Anti-abortion. Suitland, Maryland. A bomb goes off beside the Metropolitan Family Planning center at 4:26 a.m. A hair salon and IRS offices are damaged, but the clinic, which is located on the 5th floor, sustains no damage.

December 25, 1984. *Bombing/explosive.* Anti-abortion. Pensacola, Florida. The office of Dr. Bagenholm, who performs abortions, is bombed at 3:30 a.m., causing approximately $100,000 in damage. There was picketing prior to the bombing.

December 25, 1984. *Bombing/explosive.* Anti-abortion. Pensacola, Florida. The West Florida Women's Clinic is bombed at 3:30 a.m.; the building is completely destroyed.

December 25, 1984. *Bombing/explosive.* Anti-abortion. Pensacola, Florida. The Ladies Center is bombed at 3:30 a.m., causing an estimated damage of $75,000–$100,000.

January 1985. *Bombing/incendiary.* White racist. Cobb County, Georgia. A black home in a white neighborhood is fire-bombed.

January 1985. *Shooting.* White racist. Tallapoosa, Georgia. Shots are fired into a black woman's car.

January 1, 1985. *Bombing/explosive.* Anti-abortion. Washington, D.C. A few minutes after midnight, the Hillcrest Women's Surgi-Center is bombed, causing an estimated damage of $60,000. Windows across the street are broken.

January 23, 1985. *Rocket fired.* Puerto Rican nationalist, Macheteros. San Juan, Puerto Rico. A rocket is fired at the United States Courthouse in Old San Juan, Puerto Rico. It is a joint action by the Macheteros and the Organization of Volunteers for the Revolution.

February 1985. *Shooting.* White racist. Iredell, North Carolina. Shots fired into a black home wound three people.

February 1985. *Bombing/explosive.* White racist. Weslaco, Texas. The Hispanic mayor's house is bombed.

February 1, 1985. *Arson.* Islamic, Al-Fuqra. Leetsdale, Colorado. A fire breaks out at a power station.

February 18, 1985. *Attempted bombing.* Jewish, Jewish Defense League. New York City, New York. A bomb is placed under a Soviet diplomat's car.

February 22, 1985. *Arson.* Anti-abortion. Mesquite, Texas. At 10:30 p.m. someone breaks a window in the waiting room of the Women's Clinic of Mesquite, pours in gasoline, and lights a match. The entire shopping center where the clinic is located burns down, and two firefighters are injured. The damage is estimated to be $1.5 million.

February 23, 1985. *Bombing/explosive.* Revolutionary leftist. New York City, New York. Responsibility for the bombing of the Police Benevolent Association is claimed by the Red Guerrilla Defense.

March 1985. *Shooting.* Rightist, Nazis. Chicago, Illinois. Kevin Zornes, a police informer, is murdered by members of a neo-Nazi gang.

March 16, 1985. *Bombing/incendiary.* Anti-abortion. San Diego, California. The Birth Control Institute is firebombed. A Molotov cocktail is thrown through the lobby window, causing an estimated damage of $8000–$10,000.

March 19, 1985. *Attempted arson.* Anti-abortion. Baton Rouge, Louisiana. Delta Women's Clinic-West is the target of attempted arson. When the staff arrived, they found the building soaked with gasoline.

April 1985. *Bombing/explosive.* White racist. Northbrook, Illinois. A synagogue is pipe bombed.

April 15, 1985. *Shoot-out.* Rightist, Order/Silent Brotherhood. Ridgedale, Missouri. James Linegar, a state trooper, is killed and another state trooper is wounded after they stop a van driven by a member of the Order.

April 17, 1985. *Attempted bombing.* Anti-abortion. Granite City, Illinois. William Landing drives past The Hope Clinic for Women and throws a Molotov cocktail, which misses the building. He is arrested and charged with possession of an incendiary device with the intent to commit arson.

April 21, 1985. *Raid.* Animal rights, Animal Liberation Front. Riverside, California. The Animal Liberation Front (ALF) takes more than 1000 animals from laboratories at the University of California and destroys computer equipment. The damage is estimated at $700,000.

April 22, 1985. *Attempted bombing.* Jewish, Jewish Defense League. Venice, California. A pipe bomb is found in the theater where a Soviet film festival is being held.

May 13, 1985. *Bombing.* Black militant, MOVE. Philadelphia, Pennsylvania. In the siege of a house occupied by a radical back-to-nature group, police fire tear gas and bullets and finally bomb the house. The plastic explosives dropped on the roof cause a fire, which kills 11 members of the group.

May 15, 1985. *Bombing/explosive.* Unabomber. Berkeley, California. A bomb explodes in a computer room at Cory Hall.

May 15, 1985. *Bombing/incendiary.* Jewish, Jewish Defense League. Northridge, California. The home of a Holocaust denier is firebombed, causing $2000 in damage. "JDL" is spray-painted on the sidewalk.

June 1985. *Bombing/incendiary.* White racist. Cleveland, Ohio. An elderly black woman is killed when her home is firebombed.

June 13, 1985. *Attempted bombing.* Unabomber. Auburn, Washington. A package bomb, mailed May 8, 1985, is discovered and safely disarmed.

June 22, 1985. *Bombing/explosive.* Islamic, Al-Fuqra. Houston, Texas. Bombs destroy a mosque.

July 3, 1985. *Attempted bombing.* Puerto Rican nationalist, Volunteers for Puerto Rican Revolution. Fajardo, Puerto Rico. The Army recruiting center is the target of an attempted bombing.

July 5, 1985. *Bombing/incendiary?* Islamic, Al-Fuqra. Rockford, Illinois. The Laotian Cultural Center is attacked.

August 1985. *Shooting.* White racist. Guilford, North Carolina. A black man is wounded in a drive-by shooting.

August 13, 1985. *Bombing/explosive.* Jewish, Jewish Defense League. Patterson, New Jersey. Tscherim Soobzokov, an accused war criminal, is killed by a pipe bomb outside his home. The explosion also injures a neighbor.

August 15, 1985. *Assault.* White racist. Rulo, Nebraska. The bodies of James Thimm and Luke Stice are found in a survivalist compound. Large quantities of weapons and Posse Comitatus and Aryan Nations literature are seized.

August 15, 1985. *Bombing/explosive.* Jewish, Jewish Defense League. Boston, Massachusetts. Two police are injured while defusing a bomb that had been placed in the offices of the American-Arab Anti-Discrimination Committee.

September 1985. *Shooting.* White racist. Iredell, North Carolina. Shots are fired into a black policeman's home.

September 1985. *Assault.* Rightist, Nazis. Chicago, Illinois. Henry Hampton, a black man, is beaten to death by neo-Nazi gang members.

September 6, 1985. *Bombing/explosive.* Jewish, Jewish Defense League. New York City, New York. An accused war criminal is slightly injured by a pipe bomb placed outside his house. A passerby has both legs blown off in the explosion.

October 11, 1985. *Bombing/explosive.* Jewish, Jewish Defense League. Santa Ana, California. When a bomb explodes in his office, Alex Odeh, the director of the American-Arab Anti-Discrimination Committee, is killed, and seven others are injured. The bomb is similar to other devices used by the JDL.

October 29, 1985. *Bombing/incendiary.* Jewish, Jewish Defense League. Washington, D.C. A fire destroys the American-Arab Anti-Discrimination Committee office.

November 1985. *Arson.* White racist. Wren, Mississippi. A black home in a white neighborhood is burned to the ground.

November 1985. *Bombing/incendiary.* White racist. Dover, Delaware. The NAACP office is firebombed.

November 6, 1985. *Shooting.* Puerto Rican nationalist, Volunteers for Puerto Rican Revolution. Bayamon, Puerto Rico. Shots are fired at the Army recruiting center.

November 15, 1985. *Bombing/explosive.* Unabomber. Ann Arbor, Michigan. A package bomb, mailed to the home of a University of Michigan professor, explodes when a research assistant opens it.

December 1, 1985. *Bombing/incendiary?* Islamic, Al-Fuqra. Rockford, Illinois. A Laotian temple is attacked.

December 11, 1985. *Bombing/explosive.* Unabomber. Sacramento, California. A bomb explodes outside a computer store, killing its owner, Hugh Scrutton.

January 6, 1986. *Attempted bombing.* Jewish, Jewish Defense League. Boston, Massachusetts. A bomb is found outside an ice hockey arena before a Soviet team was due to play.

January 6, 1986. *Bombing/explosive.* Puerto Rican nationalist. Cidra, Puerto Rico. A post office is bombed.

January 6, 1986. *Bombing.* Puerto Rican nationalist. Toa Baja, Puerto Rico. A post office is bombed.

January 6, 1986. *Bombing/explosive.* Puerto Rican nationalist. Santurce, Puerto Rico. A post office is bombed.

January 6, 1986. *Bombing/explosive.* Puerto Rican nationalist. Guanica, Puerto Rico. A post office is bombed.

February 19, 1986. *Shooting.* Unknown. Los Angeles, California. Oscar Salvatierra, the business manager of a Filipino-American newspaper critical of the Philippine government, is shot to death in his home.

March 3, 1986. *Bombing/explosive.* Rightist. Glendale, California. An explosion and fire cause over $1 million in damage to the IRS office.

March 6, 1986. *Attempted bombing.* Rightist, Order/Silent Brotherhood. Hayden Lake, Idaho. The home of a Jewish businessman is the target of an attempted bombing.

March 13, 1986. *Attempted arson.* Anti-abortion. Baton Rouge, Louisiana. The Acadian Women's Center is the target of attempted arson.

March 16, 1986. *Assault.* White racist. Dallas, Texas. Fred Finch, a black civil rights activist, and his wife are stabbed to death.

March 17, 1986. *Attempted bombing.* Puerto Rican nationalist. Ponce, Puerto Rico. An Esso station is the target of an attempted bombing.

April 14, 1986. *Bombing/explosive.* Puerto Rican nationalist, Volunteers for Puerto Rican Revolution. Rio Piedras, Puerto Rico. A bomb explodes on a university campus.

April 29, 1986. *Shooting.* Puerto Rican nationalist, Volunteers for Puerto Rican Revolution. San Juan, Puerto Rico. Ex-police chief Alejandro Malave is killed in a drive-by shooting.

May 13, 1986. *Attempted arson.* Anti-abortion. Rockford, Illinois. The Northern Illinois Women's Center is the target of attempted arson.

May 14, 1986. *Sabotage, vandalism, and property destruction.* Environmental, Earth Liberation Front. Phoenix, Arizona. Power lines are sabotaged.

May 19, 1986. *Bombing/incendiary.* Animal rights, Animal Liberation Front. Gilroy, California. A laboratory is firebombed, causing $165,000 in damage.

May 20, 1986. *Attempted arson.* Anti-abortion. Toledo, Ohio. The Center for Choice is the target of attempted arson.

May 20, 1986. *Bombing/incendiary.* Black militant, Yahweh cult. Miami, Florida. Six houses are firebombed, allegedly by Yahweh members who had clashed with residents a few days earlier. Four people are injured.

May 22, 1986. *Assault.* Black militant, Yahweh cult. Miami, Florida. Clair Walters, an ex-member of the Yahweh cult, has her throat slit.

May 28, 1986. *Assault.* Islamic, Al-Fuqra. Bethany, West Virginia. A leader of the Hare Krishna temple in Philadelphia is assaulted.

June 1986. *Bombing/incendiary.* White racist. Baltimore, Maryland. A black home in a white neighborhood is firebombed.

June 9, 1986. *Attempted bombing.* Anti-abortion. Wichita, Kansas. The Women's Health Care Services Clinic is the target of an attempted bombing.

June 14, 1986. *Arson.* Anti-abortion. Manchester, Missouri. The Reproductive Health Services Clinic is set on fire.

June 16, 1986. *Arson.* Jewish. Washington, D.C. Arson at the offices of a Palestinian organization causes $60,000 in damage.

July 1986. *Bombing/explosive.* White racist. Chicago, Illinois. The IRS office is bombed.

August 1986. *Robbery.* Rightist, Aryan Nations. Rossville, Illinois. A bank is robbed by Aryan Nations members; $44,000 is taken.

August 7, 1986. *Bombing/explosive.* Rightist, Order/Silent Brotherhood. Kootenai, Idaho. A Jewish business is pipe bombed.

September 3, 1986. *Bombing.* Jewish, Jewish Defense League. New York City, New York. A tear-gas bomb goes off in the Metropolitan Opera House during a performance by the Soviet ballet. Twenty-six people are treated for injuries sustained from the tear gas.

September 16, 1986. *Bombing/explosive.* Rightist, Order/Silent Brotherhood. Coeur D'alene, Idaho. A pipe bomb explodes at the house of a Catholic priest who had spoken out against right-wing extremism.

September 18, 1986. *Bombing/incendiary.* Puerto Rican nationalist. Toa Baja, Puerto Rico. The Army recruiting office is firebombed.

September 21, 1986. *Bombing/explosive.* White racist/rightist, Order/Silent Brotherhood. Coeur D'alene, Idaho. Four buildings are bombed as a diversion for a planned bank robbery.

September 27, 1986. *Robbery.* White racist/rightist, White Peoples Party. Fayetteville, North Carolina. A Pizza Hut is robbed by a member of the White Peoples Party.

October 20, 1986. *Bombing/incendiary.* Jewish, Jewish Defense League. New York City, New York. Lincoln Center is firebombed before a Soviet orchestra is to perform.

October 26, 1986. *Sabotage, vandalism, and property destruction.* Animal rights, Animal Liberation Front. Eugene, Oregon. The ALF frees animals from the University of Oregon's research facility and causes $50,000 in damage.

October 28, 1986. *Bombing/explosive.* Puerto Rican nationalist, Macheteros. Fajardo, Puerto Rico. The Macheteros, in conjunction with the Armed Forces of Popular Resistance and the Organization of Volunteers for the Puerto Rican Revolution, claim credit for two bombings of military installations in Puerto Rico. The bombings are to protest Nicaraguan Contras being trained in Puerto Rico and commercial logging in a rain forest preserve.

October 29, 1986. *Bombing/explosive.* Anti-abortion. New York City, New York. The Eastern Women's Center is bombed.

October 30, 1986. *Shooting.* Black militant, Yahweh cult. Miami, Florida. Anthony Brown and Rudolph Broussard are shot to death by members of the Yahweh cult. The two men were resisting eviction from their apartment complex, which had just been purchased by the cult.

October 31, 1986. *Arson.* Anti-abortion. Rockford, Illinois. The Northern Illinois Women's Center is set on fire.

November 11, 1986. *Attempted bombing.* Anti-abortion. Queens, New York. The Women's Medical Office is the target of an attempted bombing.

November 25, 1986. *Arson.* Anti-abortion. Rockford, Illinois. The Northern Illinois Women's Center is set on fire.

December 1, 1986. *Arson.* Anti-abortion. Kalamazoo, Michigan. The Reproductive Health Care Center of Planned Parenthood is set on fire.

December 4, 1986. *Attempted bombing.* Anti-abortion. Lathrup Village, Michigan. The Woman's Care Clinic of Southfield is the target of an attempted bombing.

December 10, 1986. *Arson.* Anti-abortion. Rockford, Illinois. The Northern Illinois Women's Center is set on fire.

December 14, 1986. *Attempted bombing.* Anti-abortion. New York City, New York. Planned Parenthood of New York City–Margaret Sanger Center is the target of an attempted bombing.

December 27, 1986. *Arson.* Anti-abortion. Riverside, California. Planned Parenthood of San Diego and Riverside Counties is set on fire.

December 28, 1986. *Bombing/explosive.* Puerto Rican nationalist, Macheteros. Yauco, Puerto Rico. A National Guard truck is bombed.

December 28, 1986. *Attempted bombing.* Puerto Rican nationalist, Macheteros. Guayama, Puerto Rico. A post office is the target of an attempted bombing.

January 6, 1987. *Arson.* Anti-abortion. Rockford, Illinois. The Northern Illinois Women's Center is set on fire.

January 17, 1987. *Shooting.* White racist/rightist, White Peoples Party. North Carolina. Three people in a gay bookstore are shot and killed by members of the White Peoples Party.

January 27, 1987. *Arson.* Anti-abortion. Minneapolis, Minnesota. The Midwest Health Center for Women is set on fire.

February 12, 1987. *Attempted bombing.* Anti-abortion. Indianapolis, Indiana. The Clinic for Women is the target of an attempted bombing.

February 18, 1987. *Shooting.* Unknown. Chicago, Illinois. Frank Masic, a Croatian radio broadcaster, is murdered.

February 20, 1987. *Bombing/explosive.* Unabomber. Salt Lake City, Utah. A bomb explodes outside a computer store when an employee tries to pick it up.

February 23, 1987. *Attempted bombing.* Anti-abortion. Cincinnati, Ohio. The Margaret Sanger Center is the target of an attempted bombing.

March 2, 1987. *Attempted bombing.* Rightist. Laguna, California. Pipe bombs are found at the IRS building, allegedly planted by the Arizona Patriots.

March 8, 1987. *Attempted arson.* Anti-abortion. Toledo, Ohio. The Toledo Medical Services is the target of attempted arson.

April 15, 1987. *Arson.* Animal rights, Animal Liberation Front. Davis, California. A research laboratory at the University of

California is set on fire, causing damage estimated at over $5 million.

April 19, 1987. *Bombing/explosive.* Rightist, Aryan Nations. Missoula, Montana. An unoccupied police vehicle is bombed. Responsibility for the attack is claimed by Aryan Nations.

May 1, 1987. *Bombing/explosive.* Cuban, Omega7. Miami, Florida. A business shipping medical supplies to Cuba is bombed.

May 2, 1987. *Bombing/explosive.* Cuban, Omega7. Hialeah, Florida. A business shipping medical supplies to Cuba is bombed.

May 25, 1987. *Bombing/explosive.* Cuban, Omega7. Miami, Florida. A business shipping medical supplies to Cuba is bombed.

May 27, 1987. *Bombing/explosive.* Puerto Rican nationalist, Guerrilla Forces of Liberation. Ponce, Puerto Rico. Government offices are pipe bombed.

May 27, 1987. *Bombing/explosive.* Puerto Rican nationalist, Guerrilla Forces of Liberation. Caguas, Puerto Rico. A pipe bomb explodes in a department store.

May 27, 1987. *Bombing/explosive.* Puerto Rican nationalist, Guerrilla Forces of Liberation. Mayaguez, Puerto Rico. A bank is bombed.

June 2, 1987. *Bombing/incendiary.* Animal rights, Animal Liberation Front. St. Louis, Missouri. A firebomb attack on Hallmark Furs causes $1 million in damage.

June 8, 1987. *Arson.* Anti-abortion. Toledo, Ohio. The Toledo Medical Services is set on fire.

June 30, 1987. *Attempted bombing.* Jewish, Jewish Defense League. New York City, New York. A bomb is found in a trash basket at Lincoln Center before a performance by the Bolshoi Ballet.

July 27, 1987. *Attempted bombing.* Anti-abortion. San Diego, California. The Family Planning Associates Medical Group is the target of an attempted bombing.

July 30, 1987. *Bombing/explosive.* Cuban. Miami, Florida. A pipe bomb explodes outside Machi Community Services, a business that trades with Cuba.

August 27, 1987. *Bombing/explosive.* Cuban. Hialeah, Florida. A pipe bomb explodes outside a business that sends medical supplies to Cuba.

September 1, 1987. *Arson.* Animal rights, Animal Liberation Front. Santa Clara, California. A fire at San Jose Valley Veal & Beef Company causes $10,000 in damage.

September 14, 1987. *Attempted arson.* Anti-abortion. St. Paul, Minnesota. Planned Parenthood of Minnesota is the target of attempted arson.

September 17, 1987. *Arson.* Anti-abortion. Robbinsdale, Minnesota. Robbinsdale Clinic is set on fire.

October 5, 1987. *Attempted arson.* Anti-abortion. St. Paul, Minnesota. Planned Parenthood of Minnesota is the target of attempted arson.

November 9, 1987. *Sabotage, vandalism, and property destruction.* Environmental/ animal rights, Evan Mecham Eco-Terrorist International Conspiracy. Flagstaff, Arizona. Sabotage occurs at a ski resort, causing over $20,000 in damage.

November 28, 1987. *Bombing/explosive.* Revolutionary leftist. Livermore, California. Responsibility for an explosion in the parking lot of a nuclear laboratory is claimed by the Nuclear Liberation Front.

November 28, 1987. *Arson.* Animal rights, Animal Liberation Front. Santa Clara, California. A fire at the Melani poultry distribution company causes $200,000 in damage.

December 4, 1987. *Assault.* White racist, Skinheads. Tampa, Florida. Skinheads murder Isaiah Walker, a black man.

December 23, 1987. *Attempted arson.* Anti-abortion. Montgomery, Alabama. The Beacon Women's Center is the target of attempted arson.

January 1988. *Attempted arson.* Anti-abortion. Everett, Washington. Planned Parenthood of Everett is the target of attempted arson.

January 2, 1988. *Bombing/explosive.* Cuban. Miami, Florida. A business that ships medical supplies to Cuba is pipe bombed.

January 12, 1988. *Bombing/incendiary.* Puerto Rican nationalist, Pedro Albizu Campos Revolutionary Force. Rio Piedras, Puerto Rico. A bank is firebombed.

January 12, 1988. *Bombing/incendiary.* Puerto Rican nationalist, Pedro Albizu Campos Revolutionary Force. Rio Piedras, Puerto Rico. A Mexican travel agency is firebombed.

January 28, 1988. *Shoot-out.* Latter Day Saints/Mormon Sects. Marion, Utah. A 13-day siege, which began after the bombing of a Mormon church on January 16, ends in a shoot-out that leaves one police officer dead and a Mormon polygamist leader seriously wounded.

April 21, 1988. *Assault.* White racist, Skinheads. Halifax, North Carolina. A black man is assaulted and killed by Skinheads.

May 1988. *Attempted bombing.* Anti-abortion. Pensacola, Florida. The Ladies Center is the target of an attempted bombing.

May 3, 1988. *Bombing/explosive.* Cuban. Miami, Florida. The Cuban Museum of Arts and Culture is bombed.

May 5, 1988. *Shooting.* White racist. Louisville, Kentucky. David Price, a black man, is killed in a drive-by shooting.

May 6, 1988. *Bombing/explosive.* Cuban. Miami, Florida. A pipe bomb explodes under the car of a board member of the Cuban Museum of Arts and Culture. The museum had exhibited works by artists still living in Cuba.

May 26, 1988. *Bombing/explosive.* Cuban. Coral Gables, Florida. The home of the director of the Institute of Cuban Studies is bombed.

June 1988. *Attempted arson.* Anti-abortion. Long Beach, California. The Women's Family Planning Abortion Counseling Clinic is the target of attempted arson.

June 23, 1988. *Robbery.* Animal rights, Animal Liberation Front. Santa Rosa, California. Two calves are stolen from a veal farm.

June 27, 1988. *Shooting.* Latter Day Saints/Mormon Sects. Utah. Four defectors from a polygamist Mormon cult are murdered.

July 14, 1988. *Assault.* White racist, Ku Klux Klan. Kingston, New York. The body of a young black woman, Anna Kithcart, is found beaten and strangled to death, with the letters KKK cut into her back.

July 22, 1988. *Bombing/explosive.* Puerto Rican nationalist, Macheteros. Caguas, Puerto Rico. An Army recruiting center is pipe bombed.

August 22, 1988. *Bombing/explosive.* White racist. Atlanta, Georgia. Eight people are injured when the NAACP headquarters is bombed.

September 5, 1988. *Bombing/explosive.* Cuban. Miami, Florida. A business shipping supplies to Cuba is pipe bombed.

September 17, 1988. *Shooting.* Islamic, Al-Fuqra. Augusta, Georgia. A Hindu doctor is shot to death in front of a hospital.

September 18, 1988. *Bombing/explosive.* Cuban. Miami, Florida. The residence of the leader of the Reunion Flotilla is bombed. The group organizes visits to Cuba.

September 19, 1988. *Bombing/explosive.* Rightist, Up the IRS. Los Angeles, California. A bomb explodes in a car parked in an IRS garage.

September 25, 1988. *Sabotage, vandalism, and property destruction.* Environmental/animal rights. Grand Canyon, Arizona. Power lines are sabotaged by the Evan Mecham Eco-Terrorist International Conspiracy.

October 1988. *Arson.* Anti-abortion. Long Beach, California. The Women's Family Planning Abortion Counseling Clinic is set on fire.

October 8, 1988. *Sabotage, vandalism, and property destruction.* White racist/rightist, Skinheads. Dallas, Texas. Confederate Hammerskins vandalize Temple Shalom Synagogue and an Islamic mosque.

November 1, 1988. *Bombing/explosive.* Puerto Rican nationalist, Pedro Albizu Campos Revolutionary Force. Rio Piedras, Puerto Rico. The General Electric office is bombed.

November 10, 1988. *Attempted bombing.* Animal rights, Animal Liberation Front. Norwalk, Connecticut. Fran Truitt attempts to murder corporate executive Leon Hirsch by planting a bomb under Hirsch's car. His firm used dogs to demonstrate the use of surgical staples.

November 13, 1988. *Assault.* White racist, White Aryan Resistance. Portland, Oregon. Skinheads linked to the White Aryan Resistance beat an Ethiopian immigrant, Mulugeta Seraw, to death.

December 1988. *Bombing/explosive.* Puerto Rican nationalist, Pedro Albizu Campos Revolutionary Force. Puerto Rico. U.S. corporation offices are bombed.

December 10, 1988. *Shooting.* White racist, Skinheads. Reno, Nevada. Tony Montgomery, a black man, is shot and killed in a drive-by shooting.

December 25, 1988. *Arson.* Anti-abortion. Dallas, Texas. The Metro-Plex Gynecological Group is set on fire.

December 25, 1988. *Arson.* Anti-abortion. Dallas, Texas. The North Dallas Women's Clinic is set on fire.

December 25, 1988. *Arson.* Anti-abortion. Dallas, Texas. The Fairmount Center is set on fire.

January 1989. *Attempted bombing.* Anti-abortion. New Orleans, Louisiana. The Delta Women's Center is the target of an attempted bombing; no damage is reported.

January 29, 1989. *Arson.* Animal rights, Animal Liberation Front. Sacramento, California. Arson at a livestock firm causes $250,000 in damage.

February 24, 1989. *Bombing/explosive.* Cuban. Miami, Florida. A business shipping supplies to Cuba is pipe bombed.

February 28, 1989. *Bombing/incendiary.* Islamic. Berkeley, California. Two bookstores selling *The Satanic Verses* written by Salman Rushdie are firebombed.

February 28, 1989. *Bombing/incendiary.* Islamic. New York City, New York. A bookstore selling *The Satanic Verses* written by Salman Rushdie is firebombed.

March 1989. *Arson.* Anti-abortion. Ocala, Florida. The All Women's Health Center is set on fire, causing an estimated damage of $60,000.

March 10, 1989. *Bombing/explosive.* Unknown. La Jolla, California. A pipe bomb explodes under a van belonging to the wife of a naval commander. He had been in command of the *USS Vincennes,* which shot down an Iranian passenger plane in 1988.

March 26, 1989. *Bombing/explosive.* Cuban. Miami, Florida. A business shipping supplies to Cuba is pipe bombed.

April 1989. *Arson.* Anti-abortion. Fort Myers, Florida. The Fort Myers Women's Health Center is set on fire, causing an estimated damage of $50,000.

April 1989. *Arson.* Anti-abortion. Ocala, Florida. The All Women's Health Center is set on fire, causing an estimated damage of $190,000.

April 2, 1989. *Arson.* Animal rights, Animal Liberation Front. Tucson, Arizona. Two university laboratories are set on fire, causing over $100,000 in damage. More than 1000 lab animals were released.

June 19, 1989. *Bombing/explosive.* Puerto Rican nationalist, Macheteros. Bayamon, Puerto Rico. The Army recruiting office is pipe bombed.

July 1989. *Arson.* Anti-abortion. Concord, New Hampshire. The Concord Feminist Health Center is set on fire, causing an estimated damage of $5000.

July 4, 1989. *Arson.* Animal rights, Animal Liberation Front. Lubbock, Texas. ALF members break into a lab at the University of Texas, destroying equipment and freeing lab animals, causing $70,000 in damage.

August 10, 1989. *Shooting.* Jewish, Jewish Defense Organization. Manhattan, New York. The leader of the Jewish Defense Organization fires into the street apparently at the leader of the JDL. He wounds a bystander.

August 19, 1989. *Shooting.* Unknown. Fresno, California. A Vietnamese activist is wounded in an apparent assassination attempt.

September 1989. *Bombing/explosive.* Anti-abortion. Kalamazoo, Michigan. Planned

Parenthood of Kalamazoo is bombed, causing an estimated damage of $5000.

September 1989. *Arson.* Anti-abortion. Pittsburgh, Pennsylvania. The Allegheny Reproductive Health Center is set on fire, causing an estimated damage of $10,000.

September 10, 1989. *Bombing/explosive.* Cuban. Hialeah, Florida. A business that ships supplies to Cuba is pipe bombed.

October 1989. *Arson.* Anti-abortion. Fairfield, New Jersey. The North Jersey Women's Health clinic is set on fire, causing an estimated damage of $5000.

December 1989. *Bombing/explosive.* Anti-abortion. Independence, Missouri. The Planned Parenthood of Greater Kansas City clinic is bombed, causing an estimated damage of $50,000.

December 16, 1989. *Bombing/explosive.* Rightist, Americans for a Competent Judiciary. Birmingham, Alabama. A federal judge, Robert Vance, is killed by a letter bomb mailed to his house.

December 18, 1989. *Bombing/explosive.* Rightist, Americans for a Competent Judiciary. Savannah, Georgia. Robert Robinson, a black civil rights lawyer, is killed by a , is killed by a letter bomb letter bomb mailed to his office.

December 18, 1989. *Attempted bombing.* Rightist, Americans for a Competent Judiciary. Atlanta, Georgia. A package bomb mailed to a federal courthouse is intercepted and disarmed.

December 19, 1989. *Attempted bombing.* Rightist, Americans for a Competent Judiciary. Jacksonville, Florida. A package bomb mailed to the NAACP office is

disarmed. This was the last of four letter bombs from "Americans for a Competent Judiciary." Roy Moody, a petty criminal, was found guilty of mailing the devices.

1990. *Shooting.* White racist, Ku Klux Klan. Nashville, Tennessee. Shots are fired at a synagogue.

January 1990. *Vandalism.* Anti-abortion. Memphis, Tennessee. A concrete block is thrown through the window of the Memphis Center for Reproductive Health, causing an estimated damage of $3000.

January 1990. *Attempted arson.* Anti-abortion. Kansas City, Kansas. The Aid for Women Center is the target of attempted arson.

January 12, 1990. *Bombing/explosive.* Puerto Rican nationalist, Pedro Albizu Campos Revolutionary Force. Carolina, Puerto Rico. Pipe bombs explode outside a Westinghouse office.

January 12, 1990. *Bombing/explosive.* Puerto Rican nationalist, Pedro Albizu Campos Revolutionary Force. Santurce, Puerto Rico. Pipe bombs explode outside a Navy recruiting office.

January 14, 1990. *Robbery.* Animal rights, Animal Liberation Front. University of Pennsylvania, Pennsylvania. The ALF takes files, videotapes, slides, and computer disks from the office of a researcher.

January 31, 1990. *Assault.* Islamic, Al-Fuqra. Tucson, Arizona. Imam Rashid Khalifa, leader of an area mosque, is stabbed to death by members of the al-Fuqra sect.

February 22, 1990. *Attempted bombing.* Rightist, Up the IRS. Los Angeles, California. A pickup truck parked near an IRS office and loaded with explosives catches fire but does not explode. "Up the IRS" claims responsibility.

March 30, 1990. *Bombing/incendiary?* Islamic, Al-Fuqra. Quincy, Massachusetts. The Islamic Center of Quincy is attacked.

April 22, 1990. *Sabotage, vandalism, and property destruction.* Environmental, Earth Liberation Front. Santa Cruz, California. Power lines are sabotaged by Earth Action, a militant environmentalist group.

April 28, 1990. *Bombing/explosive.* Unknown. Leesburg, Virginia. A mail bomb addressed to Rev. Pat Robertson injures a guard.

May 1990. *Arson.* Anti-abortion. Portland, Oregon. The Lovejoy Surgicenter is set on fire, causing an estimated damage of $15,000.

May 1990. *Arson.* Anti-abortion. Syracuse, New York. A fire at the Planned Parenthood of Syracuse building causes damage of $570.

May 1990. *Vandalism.* Anti-abortion. Pittsburgh, Pennsylvania. The roof of the Allegheny Reproductive Health Services is damaged with an ax; the estimated damage is $50,000.

May 1990. *Vandalism.* Anti-abortion. Reno, Nevada. The West End Women's Medical Group has anti-abortion slogans painted on the walls and the stairs. The damage is estimated at $1400.

May 24, 1990. *Bombing/explosive.* Unknown. Oakland, California. A homemade pipe bomb explodes in a car belonging to Judi Bari, an environmental activist and a member of Earth First. Police arrest Bari

and her companion, Darryl Cherney, both of whom were injured in the explosion, and charge them with transporting the bomb. Twelve years later, Bari and Cherney were awarded $4.4 million in a civil suit that claimed that their civil rights had been violated by police.

May 27, 1990. *Arson.* Puerto Rican nationalist. Mayaguez, Puerto Rico. National Guard vehicles are set on fire.

June 14, 1990. *Bombing/explosive.* Cuban. Miami, Florida. The Cuban Museum of Arts and Culture is bombed. The museum had exhibited works by artists still living in Cuba.

July 1990. *Bombing/explosive.* White racist. Georgia. The home of an NAACP official is bombed.

July 1990. *Sabotage, vandalism, and property destruction.* Anti-abortion. Atlanta, Georgia. A noxious chemical is poured into the ventilation system at the Atlanta Surgi Center, causing $2000 worth of damage.

September 1990. *Bombing/explosive.* Anti-abortion. Worcester, Massachusetts. Planned Parenthood of Central Massachusetts is bombed, causing an estimated damage of $500.

September 1990. *Arson.* Anti-abortion. Concord, California. Planned Parenthood of Shasta Diablo is set on fire, causing an estimated damage of $90,000.

September 15, 1990. *Bombing/explosive.* White racist, White Aryan Resistance. San Diego, California. The federal courthouse building, which also houses the FBI and the IRS, is bombed. The investigation focuses on the White Aryan Resistance.

September 17, 1990. *Bombing/explosive.* Puerto Rican nationalist, Pedro Albizu Campos Revolutionary Force. Arecibo, Puerto Rico. A Citibank branch is bombed.

September 17, 1990. *Bombing/explosive.* Puerto Rican nationalist, Pedro Albizu Campos Revolutionary Force. Vega Baja, Puerto Rico. A U.S. owned factory is bombed.

October 1990. *Sabotage, vandalism, and property destruction.* Anti-abortion. Pittsburgh, Pennsylvania. A noxious chemical is flushed into the water of the Women's Health Services, causing $12,000 worth of damage.

October 1990. *Sabotage, vandalism, and property destruction.* Anti-abortion. Philadelphia, Pennsylvania. The safety glass on the front door of the Northeast Women's Center is broken, causing an estimated $1500 in damage.

November 1990. *Arson.* Anti-abortion. Fort Wayne, Indiana. The Fort Wayne Women's Health Organization is set on fire, causing an estimated damage of $10,000.

November 5, 1990. *Shooting.* Islamic. New York City, New York. Rabbi Meir Kahane, founder of the Jewish Defense League, is shot to death by El Sayyid Nosair. Nosair is a follower of Sheikh Omar Abdel Rahman, who later is linked to the World Trade Center bombing of 1993.

December 1990. *Sabotage, vandalism, and property destruction.* Anti-abortion. South Bend, Indiana. The roof of the Women's Pavilion is vandalized, causing damage estimated at $3000.

January 1991. *Shooting.* Anti-abortion. Little Rock, Arkansas. A shotgun is fired through the window of the Little Rock Family Planning clinic.

January 10, 1991. *Arson.* White racist. North Hollywood, California. A firebomb guts a synagogue, causing damage estimated at $120,000.

January 11, 1991. *Bombing/incendiary?* Islamic, Al-Fuqra. San Diego, California. The Islamic Cultural Center of San Diego is attacked.

February 1991. *Arson.* Anti-abortion. Columbus, Ohio. Planned Parenthood of Central Ohio is set on fire, causing damage estimated at $75,000.

February 1991. *Arson.* Anti-abortion. Columbus, Ohio. The Capital Care Women's Center is set on fire, causing damage estimated at $250,000.

February 3, 1991. *Arson.* Puerto Rican nationalist. Mayaguez, Puerto Rico. National Guard trucks are set on fire.

February 18, 1991. *Arson.* Puerto Rican nationalist. Sabana, Puerto Rico. National Guard trucks are set on fire.

February 18, 1991. *Shooting.* Unknown. Miami, Florida. Jean Claude Olivier, a Haitian dissident, is gunned down on the street.

March 1991. *Arson.* Anti-abortion. Greensboro, North Carolina. The Piedmont Carolina Medical Clinic is set on fire, causing an estimated damage of $100,000.

March 1991. *Arson.* Anti-abortion. Greensboro, North Carolina. The Women's Pavilion is the target of arson.

March 1, 1991. *Shooting.* Islamic. Brooklyn, New York. Mustafa Shalabi is found dead in his house. He had been in a dispute with Sheik Omar Abdel Rahman, the spiritual leader of the 1993 World Trade Center bombers.

March 11, 1991. *Arson.* White racist. Los Angeles, California. Temple Adat Elohim is damaged by fire, causing minor damage.

March 15, 1991. *Shooting.* Unknown. Miami, Florida. Fritz Dor, a broadcaster and Haitian dissident, is gunned down as he leaves his office.

March 17, 1991. *Arson.* Puerto Rican nationalist. Carolina, Puerto Rico. A jet plane on the Air Force National Guard base is set on fire.

March 30, 1991. *Arson.* White racist. Los Angeles, California. A synagogue is damaged by fire, causing $8000 in damage.

April 1991. *Arson.* Anti-abortion. Woodbridge, New Jersey. A fire is set at the Medical Care Center at Woodbridge, causing an estimated damage of $500,000.

April 1, 1991. *Bombing/explosive.* Rightist, Up the IRS. Fresno, California. Ten pipe bombs are launched at an IRS office from a nearby field. Up the IRS claims responsibility.

April 14, 1991. *Attempted bombing.* Anti-abortion. Columbus, Ohio. The Founder's Women's Health Center is the target of an attempted bombing.

May 1991. *Arson.* Anti-abortion. Mobile, Alabama. The Bay City Women's Medical Center is set on fire, causing an estimated damage of $80,000.

June 1991. *Shooting.* White racist, Skinheads. Fort Worth, Texas. Donald Thomas, a black man, is killed in a drive-by shooting by Confederate Hammerskins.

June 1991. *Arson.* Animal rights, Animal Liberation Front. Millville, Utah. A coyote research lab is set on fire.

June 1991. *Arson.* Animal rights, Animal Liberation Front. Edmonds, Washington. A mink feed facility is torched, causing $500,000 in damage.

June 10, 1991. *Bombing/incendiary.* Animal rights, Animal Liberation Front. Corvallis, Oregon. Incendiary devices are set off at Oregon State University's experimental mink farm, causing $62,000 in damage.

July 6, 1991. *Bombing/incendiary.* Puerto Rican nationalist. Borinquen, Puerto Rico. An airplane is bombed and set on fire.

August 1991. *Arson.* Anti-abortion. Fayetteville, North Carolina. The Carolina Women's Medical Center is set on fire, causing an estimated damage of $50,000.

August 12, 1991. *Arson.* Animal rights, Animal Liberation Front. Pullman, Washington. A university campus coyote research lab is set on fire.

September 1991. *Arson.* Anti-abortion. Aurora, Illinois. The office of a doctor who performs abortions is set on fire, causing an estimated damage of $175,000–$200,000.

December 1991. *Assault.* White racist/rightist, Skinheads. Houston, Texas. Garrett Douglas, a homeless black man, is murdered.

December 15, 1991. *Arson.* Animal rights, Animal Liberation Front. Yamhill, Oregon. Fire at a mink facility causes $96,000 in damage.

December 24, 1991. *Assault.* White racist, Skinheads. Birmingham, Alabama. Aryan National Front Skinheads stab a black man to death.

December 28, 1991. *Shooting.* Anti-abortion. Springfield, Missouri. A man opens fire with a shotgun in an abortion clinic, wounding two people.

January 1992. *Arson.* Anti-abortion. Beaumont, Texas. Women's Community Health Center is set on fire, causing an estimated damage of $300,000.

January 1992. *Arson.* Anti-abortion. Helena, Montana. Intermountain Planned Parenthood is set on fire, causing an estimated damage of $75,000.

February 2, 1992. *Arson.* Animal rights, Animal Liberation Front. Great Lakes, Michigan. Arson at Michigan State University causes $100,000 in damage.

February 26, 1992. *Attempted bombing.* Jewish. New York City, New York. A pipe bomb is planted in the Syrian Mission to the UN.

February 28, 1992. *Arson.* Animal rights, Animal Liberation Front. East Lansing, Michigan. Arson at the mink research center at Michigan State University causes $1.2 million in damage.

March 9, 1992. *Sabotage, vandalism, and property destruction.* Anti-abortion. Aurora, Colorado. Chemical vandalism causes an estimated damage of $1500 at the Mayfair Women's Clinic.

March 25, 1992. *Sabotage, vandalism, and property destruction.* Anti-abortion. Dallas, Texas. Chemical vandalism attacks on the Routh Street Clinic, Dallas Medical Ladies Pavilion, North Park Medical Group, and A to Z Women's Center cause an estimated damage of $25,000.

April 1992. *Arson.* Anti-abortion. Columbus, Ohio. Founder's Clinic is set on fire, causing an estimated damage of $1000.

April 1992. *Arson.* Anti-abortion. Ashland, Oregon. Catalina Medical Center is set on fire, causing an estimated damage of $225,000.

April 1992. *Arson.* Anti-abortion. Fargo, North Dakota. Fargo Women's Health Organization is set on fire, causing an estimated damage of $2000.

April 4, 1992. *Sabotage, vandalism, and property destruction.* Anti-abortion. Omaha, Nebraska. Chemical vandalism at the Women's Medical Center of Nebraska results in an estimated damage of $1000.

April 15, 1992. *Sabotage, vandalism, and property destruction.* Anti-abortion. Ann Arbor, Michigan. Chemical vandalism at Planned Parenthood Mid-Michigan results in an estimated damage of $5000.

April 17, 1992. *Sabotage, vandalism, and property destruction.* Anti-abortion. Livonia, Michigan. Chemical vandalism at the Women's Advisory Center results in an estimated damage of $1000.

April 18, 1992. *Assault.* White racist, Skinheads. Birmingham, Alabama. Benny Rembert, a homeless black man, is murdered by Aryan National Front Skinheads.

April 28, 1992. *Sabotage, vandalism, and property destruction.* Anti-abortion. Louisville, Kentucky. Chemical vandalism at the EMW Women's Surgi-Center causes an estimated damage of $800.

May 14, 1992. *Sabotage, vandalism, and property destruction.* Anti-abortion. Memphis, Tennessee. A butyric acid attack at the Memphis Area Medical Center for Women, Memphis Center for Reproduction Health results in an estimated damage of $225,000.

June 1992. *Arson.* Anti-abortion. Redding, California. Redding Feminist Women's Health Center is set on fire, causing an estimated damage of $70,000.

June 3, 1992. *Sabotage, vandalism, and property destruction.* Anti-abortion. Chicago, Illinois. Chemical vandalism at Family Planning Associates causes an estimated damage of $5000.

June 8, 1992. *Sabotage, vandalism, and property destruction.* Anti-abortion. Overland, Kansas. Chemical vandalism at the Comprehensive Health for Women causes an estimated damage of $500.

June 18, 1992. *Sabotage, vandalism, and property destruction.* Anti-abortion. Chicago, Illinois. Chemical vandalism at the American Women's Medical Center causes an estimated damage of $1500.

June 21, 1992. *Attempted arson.* Anti-abortion. Kansas City, Missouri. Planned Parenthood, Kansas City is the target of attempted arson.

June 30, 1992. *Sabotage, vandalism, and property destruction.* Anti-abortion. Downers Grove, Illinois. Chemical vandalism at the Access Health Center causes an estimated damage of $2000.

July 1992. *Arson.* Anti-abortion. Newport Beach, California. The Family Planning Association building is set on fire, causing an estimated damage of $9000.

July 10, 1992. *Sabotage, vandalism, and property destruction.* Anti-abortion. Toledo, Ohio. Three separate incidents of chemical vandalism to the Toledo Medical Services, Center for Choice, and the Women's Clinic cause an estimated damage of $20,000.

July 10, 1992. *Sabotage, vandalism, and property destruction.* Anti-abortion. Detroit, Michigan. Chemical vandalism at the Women's Health Services causes an estimated damage of $3000.

August 1992. *Arson.* Anti-abortion. Portland, Oregon. Lovejoy Surgicenter is set on fire, causing an estimated damage of $2000.

August 1992. *Arson.* Anti-abortion. Sacramento, California. Sacramento Feminist Women's Health Center is set on fire, causing an estimated damage of $5000.

August 11, 1992. *Arson.* Animal rights, Animal Liberation Front. Minneapolis, Minnesota. Trucks belonging to Swanson Meats are set on fire, causing damage estimated at $100,000.

August 22, 1992. *Shoot-out.* White racist. Ruby Ridge, Idaho. During an 11-day siege of Randy Weaver's home by the FBI, three people are killed. His 14-year-old son Sammy is shot by U.S. Marshalls. In the ensuing firefight, a U.S. Marshall is killed. The next day, his wife, Vicki, is killed by an FBI sniper while holding her baby daughter in her arms.

September 1992. *Arson.* Anti-abortion. Reno, Nevada. The West End Women's Medical Group building is set on fire, causing an estimated damage of $5600.

September 1992. *Arson.* White racist/rightist, Skinheads. Salem, Oregon. Two gays are killed when their house is set on fire by Skinheads.

September 1992. *Arson.* Anti-abortion. Albuquerque, New Mexico. Abortion & Reproductive Health Services is set on fire, causing an estimated damage of $500.

September 6, 1992. *Arson.* Anti-abortion. Richmond, Virginia. Richmond Medical Center for Women is set on fire, causing an estimated damage of $40,000.

September 9, 1992. *Sabotage, vandalism, and property destruction.* Anti-abortion. Houston, Texas. Two separate incidents of chemical vandalism at Planned Parenthood and the Aaron Women's Center cause an estimated damage of $500.

September 14, 1992. *Sabotage, vandalism, and property destruction.* Anti-abortion. Detroit, Ann Arbor, and Grand Rapids, Michigan. There is a rash of incidents in which chemicals are sprayed into clinics. The clinics attacked include the Northland Family Planning Clinic West, Heritage Clinic, Planned Parenthood of Mid-Michigan, and 10 others. The total damage is $40,000.

September 16, 1992. *Arson.* Anti-abortion. Eugene, Oregon. Eugene Feminist Women's Health Center is set on fire, causing an estimated damage of $2000.

September 16, 1992. *Sabotage, vandalism, and property destruction.* Anti-abortion. Reno, Nevada. Four incidents of chemical vandalism at the West End Women's Medical Group cause an estimated damage of $2000.

September 16, 1992. *Sabotage, vandalism, and property destruction.* Anti-abortion. Troy, Sterling Heights, Bloomfield Hills, Michigan. Six incidents of chemical vandalism occur at the Birth Control Center, Womancare, Somerset Medical, Woman's Choice, Midwest Gynecology, and the Women's Center, causing an estimated damage of $60,000.

October 24, 1992. *Arson.* Animal rights, Animal Liberation Front. Millville, Utah. A coyote research lab is set on fire.

November 1992. *Arson.* Anti-abortion. Westmont, Illinois. Concord Medical Clinic is set on fire, causing an estimated damage of $2500.

November 1992. *Arson.* Anti-abortion. Sacramento, California. Alhambra Abortion Center is set on fire, causing an estimated damage of $175,000.

November 19, 1992. *Attempted bombing.* Mexican Revolutionary Movement. Urbana, Illinois. The Mexican Revolutionary Movement attempts unsuccessfully to firebomb a conference on the future of Latin America, with business leaders and academics from the U.S. and Mexico in attendance.

December 1992. *Arson.* Anti-abortion. Fresno, California. The office of a doctor who performs abortions is set on fire, causing an estimated damage of $50,000.

December 10, 1992. *Attempted bombing.* Puerto Rican nationalist. Chicago, Illinois. The Marine recruiting office is the target of an attempted pipe bombing.

January 17, 1993. *Arson.* Croatian. Chicago, Illinois. A fire is started at the Serbian National Defense Council building.

January 25, 1993. *Shooting.* Islamic. Langley, Virginia. While in their cars, five individuals working for the CIA are shot outside CIA headquarters. Lansing Bennet and Frank Darling are killed in the attack. The shooter, Mir Aimal Kansi, fled to Pakistan but was captured three and a half years later. Reportedly, he was betrayed by his own bodyguards for the $3.5 million reward offered by the CIA.

February 1993. *Arson.* Anti-abortion. Corpus Christi, Texas. The Reproductive Services clinic is set on fire, causing an estimated damage of $1 million.

February 1993. *Arson.* Anti-abortion. Venice, Florida. The Venice Women's Health Center is set on fire, causing an estimated damage of $300,000.

February 1993. *Sabotage, vandalism, and property destruction.* Anti-abortion. San Antonio, Texas. The Reproductive Services clinic is the target of a butyric acid attack.

February 26, 1993. *Bombing/explosive.* Islamic. New York City, New York. A massive explosion in the garage below the World Trade Center kills six people and injures over a thousand. At least 50,000 tourists and workers had to be evacuated from the complex. The FBI arrested four radical Muslims, who were tried and convicted in 1994. The conspirators were each sentenced to 240 years without parole.

The judge said that the length of their sentences was calculated by adding up the six victims' life expectancies. The six victims were William Macko, 47, Stephen Knapp, 48, Monica Smith, 35, Robert Kirkpatrick, 61, Wilfredo Mercado, 35, and John Digiovanno, 45. The alleged mastermind behind the plot, Ramzi Yousef, fled to Pakistan the day after the bombing but was captured two years later.

March 1993. *Arson.* Anti-abortion. Missoula, Montana. The Blue Mountain Clinic is set on fire, causing an estimated damage of $250,000.

March 1993. *Sabotage, vandalism, and property destruction.* Anti-abortion. San Diego, California. The Womancare Clinic, Planned Parenthood San Diego/Riverside, and eight other clinics are attacked with butyric acid, causing an estimated damage of $100,000.

March 1993. *Sabotage, vandalism, and property destruction.* Anti-abortion. Dallas, Texas. Tear gas is sprayed into Dallas Medical Ladies' Pavilion.

March 9, 1993. *Shooting.* Unknown. Miami, Florida. Daniel Buron, a Haitian dissident, is gunned down on the street.

March 10, 1993. *Shooting.* Anti-abortion. Pensacola, Florida. Dr. David Gunn, Pensacola Medical Services, is murdered by Michael Griffin. After shooting Dr. Gunn in the back three times, Griffin surrendered to police, who were at the clinic to monitor an anti-abortion demonstration.

March 16, 1993. *Assault.* White racist, Skinheads. St. Louis, Missouri. Kevin Poke, a black man, is murdered by Skinheads.

April 19, 1993. *Shoot-out.* Other domestic. Waco, Texas. After a 51-day siege, federal agents storm the Branch Davidian compound. Ninety-two people are killed, including four federal agents.

April 26, 1993. *Assault.* Jewish, Jewish Defense Organization. Washington, D.C. A man waving a Palestinian flag outside the United States Holocaust Memorial Museum is beaten with a pipe by members of the Jewish Defense Organization.

May 1993. *Sabotage, vandalism, and property destruction.* Anti-abortion. South Bend, Indiana. A chemical attack on the Women's Pavilion causes an estimated damage of $100,000.

May 1993. *Arson.* Anti-abortion. Forest Grove, Oregon. The Bours Health Center is set on fire, causing an estimated damage of $5000.

May 27, 1993. *Arson.* Anti-abortion. Boise, Idaho. The Women's Health Center is set on fire, causing an estimated damage of $100,000.

June 22, 1993. *Bombing/explosive.* Unabomber. Tiburon, California. A package bomb, mailed to the home of a University of California geneticist, Dr. Charles Epstein, explodes when he opens it.

June 24, 1993. *Bombing/explosive.* Unabomber. New Haven, Connecticut. A package bomb mailed to the office of David Gelernter, a computer science professor, explodes when he opens it.

June 24, 1993. *Attempted bombing.* Islamic. New York City, New York. The FBI arrests eight Islamic extremists on charges of planning a series of bombings and murders in New York. Targets were the UN

Building, federal buildings, two commuter tunnels, and the Diamond District.

July 1993. *Attempted bombing.* Anti-abortion. Chicago, Illinois. Family Planning Associates is the target of an attempted bombing.

July 1993. *Attempted bombing.* Anti-abortion. Lancaster, Pennsylvania. Planned Parenthood, Lancaster is the target of an attempted bombing.

July 13, 1993. *Assault.* White racist, Skinheads. Atlantic City, New Jersey. An elderly black man is beaten to death by Skinheads.

July 20, 1993. *Bombing/explosive.* White racist, Skinheads. Tacoma, Washington. The NAACP headquarters is bombed by American Front Skinheads.

July 22, 1993. *Bombing/explosive.* White racist, Skinheads. Seattle, Washington. A gay bar is bombed by American Front Skinheads.

July 25, 1993. *Bombing/incendiary.* White racist. Sacramento, California. The NAACP office is firebombed, totally destroying it.

July 25, 1993. *Bombing/incendiary.* White racist. Sacramento, California. A Molotov cocktail is thrown at Congregation B'Nai Israel Synagogue.

August 1993. *Sabotage, vandalism, and property destruction.* Anti-abortion. Milwaukee, Wisconsin. Imperial Health Center is the target of a chemical vandalism attack.

August 19, 1993. *Shooting.* Anti-abortion. Wichita, Kansas. Dr. George Tiller, a doctor who performs abortions, is shot and wounded by Rachelle Shannon, an anti-abortion activist.

September 1993. *Bombing.* Anti-abortion. Newport Beach, California. Family Planning Associates is bombed, causing an estimated damage of $3500.

September 1993. *Arson.* Anti-abortion. Bakersfield, California. Family Planning Associates is set on fire, causing an estimated damage of $1.4 million.

September 1993. *Bombing/explosive.* Anti-abortion. Lancaster, Pennsylvania. Planned Parenthood, Lancaster is bombed, causing an estimated damage of $130,000.

September 1993. *Sabotage, vandalism, and property destruction.* Anti-abortion. Appleton, Wisconsin. Chemical vandalism at Planned Parenthood Appleton North causes an estimated damage of $40,000.

September 8, 1993. *Assault.* White racist, Skinheads. Orange County, California. Tina Rodriguez, a black woman, is beaten to death by Skinheads.

September 27, 1993. *Arson.* Anti-abortion. Peoria, Illinois. National Health Care Services is set on fire, causing an estimated damage of $10,000.

October 1993. *Arson.* Anti-abortion. Houston, Texas. West Loop Clinic is set on fire, causing an estimated damage of $50,000.

October 5, 1993. *Bombing/incendiary.* White racist. Sacramento, California. The firebombing of the Japanese-American civil rights office is claimed by the Aryan Liberation Front, which also claimed responsibility for other bombings in July 1993.

October 9, 1993. *Bombing/incendiary.* White racist. Sacramento, California. The home of James Yee, a Chinese-American member of the City Council, is fire-bombed.

October 31, 1993. *Bombing/explosive.* White racist. Reno, Nevada. The Bureau of Land Management office is bombed.

November 1993. *Arson.* Anti-abortion. Ventura, California. An arson attack on Family Planning Associates causes damage of $500.

November 1993. *Attempted bombing.* Anti-abortion. York, Pennsylvania. Hillcrest Women's Medical Center is the target of an attempted bombing.

November 27, 1993. *Bombing/incendiary.* Animal rights, Animal Liberation Front. Chicago, Illinois. Incendiary devices placed in four department stores cause minor damage.

December 7, 1993. *Shooting.* Black militant. Long Island, New York. Colin Ferguson, a black man, opens fire with a handgun on a crowded commuter train. Six people are killed and 17 are wounded. All the victims are whites or Asians. Handwritten notes found on Ferguson express his hatred of whites and Asians.

January 5, 1994. *Attempted bombing.* Jewish, Jewish Defense League. New York City, New York. Explosive devices are found outside a building housing pro-peace Jewish organizations.

March 1994. *Arson.* Environmental, Earth Liberation Front. Olympia, Washington. Two fires cause $8000 in damage to Allan Wirkkala Logging Company.

March 1, 1994. *Shooting.* Islamic. New York City, New York. A Lebanese immigrant, Rashid Baz, fires on a van full of Hasidic students, killing Ari Halberstam and wounding two other students. At his trial, it was claimed that the attack was in response to the massacre of Muslim worshippers by a Jewish extremist in the Israeli-occupied West Bank a few days earlier.

March 16, 1994. *Shooting.* Unknown. Miami, Florida. A Haitian dissident is assassinated. He was a supporter of ex-President Aristide.

April 1994. *Sabotage, vandalism, and property destruction.* Anti-abortion. Syracuse, New York. Two separate incidents of chemical vandalism occur at the offices of Dr. Jack Yoffa and Planned Parenthood of Syracuse.

April 1994. *Arson.* Environmental, Earth Liberation Front. Snoqualmie, Washington. Fire causes $50,000 in damage to a logging company.

July 1994. *Attempted bombing.* Anti-abortion. Philadelphia, Pennsylvania. Northeast Women's Center is the target of an attempted bombing.

July 7, 1994. *Assault.* White racist, Skinheads. West Hollywood, California. A Hasidic Jew is assaulted with a lead pipe by a Skinhead.

July 27, 1994. *Arson.* Environmental, Earth Liberation Front. Olympia, Washington. Fire destroys logging equipment valued at more than $200,000.

July 29, 1994. *Shooting.* Anti-abortion. Pensacola, Florida. At the Ladies Center, Dr. John Britton and escort Jim Barrett are shot and killed by anti-abortion extremist Paul Hill. Escort June Barrett is injured.

July 31, 1994. *Bombing/explosive.* Anti-abortion. Falls Church, Virginia. Commonwealth Women's Clinic is bombed, causing an estimated damage of $10,000.

July 31, 1994. *Arson.* Environmental, Earth Liberation Front. Olympia, Washington. The torching of a log skidder, two fire trucks, and a bulldozer cause $80,000 in damage.

August 1994. *Bombing/explosive.* White racist, White Aryan Resistance. California. The Fair Housing Department offices are bombed.

August 1994. *Arson.* Anti-abortion. Brainerd, Minnesota. Planned Parenthood is set on fire, causing an estimated damage of $500,000.

August 1994. *Bombing/explosive.* White racist, White Aryan Resistance. California. The NAACP office is bombed.

August 1994. *Attempted bombing.* Anti-abortion. St. Albans, Vermont. Planned Parenthood of Northern New England is the target of an attempted bombing.

August 1994. *Bombing/explosive.* White racist, White Aryan Resistance. California. Two Asian homes are bombed.

August 1994. *Assault.* White racist, Skinheads. California. A black man is stabbed by Skinheads.

August 1994. *Assault.* White racist, Skinheads. California. Jody Robinson, a black man, is tortured and murdered by Skinheads.

September 4, 1994. *Bombing/incendiary.* Cuban. Florida. The *Replica* magazine office is firebombed after an editorial calls for dialogue with Castro.

September 17, 1994. *Assault.* White racist, Skinheads. Huntingdon Beach, California. Vernon Floury, a black man, is murdered by Skinheads.

October 1994. *Arson.* Anti-abortion. Redding, California. Redding Feminist Women's Health Center is set on fire, causing an estimated damage of $5000.

October 1994. *Arson.* Anti-abortion. Chico, California. Planned Parenthood is set on fire, causing an estimated damage of $35,000.

October 1994. *Attempted bombing.* Anti-abortion. San Jose, California. Women's Community Clinic is the target of an attempted bombing, causing an estimated damage of $500.

October 1994. *Shooting.* White racist, Skinheads. Lubbock, Texas. Melvin Johnson, a black man, is killed in a drive-by shooting.

October 1994. *Arson.* Anti-abortion. Kalispell, Montana. A doctor's office is set on fire, causing an estimated damage of $75,000–$100,000.

October 25, 1994. *Robbery.* Rightist, Aryan Republican Army. Columbus, Ohio. A bank is robbed. This is the first bank robbery by the Midwest Bank Robbers, also known as the Aryan Republican Army.

November 1994. *Bombing/explosive.* Anti-abortion. San Rafael, California. A bomb explodes in the parking lot of Planned Parenthood.

December 1994. *Shooting.* Anti-abortion. Norfolk, Virginia. Shots are fired into the lobby of Hillcrest Clinic. No one is injured.

December 1994. *Bombing/explosive.* Anti-abortion. Rapid City, South Dakota. Planned Parenthood is bombed. The new facility had not yet opened. The estimated damage is $1000.

December 1994. *Attempted arson.* Anti-abortion. Kansas City, Missouri. Planned Parenthood is the target of attempted arson.

December 1994. *Shooting.* White racist, Skinheads. Riverside, California. Rod Jackson, a black man, is shot in his driveway by a Skinhead.

December 9, 1994. *Robbery.* Rightist, Aryan Republican Army. Middleburg Heights, Ohio. A bank is robbed.

December 10, 1994. *Bombing/explosive.* Unabomber. North Caldwell, New Jersey. A package bomb mailed to the home of Thomas Mosser, a New York City advertising executive, explodes when it is opened, killing him.

December 15, 1994. *Arson.* Anti-abortion. Kansas City, Missouri. Aid for Women/Central Medical is set on fire, causing an estimated damage of $1000.

December 27, 1994. *Robbery.* Rightist, Aryan Republican Army. Maryland Heights, Missouri. A bank is robbed.

December 30, 1994. *Shooting.* Anti-abortion. Boston, Massachusetts. Shannon Lowney, a receptionist at Planned Parenthood of Greater Boston, and Leanne Nichols, a receptionist at Preterm Health

Services, are killed in two separate attacks. Five other people are injured when John Salvi fires into the clinics. All the victims were employees or volunteers at the clinics.

January 14, 1995. *Shooting.* Black militant. Guthrie, Kentucky. A group of black youths pursue a truck driven by a white man, who is flying a Confederate flag. They fire at the truck and kill the driver, Michael Westerman.

February 1995. *Arson.* Anti-abortion. San Luis Obispo, California. Planned Parenthood of Santa Barbara & San Luis Obispo is set on fire, causing an estimated damage of $25,000.

February 1995. *Arson.* Anti-abortion. Ventura, California. Family Planning Associates is set on fire, causing an estimated damage of $1000.

February 1995. *Arson.* Anti-abortion. San Francisco, California. Pregnancy Consultation Center & Buena Vista Women's Services is set on fire, causing an estimated damage of $10,000.

February 1995. *Arson.* Anti-abortion. Richmond, Virginia. Richmond Medical Center for Women is set on fire, causing an estimated damage of $500.

February 24, 1995. *Arson.* Anti-abortion. Albuquerque, New Mexico. Abortion & Reproductive Services is set on fire, causing an estimated damage of $7500.

March 1995. *Arson.* Anti-abortion. Norfolk, Virginia. Tidewater Women's Health Center is set on fire, causing an estimated damage of under $5000.

March 1995. *Bombing/explosive.* White racist. Lamoille, Nevada. The U.S. Forest Service office is bombed.

March 1995. *Sabotage, vandalism, and property destruction.* Anti-abortion. Denver, Colorado. The offices of Planned Parenthood of the Rocky Mountains are vandalized by an anti-abortion activist, David Lane, who uses a sledgehammer to destroy medical equipment, walls, and toilets.

March 29, 1995. *Robbery.* Rightist, Aryan Republican Army. Des Moines, Iowa. A bank is robbed.

March 30, 1995. *Bombing/explosive.* Rightist. Carson City, Nevada. The U.S. Forest Service office is bombed.

April 1995. *Shooting.* White racist, Skinheads. Lancaster, California. Four blacks are wounded when Skinheads fire at them.

April 14, 1995. *Bombing/incendiary.* Animal rights, Animal Liberation Front. Syracuse, New York. An incendiary device explodes at Oneata Beef Company, causing $6000 in damage.

April 19, 1995. *Bombing/explosive.* Rightist. Oklahoma City, Oklahoma. A truck bomb destroys the Alfred P. Murrah Federal Building, killing 168 people, including 19 children. Timothy McVeigh carried out the bombing in retaliation for the Branch Davidian deaths at Waco, Texas, on April 19, 1993.

April 24, 1995. *Bombing/explosive.* Unabomber. Sacramento, California. A package bomb mailed to the lobbying offices of the private California Forestry Association explodes when it is opened, killing the association's president, Gilbert P. Murray.

May 1995. *Bombing/explosive.* Anti-abortion. Canton, Ohio. At Planned Parenthood of Stark County, a bomb explodes in the medical director's mailbox, causing minor damage.

May 1995. *Assault.* White racist, Skinheads. Lancaster, California. A black man is stabbed by Skinheads.

June 1995. *Assault.* White racist, Skinheads. Lancaster, California. A black woman is badly beaten by Skinheads.

June 15, 1995. *Arson.* Animal rights, Animal Liberation Front. Murray, Utah. Tandy Leather Company is torched, causing $300,000 in damage.

June 20, 1995. *Arson.* White racist, Ku Klux Klan. Greeleyville, South Carolina. A black church is set on fire.

June 21, 1995. *Arson.* White racist, Ku Klux Klan. Bloomville, South Carolina. A black church is set on fire.

June 25, 1995. *Shooting.* Rightist, Militia. Ohio. Michael Hill, a Militia member, is shot and killed by police.

August 1995. *Arson.* Anti-abortion. St. Petersburg, Florida. All Women's Center is set on fire, causing an estimated damage of $250,000.

August 1995. *Attempted arson.* Anti-abortion. Grants Pass, Oregon. Planned Parenthood is the target of attempted arson.

August 4, 1995. *Bombing/explosive.* White racist. Carson City, Nevada. A U.S. Forest Service vehicle is destroyed by a bomb.

August 16, 1995. *Robbery.* White racist/rightist, Aryan Republican Army. Bridgeton, Missouri. A bank is robbed.

August 30, 1995. *Robbery.* Rightist, Aryan Republican Army. Madison, Wisconsin. A bank is robbed.

September 18, 1995. *Arson.* Anti-abortion. Jackson, Wyoming. Emergicare clinic is set on fire, causing an estimated damage of $30,000.

October 9, 1995. *Sabotage, vandalism, and property destruction.* Rightist, Sons of the Gestapo. Hyder, Arizona. The sabotage of railway tracks results in an Amtrak train derailment. Michael Bates is killed, and 78 other passengers are injured. A note claiming responsibility was signed "Sons of the Gestapo."

October 26, 1995. *Bombing/explosive.* Rightist. Buffalo Creek, Colorado. The U.S. Forest Service office is bombed.

November 1995. *Arson.* Anti-abortion. St. Petersburg, Florida. All Women's Center is set on fire, causing an estimated damage of $2000.

December 7, 1995. *Shooting.* White racist. North Carolina. A black couple, Jackie Burden and Michael James, is shot and killed by Skinhead soldiers in what is alleged to be an initiation rite.

December 17, 1995. *Attempted bombing.* Rightist. Reno, Nevada. A bomb is discovered in the parking lot of the IRS building.

December 19, 1995. *Robbery.* Rightist, Aryan Republican Army. Sylvania, Ohio. A bank is robbed.

December 24, 1995. *Bombing.* Animal rights, Animal Liberation Front. Eugene, Oregon. Explosive devices explode under three Dutch Girl Ice Cream trucks, causing $15,000 in damage.

1996. *Arson.* Environmental, Earth Liberation Front. Oak Ridge, Tennessee. Arson at the park ranger headquarters causes $9 million in damage.

January 1996. *Robbery.* Rightist. Tilly, Arkansas. A gun dealer, William Mueller, his wife, Nancy, and their eight-year-old daughter are tortured and murdered during a robbery committed by Chevie Kehoe, who planned to create an Aryan Peoples Republic.

January 4, 1996. *Bombing/explosive.* Rightist. Opelika, Alabama. An explosion injures the neighbor of a recently retired BATF agent.

January 6, 1996. *Assault.* White racist. Houston, Texas. Fred Mangione, a gay man, is stabbed to death by two members of the neo-Nazi German Peace Corps.

January 28, 1996. *Assault.* White racist, Skinheads. Austin, California. A Vietnamese man is stabbed to death by Skinheads.

February 1996. *Assault.* White racist, Skinheads. Huntingdon Beach, California. An American Indian is stabbed by Skinheads.

March 1996. *Assault.* White racist, Skinheads. Redlands, California. Skinheads assault an American Indian, beating him severely.

April 1, 1996. *Bombing/explosive.* Rightist. Spokane, Washington. A pipe bomb explodes in a newspaper office.

April 1, 1996. *Robbery.* Rightist. Spokane, Washington. A bank is robbed by the Phineas Priesthood; $108,000 is taken.

April 12, 1996. *Shooting.* White racist. Jackson, Mississippi. Larry Shoemake opens fire on a shopping center in a black neighborhood, killing one person and wounding 10. He then dies in a fire. Notes left at his home suggest the attack was racially motivated.

April 12, 1996. *Attempted bombing.* Rightist. Sacramento, California. A pipe bomb is found near a post office. A note says "Timothy McVeigh lives."

April 29, 1996. *Bombing/explosive.* Rightist, Militia. Spokane, Washington. A explosion occurs outside city hall.

May 20, 1996. *Bombing/explosive.* Rightist. Laredo, Texas. The FBI office is bombed.

June 12, 1996. *Arson.* Animal rights, Animal Liberation Front. Salt Lake City, Utah. An Egg Products store is set on fire, causing over $100,000 in damage.

July 11, 1996. *Bombing/explosive.* Cuban. Florida. A Cuban restaurant is bombed after a pro-Castro singer is booked as an entertainer.

July 12, 1996. *Bombing/explosive and robbery.* Rightist. Spokane, Washington. The Planned Parenthood office is bombed, apparently as a diversion for a bank robbery.

July 12, 1996. *Robbery.* Rightist. Spokane, Washington. A bank is robbed by men belonging to the Phineas Priesthood.

July 27, 1996. *Bombing/explosive.* Rightist, Eric Rudolph. Atlanta, Georgia. During the Summer Olympics, a pipe bomb in a knapsack detonates, killing one person, Alice Hawthorne, and injuring 111 other visitors at Centennial Olympic Park. Richard Jewell, a security guard at the park, was publicly identified as a suspect but was later exonerated. A right-wing extremist, Eric Rudolph, was later indicted for the bombing and three other terrorist attacks.

September 1996. *Bombing/explosive.* Anti-abortion. Broken Arrow, Oklahoma. The Planned Parenthood center is bombed.

October 1996. *Bombing/explosive.* White racist. Lancaster, California. A gay bar is bombed.

October 27, 1996. *Arson.* Environmental/animal rights, Earth Liberation Front/Animal Liberation Front. Willamette, Oregon. A U.S. Forest Service truck is destroyed. The damage is estimated at $15,000.

October 30, 1996. *Arson.* Environmental/animal rights, Earth Liberation Front/Animal Liberation Front. Eugene, Oregon. Arsonists destroy U.S. Forest Service Oakridge Ranger Station. The damage is estimated at $5.3 million.

November 1996. *Shooting.* White racist, Ku Klux Klan. South Carolina. Klansmen shoot at and wound three blacks.

November 12, 1996. *Bombing/incendiary.* Animal rights, Animal Liberation Front. Bloomington, Minnesota. The firebombing of a fur store causes $2 million in damage.

December 1996. *Arson.* White racist, Ku Klux Klan. South Carolina. A black church is set on fire.

January 16, 1997. *Bombing/explosive.* Rightist, Eric Rudolph. Atlanta, Georgia. A bomb explodes outside an abortion clinic, and an hour later a second bomb explodes injuring seven people, including the police officers who had responded to the blast.

January 19, 1997. *Bombing/explosive.* Anti-abortion. Tulsa, Oklahoma. Two bombs explode behind Reproductive Services, an abortion clinic.

February 2, 1997. *Shooting.* Anti-abortion. Tulsa, Oklahoma. Shots are fired at an abortion clinic.

February 13, 1997. *Attempted bombing.* Jewish. Jacksonville, Florida. A bomb is found in a synagogue shortly before Shimon Peres, former Israeli prime minister, is to give a speech.

February 15, 1997. *Shoot-out.* Rightist. Wilmington, Ohio. Chevie Kehoe and his brother Cheyne, wanted in connection with a triple murder of a year earlier, are stopped by police. In the shoot-out that follows no one is hurt, but a short time later when police try to arrest the brothers, a passerby is wounded.

February 21, 1997. *Bombing/explosive.* Rightist, Eric Rudolph. Atlanta, Georgia. Five people are injured when a bomb explodes outside a gay nightclub. A second bomb is discovered and is safely detonated by police. Law enforcement officials noted the similarity to the January 16 attack on an abortion clinic. The bombs were also similar in that they contained nails and shrapnel as did the Centennial Olympic Park bomb. A letter postmarked the next day claimed responsibility for both attacks on behalf of the Army of God.

February 24, 1997. *Shooting.* Islamic. New York City, New York. A Palestinian opens fire from the Empire State Building with a semiautomatic pistol, killing a Danish tourist and wounding six other people. He then shoots himself. In a letter he wrote that he was taking revenge against the enemies of the Palestinian people.

March 11, 1997. *Bombing.* Animal rights, Animal Liberation Front. Utah. Five pipe bombs explode at Fur Breeders Agricultural Cooperative, causing $1 million in damage.

March 18, 1997. *Arson.* Animal rights, Animal Liberation Front. Ogden, Utah. Montgomery Furs is torched while the night watchman is inside.

March 18, 1997. *Arson.* Animal rights, Animal Liberation Front. California. A fire is set at a University of California laboratory.

April 26, 1997. *Shooting.* White racist. Dallas, Texas. Shots are fired at a synagogue.

April 27, 1997. *Kidnapping and shoot-out.* Rightist. Fort Davis, Texas. A siege of the compound of the Republic of Texas, which begins after a local couple is kidnapped, ends peacefully. The separatists claim that Texas is not a part of the USA.

May 3, 1997. *Shoot-out.* Rightist. Davis Mountains, Texas. In a shoot-out, Mike Matson is killed by state police after he and another man flee from the Republic of Texas compound.

May 30, 1997. *Sabotage, vandalism, and property destruction.* Animal rights, Animal Liberation Front. Oregon. The ALF releases 10,000 mink. The animals are valued at $750,000.

June 1997. *Arson.* Animal rights, Animal Liberation Front. Redmond, California. Arson at a slaughterhouse causes damage estimated at $1.3 million.

July 4, 1997. *Sabotage, vandalism, and property destruction.* Environmental/animal rights, Earth Liberation Front/Animal Liberation Front. Cle Elum, Washington. The Earth Liberation Front (ELF) and the ALF release 6000 mink from a fur farm.

July 21, 1997. *Arson.* Environmental/animal rights, Earth Liberation Front/Animal Liberation Front. Redmond, Oregon. A horse slaughter plant is burned down, causing over $1 million in damage.

July 31, 1997. *Shoot-out.* Islamic. Brooklyn, New York. Three men are arrested after a shoot-out with police and are charged with planning attacks on the subway system. Five bombs were found in their apartment.

August 16, 1997. *Arson.* Animal rights, Animal Liberation Front. West Jordan, Utah. A McDonald's restaurant is burned down, causing $400,000 in damage.

August 19, 1997. *Arson.* Animal rights, Animal Liberation Front. Fort Collins, Colorado. A pharmaceutical company is the target of arson.

August 26, 1997. *Arson.* Animal rights, Animal Liberation Front. Howell, New Jersey. Meat trucks are torched, causing damage of $60,000.

October 28, 1997. *Shooting.* Anti-abortion. Rochester, New York. A doctor who performs abortions is shot and wounded while sitting in his home.

November 12, 1997. *Shoot-out.* White racist, Skinheads. Denver, Colorado. Bruce VanderJagt, a policeman, is shot and killed by a Skinhead after a car chase. The Skinhead then commits suicide.

November 18, 1997. *Shooting.* White racist, Skinheads. Denver, Colorado. A Skinhead shoots and kills Oumar Dia, a West African immigrant, while he was waiting at a bus stop. The Skinhead said, "This is white territory; this is what happens when you come here."

November 29, 1997. *Robbery.* Environmental/animal rights, Earth Liberation Front/Animal Liberation Front. Burns, Oregon. Four hundred horses are released, causing damage of $474,000.

1998. *Arson.* Environmental, Earth Liberation Front. Washington. A fire at federal wildlife offices causes $1.9 million in damage.

January 9, 1998. *Bombing/explosive.* White racist. Los Angeles, California. A black home is bombed.

January 29, 1998. *Bombing/explosive.* Rightist, Eric Rudolph. Birmingham, Alabama. An explosion at an abortion clinic kills Robert Sanderson, a security guard, and seriously injures Emily Lyons, a nurse. A witness sees a man leaving the scene of the attack and takes down the license plate of his truck. The truck is traced to Eric Rudolph. Rudolph evades a massive manhunt before being apprehended in 2003.

March 13, 1998. *Bombing/explosive.* Puerto Rican nationalist, Macheteros. Arecibo, Puerto Rico. An explosion causes considerable damage at an aqueduct construction site.

May 4, 1998. *Arson.* Animal rights, Animal Liberation Front. Wimauma, Florida. A slaughterhouse is burned down.

May 9, 1998. *Shooting.* White racist. Rutherford, North Carolina. Shots are fired into a black home.

May 29, 1998. *Shooting.* Rightist. Cortez, Colorado. A police officer, Dale Claxton, is shot and killed by three camouflage-clad men, when he stops their truck. Two sheriff's deputies are wounded in the subsequent chase. The three men were identified as survivalists; pipe bombs were found in their abandoned truck.

June 4, 1998. *Shooting.* Rightist. Bluff, Utah. A sheriff's deputy is shot and wounded by a camouflage-clad gunman. The body of Robert Mason, one of the three survivalists wanted for the murder of police officer Dale Claxton the previous week, was discovered 300 yards away. Pipe bombs were attached to Mason's body, and he had apparently shot himself in the head. A massive manhunt by 200 National Guard troops and 300 law enforcement officers failed to capture the other two men who disappeared into the Utah wilderness.

June 1998. *Robbery.* White racist, Joseph Paul Franklin. USA. Joseph Paul Franklin is allegedly responsible for a total of 16 robberies in several states, while on his racist shooting spree.

June 9, 1998. *Bombing/explosive.* Puerto Rican nationalist, Macheteros. Rio Piedras, Puerto Rico. Banco Popular is bombed. A communiqué by the Macheteros states that the bombing is because the bank was involved in the sale of the Puerto Rico Telephone Company to a multinational corporation.

June 9, 1998. *Bombing/explosive.* Puerto Rican nationalist, Macheteros. Santa Isabel, Puerto Rico. A branch of Banco Popular is bombed.

June 10, 1998. *Assault.* White racist. Jasper, Texas. James Byrd Jr., a black man, is savagely beaten and then dragged behind a pickup truck until he dies. His three killers had links to the prison-based Aryan Brotherhood.

June 21, 1998. *Arson.* Environmental/animal rights, Earth Liberation Front/Animal Liberation Front. Olympia, Washington. Arsonists attack the U.S. Department of Agriculture Animal Damage Control building, causing $1.9 million in damage in research and $400,000 in damage to the facilities.

July 24, 1998. *Shooting.* Quasi-terrorist. Washington, D.C. Two Capitol police officers are shot and killed by a mentally disturbed individual.

August 1998. *Bombing/incendiary.* White racist, Skinheads. Riverdale, Georgia. The NAACP office is firebombed.

August 18, 1998. *Sabotage, vandalism, and property destruction.* Animal rights, Animal Liberation Front. Pearl Lake, Minnesota. The ALF releases 2500 mink from a mink ranch.

August 20, 1998. *Sabotage, vandalism, and property destruction.* Animal rights, Animal Liberation Front. Jewell, Iowa. The ALF releases 2500 mink from a fur farm.

August 27, 1998. *Sabotage, vandalism, and property destruction.* Environmental/animal rights, Earth Liberation Front/Animal Liberation Front. Beloit, Wisconsin. The ELF and the ALF release 3000 mink from a fur farm.

August 28, 1998. *Sabotage, vandalism, and property destruction.* Environmental/animal rights, Earth Liberation Front/Animal Liberation Front. Rochester, Minnesota. The ELF and the ALF release 2800 mink from a fur farm.

October 19, 1998. *Arson.* Environmental, Earth Liberation Front. Vail, Colorado. Multiple fires are set at Vail Mountain Ski Resort, causing $12 million in damage.

October 23, 1998. *Shooting.* Anti-abortion. Amherst, New York. Barnett Slepian, a doctor who performed abortions, is killed in his house by a single shot fired through his kitchen window. The sniper, James Kopp, is arrested in France after a two-year manhunt.

December 26, 1998. *Arson.* Environmental, Earth Liberation Front. Medford, Oregon. An arson attack at the headquarters of U.S. Forest Industries causes $500,000 in damage.

March 27, 1999. *Bombing/incendiary.* Animal rights, Animal Liberation Front. Franklin, New Jersey. Circus vehicles are destroyed by firebombs.

April 5, 1999. *Sabotage, vandalism, and property destruction.* Animal rights, Animal Liberation Front. Minnesota. Neurology laboratories are vandalized, causing $700,000 in estimated damage.

May 1999. *Arson.* Environmental, Earth Liberation Front. Cle Elum, Washington. Arson at a chip mill causes $65,000 in damage.

May 9, 1999. *Arson.* Animal rights, Animal Liberation Front. Eugene, Oregon. A fire at a meat company causes $350,000 in damage.

June 18, 1999. *Arson.* White racist. Sacramento, California. Three synagogues are set on fire early in the morning, causing damage estimated at $1 million.

July 1, 1999. *Bombing/incendiary.* White racist. Sacramento, California. An abortion clinic is firebombed.

July 3, 1999. *Shooting.* White racist. Chicago, Illinois. Over the Fourth of July weekend Benjamin Smith, a member of the white supremacist World Church of the Creator, goes on a shooting spree in the Chicago area, which leaves two dead and eight wounded. The two persons killed were Ricky Byrdsong, a black man, and Won Joon Yoon, an Asian man. The wounded include six Jews who were leaving a synagogue. Smith kills himself afterwards.

July 3, 1999. *Shooting.* White racist. Redding, California. A gay couple is murdered by two neo-Nazi brothers. The brothers had firebombed three synagogues and an abortion clinic in the previous month.

July 10, 1999. *Bombing/incendiary.* Animal rights, Animal Liberation Front. Howell, New Jersey. A meatpacking facility closes down after three trucks are destroyed by firebombs.

August 7, 1999. *Arson.* Environmental, Earth Liberation Front. Escanaba, Michigan. The fishing boat of a veterinarian who works with the fur industry is destroyed by fire.

August 9, 1999. *Arson.* Animal rights, Animal Liberation Front. Plymouth, Wisconsin. A fire destroys the United Feed mill, a supplier of feed to fur farms, causing damage at $1.5 million.

August 9, 1999. *Sabotage, vandalism, and property destruction.* Animal rights, Animal Liberation Front. Plymouth, Wisconsin. Three thousand mink are released.

August 10, 1999. *Shooting.* White racist. Granada Hills, California. Buford Furrow walks into a Jewish community center at 10:45 a.m. and opens fire, wounding five people, three of them children. He then drives to Van Nuys airport, abandons his van containing an extensive arsenal of weapons, and hijacks a car at gunpoint. Later that morning, he approaches a Filipino mailman, Joseph Ileto, who is delivering letters in the Chatsworth neighborhood. After talking to the mailman, he shoots and kills him. Despite a massive multi-state manhunt, police are unable to apprehend Furrow, who walks into the FBI office in Las Vegas the next morning and surrenders. Furrow said that he "wanted to send a message to America by killing Jews." Investigators found that Furrow had a history of involvement with the racist organization Aryan Nations and had been married to the widow of Robert Mathews, the founder of the Order. He also had a record of mental illness. At his trial Furrow pleaded guilty to murder, civil rights violations, and weapons charges.

August 29, 1999. *Robbery and vandalism.* Animal rights, Animal Liberation Front. Orange County, California. Forty-six dogs are stolen from Bio-Devices, Inc., and the laboratory is vandalized, causing damage estimated at $250,000.

August 31, 1999. *Bombing/explosive.* White racist. Tallahassee, Florida. Bombs explode on a black college campus.

August 31, 1999. *Arson.* Animal rights, Animal Liberation Front. Fulton, Georgia. A McDonald's restaurant is burned down.

September 22, 1999. *Bombing/explosive.* White racist. Tallahassee, Florida. After another explosion at a black college, the bomber is caught.

October 1999. *Attempted assault.* Animal rights, Animal Liberation Front? USA. Booby-trapped letters with razor blades inside the envelopes are mailed to animal researchers throughout the U.S. At least 31 letters postmarked Las Vegas, Nevada, were intercepted, and no injuries were reported.

October 16, 1999. *Sabotage, vandalism, and property destruction.* Animal rights, Animal Liberation Front. Nassau, New York. Four McDonald's restaurants are attacked, causing damage exceeding $23,000.

October 22, 1999. *Arson.* Animal rights, Animal Liberation Front. Warwick, Rhode Island. A delivery van belonging to a fur store is destroyed by fire.

November 1, 1999. *Bombing.* Animal rights, Animal Liberation Front. Seattle, Washington. A Gap store is bombed.

November 17, 1999. *Shooting.* White racist. Goshen, Indiana. Sase Richardson, a black man, is killed in a drive-by shooting.

December 14, 1999. *Attempted bombing.* Islamic. Washington. Ahmed Ressam is arrested at the U.S.–Canadian border, when bomb-making material is found in his car. He had planned to bomb the Los Angeles International Airport.

December 20, 1999. *Attempted arson.* Animal rights, Animal Liberation Front. San Francisco, California. Fulton Poultry Processors is the target of attempted arson.

December 21, 1999. *Arson.* Environmental, Earth Liberation Front. East Lansing, Michigan. A fire at Michigan State University causes $900,000 in damage.

January 3, 2000. *Bombing.* Animal rights, Animal Liberation Front. Petaluma, California. The bombing of offices, storage facilities, and trucks at Rancho Veal Corporation causes $250,000 in damage.

January 15, 2000. *Bombing.* Environmental, Earth Liberation Front. San Francisco, California. An office and two trucks are destroyed by bombs.

January 23, 2000. *Arson.* Environmental, Earth Liberation Front. Bloomington, Indiana. A new house is set on fire, causing an estimated damage of $200,000.

January 24, 2000. *Attempted arson.* Animal rights, Animal Liberation Front. Redwood, California. Primate Products medical research facility is the target of attempted arson.

February 9, 2000. *Sabotage, vandalism, and property destruction.* Environmental, Earth Liberation Front. St. Paul, Minnesota. At a university biotech laboratory 800 experimental oat plants are destroyed.

February 25, 2000. *Bombing.* Animal rights, Animal Liberation Front. Fremont, California. Trucks belonging to B&K Universal are destroyed by bombs; B&K breeds animals for research.

February 27, 2000. *Sabotage, vandalism, and property destruction.* Animal rights, Animal Liberation Front. San Francisco, California. Vandals smash 29 windows of the Neiman Marcus store, causing an estimated damage of $100,000.

March 1, 2000. *Shooting.* Black militant. Pittsburgh, Pennsylvania. Ronald Taylor shoots five whites, killing three of them, in two fast-food restaurants. Racist writings were found in his apartment.

March 25, 2000. *Sabotage, vandalism, and property destruction.* Environmental, Earth Liberation Front. Minnesota. Construction equipment is sabotaged.

March 25, 2000. *Bombing.* Animal rights, Animal Liberation Front? Chandler, Arizona. Revlon manager Richard D. Simer's finger is blown off by a package bomb. There is no claim of responsibility.

April 28, 2000. *Shooting.* White racist. Pittsburgh, Pennsylvania. In a shooting spree, Richard Bauhammers kills five people, a black, a Jew, and three Asians. He was trying to found an anti-immigrant political party.

April 30, 2000. *Sabotage, vandalism, and property destruction.* Environmental, Earth Liberation Front. Ellettsville, Indiana.

Sabotage of a highway construction site causes $75,000 in damage to logging equipment.

May 7, 2000. *Arson.* Environmental, Earth Liberation Front. Olympia, Washington. A fire guts the headquarters of a timber company, causing $150,000 in damage.

May 14, 2000. *Sabotage, vandalism, and property destruction.* Animal rights, Animal Liberation Front. Lyndeboro, New Hampshire. Five hundred mink are released.

June 2000. *Arson.* Environmental, Earth Liberation Front. Boulder, Colorado. New houses are set on fire.

June 4, 2000. *Sabotage, vandalism, and property destruction.* Environmental, Earth Liberation Front. Canby, Oregon. Sabotage at a greenhouse causes $300,000 in damage.

July 2, 2000. *Arson.* Animal rights, Animal Liberation Front. North Vernon, Indiana. Arson at the Rose Acre chicken farm destroys a feed truck and causes an estimated $100,000 in damage.

July 12, 2000. *Sabotage, vandalism, and property destruction.* Environmental, Earth Liberation Front. Long Island, New York. Sabotage occurs at Cold Spring Laboratory, a biotech lab.

July 20, 2000. *Sabotage, vandalism, and property destruction.* Environmental, Earth Liberation Front. Rhinelander, Wisconsin. Vandals hack down thousands of experimental trees, causing $1 million in damage.

July 25, 2000. *Assault.* Black militant. Alexandria, Virginia. Kevin Shifflett, an eight-year-old white boy, is stabbed to death by a black man. A handwritten note left in his hotel room said "Kill them racist white kids."

September 7, 2000. *Sabotage, vandalism, and property destruction.* Animal rights, Animal Liberation Front. New Hampton, Iowa. The largest animal release in U.S. history occurs when 14,000 mink are released.

September 9, 2000. *Arson.* Environmental, Earth Liberation Front. Bloomington, Indiana. A fire at Monroe County Republican Party Committee headquarters causes $1500 in damage.

September 30, 2000. *Sabotage, vandalism, and property destruction.* Anti-abortion. Rockford, Illinois. A Catholic priest attacks an abortion clinic with an axe.

October 18, 2000. *Sabotage, vandalism, and property destruction.* Environmental, Earth Liberation Front. Martin County, Indiana. Logging equipment is damaged, causing $55,000 in damage.

November 27, 2000. *Arson.* Environmental, Earth Liberation Front. Longmont, Colorado. A mansion is attacked by arsonists, causing damage of $500,000.

December 9, 2000. *Arson.* Environmental, Earth Liberation Front. Middle Island, New York. A fire at a condominium causes $200,000 in damage.

December 19, 2000. *Arson.* Environmental, Earth Liberation Front. Miller Place, New York. A luxury home is torched, causing $50,000 in damage.

December 25, 2000. *Arson.* Environmental, Earth Liberation Front. Monmouth, Oregon. Arson destroys a timber management office, causing $1 million in damage.

December 29, 2000. *Arson.* Environmental, Earth Liberation Front. Long Island, New York. Arsonists attack four luxury homes, causing $160,000 in damage.

January 2, 2001. *Arson.* Environmental, Earth Liberation Front. Glendale, Oregon. The offices of Superior Lumber Company are set on fire, causing $500,000 in damage.

January 15, 2001. *Sabotage, vandalism, and property destruction.* Environmental, Earth Liberation Front. Marblemount, Washington. Sand is poured into the oil in logging equipment, causing damage estimated at $100,000.

February 20, 2001. *Arson.* Environmental, Earth Liberation Front. Visalia, California. A cotton gin is set on fire at Delta and Pine Land Co.

March 30, 2001. *Arson.* Environmental, Earth Liberation Front. Eugene, Oregon. An arson attack at a Chevrolet dealership destroys 36 sport utility vehicles (SUV's), causing damage of $1 million.

April 5, 2001. *Arson.* Animal rights, Animal Liberation Front. Arlington, Washington. An egg farm is set on fire, causing $1.5 million in damage.

April 15, 2001. *Arson.* Environmental, Earth Liberation Front. Portland, Oregon. Three cement trucks are destroyed by fire, causing damage of $210,000.

April 20, 2001. *Sabotage, vandalism, and property destruction.* Animal rights, Animal Liberation Front. Snohomish,

Washington. Three hundred mink are released, causing damage of $35,000.

May 2001. *Shooting.* Quasi-terrorist. Tacoma, Washington. Shots are fired at a synagogue. The shooter was later revealed to have been John Muhammad, the "Washington sniper" who terrorized the D.C. area in October 2002.

May 21, 2001. *Arson.* Environmental, Earth Liberation Front. Clatskanie, Oregon. A tree farm is attacked by arsonists, who destroy buildings and equipment worth $500,000. The incendiary device is identical to that used in the arson attack at the University of Washington.

May 21, 2001. *Arson.* Environmental, Earth Liberation Front. Seattle, Washington. The university horticultural lab is totally destroyed by fire. The incendiary device is similar to the one used in the same day attack in Clatskanie, Oregon.

June 11, 2001. *Arson.* Environmental, Earth Liberation Front. Tucson, Arizona. Four luxury homes in Pima Canyon Estates outside Tucson are torched, causing $5 million in damage.

July 4, 2001. *Arson.* Environmental, Earth Liberation Front. Michigan. SUV's are destroyed by fire at a Ford dealership.

August 21, 2001. *Sabotage, vandalism, and property destruction.* Environmental, Earth Liberation Front. Nassau, New York. A New York laboratory is vandalized, causing $15,000 in damage.

September 8, 2001. *Arson.* Environmental/animal rights, Earth Liberation Front/Animal Liberation Front. Tucson,

Arizona. A McDonald's restaurant is set on fire, causing damage estimated at $500,000.

September 11, 2001. *Hijacking.* Islamic. USA. On Tuesday, September 11, 2001, terrorists hijack four planes filled with passengers. At 8:48 a.m. the first plane crashes into the North Tower of the World Trade Center in New York City. Fifteen minutes later the second plane flies into the South Tower. Both towers burst into flames and later collapse. Shortly before 10 a.m., the third plane crashes into the Pentagon outside Washington, D.C. The fourth plane crashes in rural Pennsylvania, after passengers attack the hijackers.

The attacks were unprecedented in terms of the number of deaths and the amount of damage which resulted. In addition to the 226 passengers on the four planes (including the 19 hijackers), almost 3000 persons lost their lives at the World Trade Center and 125 people perished at the Pentagon. The cost of the physical damage alone was over $5 billion, while the indirect economic costs were even more significant. American business was paralyzed, many stores closed, and sales were down sharply in those that remained open. Hardest hit was the airline industry, which was already in bad financial straits. The major airlines announced layoffs and warned that they might file for bankruptcy protection. As passengers canceled their flight plans a ripple effect was felt throughout other sectors of the travel industry, including hotels, resorts, convention centers, and cab and auto-rental companies. The insurance industry and financial markets suffered heavy losses. The stock market was closed for the rest of the week, but after it reopened the Dow Jones Index plunged 1370 points (14.3 percent) in the next week—

the worst decline ever. As consumer confidence fell, the economy slipped into recession.

In response to the attacks all commercial air traffic was grounded for two days. Aircraft carriers and destroyers armed with surface-to-air missiles were stationed in the coastal waters off California and New York. Fighter jets patrolled the skies over Washington and New York, and soldiers stood guard in downtown areas.

Within a few days, the 19 hijackers were identified and linked to al Qaeda, the radical Islamic network headed by Osama bin Laden. Most were Saudis, but one was Lebanese and two were from the United Arab Emirates, while the apparent leader, Mohammed Atta, was Egyptian.

Following the September 11 attacks almost 1200 Muslims were arrested as material witnesses or detained for immigration violations, the largest such operation since World War II.

On Thursday, September 20, in a speech to a joint session of Congress, President Bush demanded that the Taliban government of Afghanistan turn over Osama bin Laden. "Our war on terror," he said "will not end until every terrorist group of global reach has been found, stopped, and defeated," but he warned that it would be a long campaign. Bush declared that any country that harbored or supported terrorists would be regarded as a hostile regime. He emphasized several times that the enemy was not Islam or the Arabs. "Our enemy is a radical network of terrorists and every government that supports them." When the Taliban failed to surrender Osama, the anti-Taliban coalition within Afghanistan, the Northern Alliance, was supplied with weapons and supported by American air power. By late December, the Taliban had been overthrown and U.S. Special Forces

were searching caves along the Pakistan border for Osama bin Laden and other al-Qaeda leaders.

Domestically, in the aftermath of the attacks unprecedented new powers were granted to the government. Under the Patriot Act, law enforcement and intelligence agencies were given expanded powers to wiretap phones and monitor Internet messages, penalties were increased for terrorist-related activities, and the attorney general was given the power to detain non-citizens without charge. By executive order, President Bush created the Department of Homeland Security with the responsibility of coordinating the response to the terrorist threat.

September 20, 2001. *Arson.* Animal rights, Animal Liberation Front. Alamogordo, New Mexico. A maintenance building is burned down; the damage is estimated at over $1 million.

September 22, 2001. *Bio-terrorism.* Islamic? New York City, New York. A letter sent to the *New York Post* is not opened, but it infects an employee with an anthrax lesion on her finger. The letter, like that addressed to Tom Brokaw, is postmarked September 18, 2001, from Trenton and contains identical language: "Death to America. Death to Israel. Allah is great."

October 1, 2001. *Bio-terrorism.* Islamic? New York City, New York. A letter sent to CBS addressed to Dan Rather is opened by his assistant, who later develops an anthrax lesion.

October 5, 2001. *Bio-terrorism.* Islamic? Boca Raton, Florida. An anthrax letter sent to the offices of American Media Inc. results in the death of Robert Stevens, an editor, and hospitalization of a mailroom clerk.

October 12, 2001. *Bio-terrorism.* Islamic? New York City, New York. A letter sent to NBC addressed to Tom Brokaw is opened by his assistant, who later develops an anthrax lesion. The letter says "Death to America. Death to Israel. Allah is great."

October 15, 2001. *Bio-terrorism.* Islamic? New York City, New York. A seven-month-old baby develops anthrax 17 days after his mother, a producer at ABC News, takes him to the studio.

October 15, 2001. *Bio-terrorism.* Islamic? Washington, D.C. A letter sent to Senator Daschle's office in the Hart Senate Building infects 28 people with anthrax. The letter, like that addressed to Tom Brokaw and the *New York Post,* is postmarked from Trenton and also contains slogans: "Death to America. Death to Israel. Allah is great." The letter was posted on October 9. An investigation of the mail sent to the Senate offices found an identical letter addressed to Senator Patrick Leahy, also postmarked from Trenton on October 9.

October 15, 2001. *Arson.* Environmental, Earth Liberation Front. Litchfield, California. A barn containing hay is destroyed by a fire at the U.S. Bureau of Land Management's wild horse and burro corrals, causing damage over $85,000.

October 16, 2001. *Sabotage, vandalism, and property destruction.* Animal rights, Animal Liberation Front. Hamilton, Iowa. The ALF releases 1400 mink from a fur farm.

October 18, 2001. *Bio-terrorism.* Islamic? West Trenton, New Jersey. One postal worker develops skin lesions.

October 19, 2001. *Bio-terrorism.* Islamic? Hamilton, New Jersey. Three post office workers are infected with anthrax.

October 21, 2001. *Bio-terrorism.* Islamic? Washington, D.C. At Brentwood post office center, four workers are infected with anthrax. Two of them, Joe Curseen and Tom Morris, die.

October 24, 2001. *Sabotage, vandalism, and property destruction.* Animal rights, Animal Liberation Front. Ringwood, New Hampshire. Five hundred mink are released from a fur farm.

October 25, 2001. *Bio-terrorism.* Islamic? Washington, D.C. A mail clerk in the State Department is diagnosed with anthrax.

October 31, 2001. *Bio-terrorism.* Islamic? New York City, New York. Kathy Nguyen dies of inhalation anthrax with no obvious source of infection.

November 2001. *Bio-terrorism.* Anti-abortion. USA. Clayton Lee Wagner mails hoax anthrax letters, containing a harmless white powder to 280 abortion clinics. He is arrested a month later, after having been on the run for 10 months after escaping from an Illinois jail.

November 13, 2001. *Sabotage, vandalism, and property destruction.* Animal rights, Animal Liberation Front. San Diego, California. Files and equipment are damaged at Sierra Biomedical in La Jolla, costing $50,000.

November 21, 2001. *Bio-terrorism.* Islamic? Oxford, Connecticut. A 94-year-old woman, Ottilie Lundgren, dies of inhalation anthrax with no obvious source of infection. It is believed to be a result of cross contamination when mail addressed to her was sorted on a machine that had been exposed to mail from the Hamilton, New Jersey, center.

January 26, 2002. *Arson.* Environmental, Earth Liberation Front. St. Paul, Minnesota. Fire damages a trailer and two pieces of heavy machinery at the construction site of the Center for Microbial and Plant Genomics on a campus.

January 29, 2002. *Sabotage, vandalism, and property destruction.* Environmental/animal rights, Earth Liberation Front/Animal Liberation Front. Fairfield, Maine. A biotech plant being built for Jackson Labs, an animal testing business, is sabotaged.

March 24, 2002. *Arson.* Environmental, Earth Liberation Front. Wintergreen Gorge, Pennsylvania. A crane is destroyed by fire, causing $500,000 in damage.

April 2002. *Attempted bombing.* White racist. Walnut Creek, California. A Jewish community center is the target of an attempted bombing.

April 2002. *Assault.* White racist, Skinheads. Los Angeles, California. Four Jewish youths are attacked and injured by Skinheads.

May 3, 2002. *Bombing/incendiary.* Animal rights, Animal Liberation Front. Bloomington, Indiana. A truck at an Indiana poultry company is firebombed.

May 12, 2002. *Robbery.* Animal rights, Animal Liberation Front. Erie, Pennsylvania. Two hundred mink are stolen from a farm and abandoned.

July 4, 2002. *Shooting.* Islamic. LA Airport, California. An Egyptian immigrant opens fire at the El Al airline ticket counter, killing Victoria Hen and Jacob Aminov, and wounding three others. All victims were Israelis. The gunman left a letter saying that he was angered by Israel's treatment of Palestinians.

July 19, 2002. *Arson.* Environmental, Earth Liberation Front. Tucson, Arizona. A fire at a construction site destroys $1500 worth of materials.

August 11, 2002. *Arson.* Environmental, Earth Liberation Front. Irvine, Pennsylvania. The U.S. Forest Service Research Station is destroyed by fire, causing about $700,000 in damage.

August 18, 2002. *Sabotage, vandalism, and property destruction.* Animal rights, Animal Liberation Front. Waverly, Iowa. The ALF releases 1200 mink.

August 18, 2002. *Arson.* Environmental, Earth Liberation Front. Washtenaw, Michigan. A home is burned down; the insurance company pays $600,000.

September 28, 2002. *Sabotage, vandalism, and property destruction.* Environmental, Earth Liberation Front. Henrico, Virginia. SUV's are vandalized, causing $25,000 in damage.

October 2002. *Shooting.* Quasi-terrorist. New York City, New York. A South Korean fires shots at the UN headquarters and hands out leaflets condemning North Korea.

October 2002. *Shooting.* Quasi-terrorist. Washington, D.C. A series of shootings leaves 10 killed and 3 wounded, terrorizing the Washington, D.C., area. The snipers are John Muhammad and Lee Malvo, two black males. Although they hold black separatist beliefs, the shootings are not considered to be politically motivated.

October 6, 2002. *Sabotage, vandalism, and property destruction.* Environmental, Earth Liberation Front. Henrico, Virginia. SUV's are attacked with an axe, causing $14,000 in damage.

November 26, 2002. *Arson.* Environmental/animal rights, Earth Liberation Front/Animal Liberation Front. Erie, Pennsylvania. A fur farm is set on fire.

January 1, 2003. *Arson.* Environmental, Earth Liberation Front. Erie, Pennsylvania. Four new SUV's are set on fire, causing damage of $90,000.

February 2, 2003. *Sabotage, vandalism, and property destruction.* Animal rights, Animal Liberation Front. Villa Park, Illinois. Supreme Lobster and Seafood Company is vandalized.

February 16, 2003. *Attempted bombing.* Rightist, Militia. Santa Fe, New Mexico. A Militia member is arrested and accused of placing a pipe bomb in the mailbox of an environmental group.

March 17, 2003. *Attempted bombing.* Quasi-terrorist. Washington, D.C. A farmer protesting cuts in tobacco subsidies drives his tractor into a pond near the Lincoln Memorial and threatens to detonate a bomb. He surrenders two days later.

March 21, 2003. *Sabotage, vandalism, and property destruction.* Environmental, Earth Liberation Front. Montgomery, Alabama. The Navy recruiting station is vandalized.

March 21, 2003. *Arson.* Environmental, Earth Liberation Front. Superior, Michigan. Two homes under construction are torched, causing damage of $500,000 each.

March 22, 2003. *Arson.* Animal rights, Animal Liberation Front. Petaluma, California. Rancho Veal slaughterhouse is torched, causing $100,000 in damage.

April 4, 2003. *Arson.* Animal rights, Animal Liberation Front. Chicago, Illinois. Czimer's Game and Seafood store is torched the day after the owner and others are convicted of using the store to illegally sell tiger and leopard meat.

June 4, 2003. *Arson.* Environmental, Earth Liberation Front. Macomb, Michigan. Two homes are torched, causing an estimated damage of $700,000.

July 2003. *Sabotage, vandalism, and property destruction.* Environmental, Earth Liberation Front. Sonoma, California. Multiple attacks in July and August are directed at the homes of the two owners of new Sonoma Foie Gras specialty store, causing damage of over $60,000.

August 1, 2003. *Arson.* Environmental, Earth Liberation Front. San Diego, California. A 206 unit condominium under construction is destroyed by fire, causing $50 million in damage.

August 22, 2003. *Arson.* Environmental, Earth Liberation Front. Los Angeles, California. Four auto dealerships and a warehouse at a West Covina dealership are set on fire, causing $2.5 million in damage.

August 25, 2003. *Sabotage, vandalism, and property destruction.* Animal rights, Animal Liberation Front. Snohomish, Washington. Over 100,000 mink are released.

August 28, 2003. *Bombing.* Animal rights, Animal Liberation Front. Emeryville, California. Two bombs explode at a biotech company, Chiron Corporation.

September 9, 2003. *Arson.* Environmental, Earth Liberation Front. San Diego, California. Four homes under construction are damaged by fire, causing damage estimated at over $1 million.

September 22, 2003. *Attempted bombing.* Environmental, Earth Liberation Front. Mecosta, Michigan. A water plant is the target of an attempted bombing.

September 23, 2003. *Sabotage, vandalism, and property destruction.* Animal rights, Animal Liberation Front. LSU, Louisiana. A research lab at Louisiana State University School of Veterinary Medicine is vandalized, causing an estimated damage of hundreds of thousands of dollars.

October 5, 2003. *Sabotage, vandalism, and property destruction.* Environmental, Earth Liberation Front. Rio Cebolla, New Mexico. Construction equipment for a fish rehabilitation project is vandalized.

November 18, 2003. *Arson.* Rightist. Indiana. The Holocaust Memorial Museum is destroyed by arson. A message left at the scene says "Remember Timmy McVeigh."

February 3, 2004. *Bio-terrorism.* Unknown. Washington, D.C. After ricin is discovered in the mailroom, the Senate Office Building is closed.

February 7, 2004. *Sabotage, vandalism, and property destruction.* Environmental, Earth Liberation Front. Hollymead Town Center, Virginia. Damage to equipment at a construction site is estimated at $30,000.

April 20, 2004. *Arson.* Environmental, Earth Liberation Front. Snohomish, Washington. Three luxury homes under construction are destroyed by fire, causing damage estimated at $1 million.

May 27, 2004. *Sabotage, vandalism, and property destruction.* Environmental, Earth Liberation Front. Prairie City, Oregon. Logging equipment is vandalized, causing an estimated damage of $100,000.

June 15, 2004. *Arson.* Environmental, Earth Liberation Front. West Jordan, Utah. A storage building at Stock Building Supply is set on fire, causing damage of $1.5 million.

NAME INDEX

Main entry in which name appears is indicated in parentheses following index entry.

SUBJECT INDEX

Main entry in which subject appears is indicated in parentheses following index entry.

Abortion clinic employees killed (7/29/94), 164; (12/30/94), 165–66; (1/29/98), 171. *See also* Abortion physicians killed

Abortion clinics attacked/ threatened: anthrax hoax (11/01), 179; arson (2/23/77), 113; (5/1/77), 114; (8/18/77), 115; (11/77), 116; (2/8/78), 117; (2/15/78), 117; (2/24/78), 117; (2/15/79), 121; (4/9/81), 129; (1/23/82), 132; (1/23/82), 132; (3/29/82), 133; (10/26/82), 135; (1/14/84), 139; (3/26/84), 139; (4/19/84), 140; (9/8/84), 142; (11/11/84), 143; (2/22/85), 144; (6/14/86), 148; (10/31/86), 148; (11/25/86), 149; (12/1/86), 149; (12/10/86), 149; (12/27/86), 149; (1/6/87), 149; (1/27/87), 149; (6/8/87), 150; (9/17/87), 150; (10/88), 152; (12/25/88), 152; (12/25/88), 152; (12/25/88), 153; (3/89), 153; (4/89), 153; (4/89), 153; (7/89), 153; (9/89), 154; (10/89), 154; (5/90), 155; (5/90), 155; (5/90), 155; (11/90), 156; (2/91), 156; (2/91), 156; (3/91), 156; (3/91), 156; (4/91), 157; (5/91), 157; (8/91), 157; (9/91), 157; (1/92), 158; (1/92), 158; (4/92), 158; (4/92), 158; (4/92), 158; (6/92), 159; (7/92), 159; (8/92), 159; (8/92), 159; (9/92), 160; (9/92), 160; (9/6/92), 160; (9/16/92), 160; (11/92), 160; (11/92), 160;

(12/92), 160; (2/93), 161; (2/93), 161; (3/93), 161; (5/93), 162; (5/27/93), 162; (9/93), 163; (9/27/93), 163; (10/93), 163; (11/93), 163; (8/94), 164; (10/94), 165; (10/94), 165; (10/94), 165; (12/15/94), 165; (2/95), 166; (2/95), 166; (2/95), 166; (2/95), 166; (2/24/95), 166; (3/95), 166; (8/95), 167; (9/18/95), 167; (11/95), 167; arson attempts fail (5/12/84), 140; (10/15/84), 142; (3/19/85), 144–45; (3/13/86), 147; (5/13/86), 147; (5/20/86), 147; (3/8/87), 149; (9/14/87), 150; (10/5/87), 150; (12/23/87), 151; (1/88), 151; (6/88), 151; (1/90), 154; (6/21/92), 159; (12/94), 165; (8/95), 167; assault (2/15/78), 117; bombing (9/93), 163; bombing attempts fail (11/77), 116; (10/28/81), 131; (4/17/85), 145; (6/9/86), 147; (11/11/86), 149; (12/4/86), 149; (12/14/86), 149; (2/12/87), 149; (2/23/87), 149; (7/27/87), 150; (5/88), 151; (1/89), 153; (4/14/91), 157; (7/93), 162; (7/93), 162; (11/93), 163; (7/94), 164; (8/94), 164; (10/94), 165; bombings/explosive (6/6/82), 134; (2/17/84), 139; (3/4/84), 139; (3/16/84), 139; (6/25/84), 141; (7/4/84), 141; (7/7/84), 141; (8/20/84), 141; (9/13/84), 142; (11/5/84), 143;

(11/19/84), 143; (11/19/84), 143; (12/23/84), 143; (12/25/84), 143–44; (12/25/84), 144; (12/25/84), 144; (1/1/85), 144; (10/29/86), 148; (9/89), 153–54; (12/89), 154; (9/90), 155; (9/93), 163; (7/31/94), 164; (11/94), 165; (12/94), 165; (5/95), 167; (7/12/96), 168; (9/96), 169; (1/16/97), 169; (1/19/97), 169; (1/29/98), 171; bombings/ incendiary (5/15/78), 118; (6/10/78), 118; (6/13/78), 118; (5/29/82), 134; (12/14/82), 136; (5/26/83), 137; (7/23/83), 137; (12/3/83), 138; (2/28/84), 139; (9/7/84), 141; (9/7/84), 141–42; (9/13/84), 142; (9/20/84), 142; (3/16/85), 144; (7/1/99), 173; (7/3/99), 173; chemical vandalism (2/78), 117; (7/90), 155; (10/90), 156; (3/9/92), 158; (3/25/92), 158; (4/4/92), 158; (4/15/92), 158; (4/17/92), 158; (4/28/92), 159; (5/14/92), 159; (6/3/92), 159; (6/8/92), 159; (6/18/92), 159; (6/30/92), 159; (7/10/92), 159; (7/10/92), 159; (9/9/92), 160; (9/14/92), 160; (9/16/92), 160; (9/16/92), 160; (2/93), 161; (3/93), 161; (3/93), 161; (5/93), 162; (8/93), 162; (9/93), 163; (4/94), 164; kidnapping of owners (8/13/82), 135; shootings (1/91), 156; (12/28/91), 158; (3/10/93), 161; (8/19/93), 162–63;

About the Author

CHRISTOPHER HEWITT is Professor of Sociology at the University of Maryland Baltimore County. He has written extensively on terrorism, ethnic conflict, and political violence. His publications include *The Effectiveness of Anti-Terror Policies* (1984), *Consequences of Political Violence* (1993), *Encyclopedia of Modern Separatist Movements* (2000), and *Understanding Terrorism in America: From the Klan to Al Qaeda* (2003).